The Cutting Garden

The Cutting *Garden*

GROWING AND ARRANGING GARDEN FLOWERS

Sarah Raven

Photographs by
Pia Tryde

FRANCES LINCOLN

for Adam, Rosie, Molly and Louise

Frances Lincoln Limited
4 Torriano Mews
Torriano Avenue
London NW5 2RZ

First Frances Lincoln edition: 1996

British Library Cataloguing in Publication data
A catalogue record for this book is available from the British Library.

ISBN 0 7112 1047 0

Set in Monotype Baskerville and Gill Sans
Printed in China by Kwong Fat Offset Printing Co. Ltd

9 8 7 6 5

*Half-title page: The chartreuse-green double
Zinnia 'Envy' is one of my favourite flowers
for cutting.*

*Frontispiece: In early autumn the cutting
garden is full of hot colours, luxurious
textures and interesting shapes. Buckets of
freshly picked crabapples and white phlox
rest among pink zinnias, gloriosa daisies,
amaranthus tassels and white cosmos.*

*Title page: Tithonia rotundifolia 'Torch'
and Viburnum opulus.*

*Foreword: One or two precious late-winter
or early-spring gems, such as these aconites
and gold-laced polyanthus, a few sprigs of
winter cherry blossom and some lichened
witch hazel, bring a bright glow to your desk
on even the dullest morning.*

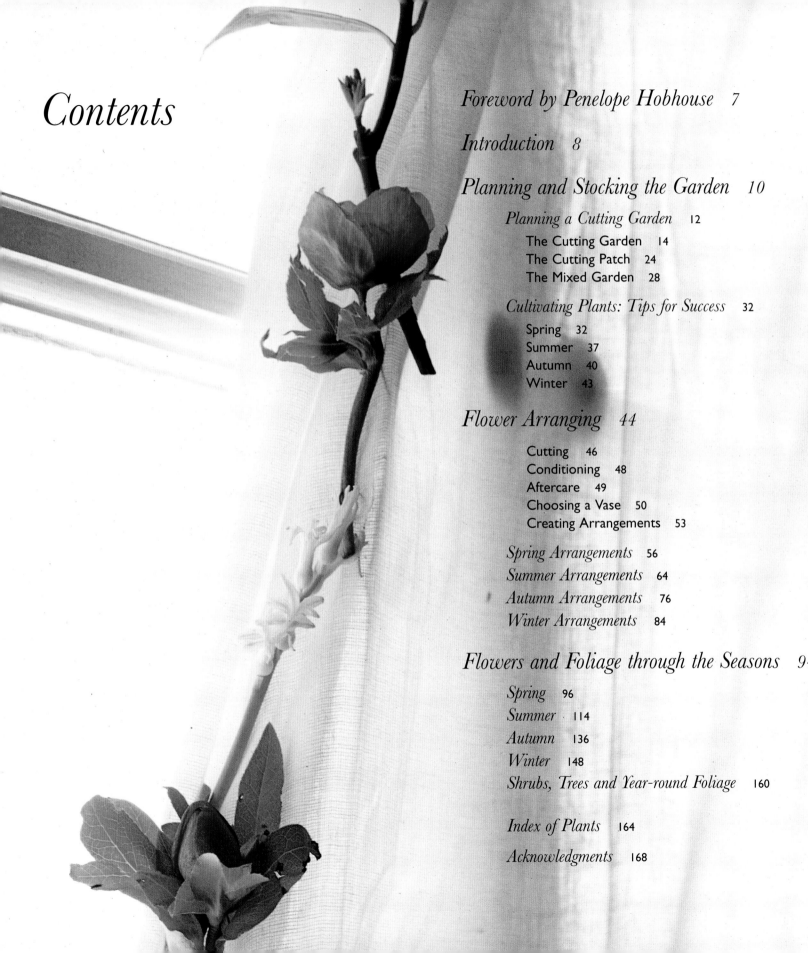

Contents

Foreword

The Cutting Garden is a beautiful, stimulating and practical book. Sarah Raven's descriptions of how to grow her flowers and foliage are not only very useful, they also make the cutting garden itself a desirable object. She designs a totally seasonal garden, producing flowers to display together in vases just as they grow and flower together in the garden. Having told the reader how to grow them in beautifully simple ways, she then suggests how to pick, prepare and arrange them. Each daily or weekly harvest from the garden reflects that exact gardening moment. Sometimes her displays are luxuriant, with clashing colours or subtle harmonies; at other times a single flower and stem provides a simple statement. This is why her approach works so well: it takes the garden and intensifies it, enriching what the moment gives her.

Professional flower arrangers can be intimidating. Often they seem rigidly controlled by an elaborate assembly of rules concerning choice of flowers as well as methods of arrangement. The rules seem designed to make the task difficult. Sometimes one can believe that the rules are invented to make judging a precise and predictable task. But Sarah Raven is a talented and innovative flower arranger who uses real garden flowers in simple, natural ways. She encourages a break with the stale formula of the commonplace (and often exotic) flowers usually found in the florist's – flown in from all corners of the world and therefore in no way reflecting the natural seasons. For her, branches from home-grown cherries, sprigs of scented viburnum or daphne, acid-green euphorbias and lady's mantle, wine-coloured perennials and summer-flowering annuals – some quite unusual –

replace artificial-looking tropicals or the more mundane 'everlastings' and spray chrysanthemums. Plants such as old man's beard, teasels and bulrushes extend her range beyond the boundaries of the cultivated flower garden. For the actual arranging she recommends a full range of schemes, from a cottage garden style to sumptuous coloured globes you might have found in the background of a Titian. While her guidelines emphasize a simplicity of approach, an escape from elaborate rules and flower show marking, her goal is often the rich and luxurious, with colour harmonies and clashes matched to nature's seasonal hues and shades.

But this is not just a romantic book. It is also eminently practical. Planning the cutting garden, growing from seed, choosing vases, the preparation of stems and flowers, all have careful explanations.

Sarah Raven is knowledgeable and inspiring. Her writing is alive and modern. Some of the book's charm comes from its evocative recommendations which, in their simplicity, seem old-fashioned. But there is a vitality to it which sets it away from what has come before. This is flower arranging for people who understand that flowers are living things, the crowning glories of the natural world. She gardens and writes for the craftsman – in a 1990s interpretation of Arts and Crafts in which real flowers, including almost forgotten favourites, grown and displayed with skill and sensitivity, and arranged with foliage picked from the garden, replace the 'factory-made' forced products to which we have become all too accustomed.

Penelope Hobhouse

Introduction

There's nothing like going out into the garden and picking flowers for the house. It's the gardener's equivalent of collecting new-laid eggs from nesting boxes. It's a personal harvest, a gathering of good and life-enhancing things that you have nurtured yourself. Gardening, as anyone knows who has ever really got their hands dirty, is not only about pretty things and lovely effects. There is a lot of planning, preparation, patience and sheer hard work necessary if that final moment is to be as glorious as you know it can be. So, in a funny way, this harvesting feels not only beautiful but earthy. You know the whole history of the flower that you are picking, you know what has gone into producing it. It is the culmination of a long haul which may well have begun the year before. The picking, in that sense, puts you in touch with nature in a way that simply looking at a flower that is growing in a garden could not.

Many people discover this pleasure and pride through growing vegetables, but for me it is an even richer experience to grow flowers for cutting. When you bring a vegetable into the house, you peel it, cook it, eat it and it has gone. Cut flowers, however, can be installed in pride of place all over the house and, as you go from room to room, you can walk through the beauty and scent of your harvest.

Of course, there is more to growing your own flowers than these rare and intense moments. The question of money comes into it. To fill the house with flowers from a florist's would be enormously expensive. That kind of cost simply doesn't need to apply if you produce your own. There obviously will be some expense, but you can be sure that it will be a fraction of what you would have spent at the florist's to get the same effect. And you can control that expense yourself: perhaps decide to grow just a few of the easy recommendations in a line or two in the vegetable patch to begin with, but then as the habit grips, as the pleasure becomes addictive, expand. One year when you know you have a wedding or party planned, or just decide you feel like having

more flowers in the house, you can try a few more. And then you will find yourself hooked!

Far more important, you can always tell garden-grown flowers from their commercially grown and shop-bought equivalents. The two are incomparable. It is like the difference between meeting someone in an office in a bland business suit and meeting that same person on holiday radiant with sun and *joie de vivre*. Commercial flowers are bred for their regularity and reliability, not for their relaxed, blowzy, open look, scent and character. A bunch of bought sweet peas may have straighter stems and a more uniform colour, but they won't fill your room with scent. An ebullient, heavily scented, double deep-magenta rose, like *R.* 'Nuits de Young' or *R.* 'Souvenir du Docteur Jamain' has no equivalent among its straight-stemmed cultivated cousins, whose heads stand with parade-ground precision in the wrap when you buy them and once released droop with just as boring a regularity.

Another wonderful thing about flowers that you have grown yourself is that you won't find yourself stuck inside the straitjacket that restricts many florists – a narrow selection of only the most reliable flowers, the stocks, the alstroemerias, the chrysanthemums and the carnations. These hard and buttony flowers last well and don't usually offend. They are, in fact, the lowest common denominator of cut flowers, the ones that the florist can rely on not to die before they are sold.

This whole problem with florists' flowers comes into focus over the question of scale. Most things you find in most florists' are smack in the middle of the mid-range, right only for the average-sized bunch. But one of the great things about your own cut flowers is the way they can swoop up and down the scale, from the boughs of whole trees dressing an entire room with their curving-over, leafy arches and the intense sappy smell of newly cut wood, through the flamboyance of a fountain of lilies or agapanthus, right down to the jewel-like, enamelled beauty of a single zinnia, or the simplicity of a few wood anemones floating in a bowl. Bunches are more fun if they are wildly over the top, more touching, somehow, if they are miniature. It is like a piano with a full keyboard. What florists can usually provide is no more than a single octave based firmly on Middle C. They won't commonly supply boughs of sweet chestnut or dramatic plants like acanthus, teasels and bulrushes, which are invaluable for a spectacular showpiece. Nor will they have the small and delicate plants which can be arranged simply on their own, like *Pulsatilla vulgaris*, a sprig of *Magnolia stellata*, or the autumn chocolate flower, *Cosmos atrosanguineus*. Only you can provide those for yourself.

You might well say that your garden already provides all of these things, and indeed pages 28–31 show how to integrate a cutting garden with growing herbs, fruit and salads in a family garden. So what need is there to have something called a cutting garden, or even a cutting patch? There is a great deal to be said for using your main garden as a source of flowers for the house, but if that is the path you decide to follow, you will inevitably make some compromises. You won't pick fritillaries because your patch of orchard grass would look denuded without them. Later in the year you will hold back from cutting those most regal of plants, tall irises, lilies, agapanthus and eremurus, because they look so grand and so stately where they are in the garden and to remove them would feel like wanton damage, an absurd piece of vandalism in your own back yard. So they stay where they are and all the pleasures from having these flowers in the house are lost. It is a double luxury to be able to have both.

With a cutting garden, or even a cutting patch, arranged in a way that allows you to see the flowers as a growing crop, that reluctance to pick will evaporate. What would have felt untouchable in the main part of the garden can be guiltlessly harvested here. Not to pick a flower, when that so obviously is what it has been grown for, even feels like wastage, allowing it, as Thomas Gray said, 'to blush unseen, And waste its sweetness on the desert air'.

A cutting garden is a place for picking, part of the garden that is in service to the house. More than that, a cutting garden provides a way of bringing together house and garden, of pulling inside and outside together. You can see the cutting garden as another of the house's rooms, where things are carefully prepared to make the house more beautiful. And you can see the produce of that room scattered on tables here and there, as the garden is brought inside. You are dissolving the walls of the house in this way, making for a flood of life and beauty that flows between inner and outer, domesticating the garden, naturalizing the home. A house filled with flowers seems to come alive. A flowery house will wear a smile on its face.

But there is something else here too: picking flowers makes you look at them. A picked flower is seen for longer and more closely than one that lives and dies in the flower bed. Partly this is because there is so much else going on in the garden that you don't look at flowers in isolation, but partly it is that out of context, maintained artificially, the actual details of these living things become apparent almost for the first time. You will stop, amazed at something like the huge yellow tulip called the 'Jewel of Spring', whose giant, thin but perfectly formed yellow petals are lined with the narrowest of red eye-liner touches along their outer rim, applied with a precision that any catwalk model would be proud of; or at the sheer bosomy richness of a peony; or at the dark snakeskin netting on the hanging head of a meadow fritillary. These things, glanced at or swept past in the garden, come into dazzlingly sharp focus if held and displayed in a vase on your desk. Cutting flowers provides a whole new, intense way of looking at them.

So this is what a cutting garden is for: bringing the undilutedly natural into the house, providing flowers that you can pick without censorship, flowers in abundance, flowers with all their foibles and their glories, flowers with the quirk of the real.

In harvesting flowers you have grown yourself you will be experiencing one of the closest relationships with the natural world that you can. I honestly don't know what life would be like if I didn't have a garden for cutting now. It has, in a way that still surprises me, become central to my life.

Planning and Stocking the Garden

Once you have been tempted to start growing your own flowers for cutting, you need to decide how much space you are going to devote to them, and this will depend above all on the size of your garden.

If you have a big garden with lots of underused space, the choice is wide open: you could opt for a small patch and cram it full of annuals (see pages 24–7), or you could go the whole hog and make a self-contained cutting garden (see pages 14–23). If, on the other hand, you are bursting at the seams and want to incorporate vegetables, children's swings and slides, a lawn and pretty herbaceous borders as well as flowers for cutting, the options are more limited: you could sacrifice one area to make a cutting patch, or you could integrate plants that are good for cutting into a mixed garden (see pages 28–31).

You will probably think next about your budget, but just as important is the question of time: the size of your cutting area must be geared to the amount of time that you are prepared to give. There is no point pretending that stocking and maintaining a garden can be done in a trice. From the moment that the days lengthen in spring, you will be mulching, pruning, sowing, dividing, weeding and watering. *Cultivating Plants: Tips for Success* (see pages 32–43) will help you get the most from your time and effort, but even a tiny cutting patch requires some commitment.

In late summer the cutting garden overflows with late-flowering annuals such as tobacco plants and cosmos, and tubers or perennials like dahlias, crocosmia, phlox, ornamental thistles and tall Verbena bonariensis. *I used to dislike the brassy orange of crocosmia, but now I enjoy using it in arrangements with deep claret dahlias and rudbeckias.*

Planning a Cutting Garden

Before you put pen to paper in designing a cutting patch or garden, you will need to work out its exact size and where to place it. These, with some other considerations such as adjacent structures and planting, will determine the form the garden takes, and what plants you can grow there.

Choosing a Site

Try to pick a prime site, in a sunny spot with good soil, because much will be demanded of this small area. Check that it does not have any fundamental problems, such as a frost pocket that will reduce your possible growing season, or a rain shadow from a nearby building that will increase the already considerable amount of watering that a cutting garden demands. You will need a convenient water source and, ideally, some form of irrigation system. Even something as basic as a leaky hose-pipe, laid along the beds and plumbed into a water butt, is a useful device.

Surveying the ground and drawing a plan

Once you have decided on your site, you should draw up a reasonably accurate plan to scale. You need to do a detailed survey of the plot, seeing how it relates to other areas of the garden, and to nearby structures. You should note on your drawing any noticeably dry or damp areas. Hedges and trees tend to suck up nutrients and water from a large surrounding area. Remember trees are the same size below ground as they are above it. Mark the shady areas, as well as those in full sun. Try to draw in the shadows thrown from surrounding buildings and shrubs and trees at different times of day. In an ideal world you would allow enough time to observe the plot through each season, taking rainfall measurements at different points in the garden, and observing how frost and prevailing winds affect existing planting. Most of us are too impatient for that, but it should be your aim. Finally, dig a good spade deep, to check your soil structure. Take a sample for pH testing. All these things will have a direct influence on what you plant and where.

Once you have incorporated this preliminary information on your ground plan, you can draw up your design for the beds and permanent structural planting, such as new hedges and trees, and hard structures such as paths and fences. Apart from matters of personal taste and finance, there are a few points worth noting.

Beds and paths

Straight lines and clean geometric shapes are easier to work with than curving ones, and they divide more naturally into smaller sections. You will need paths to give you easy access to all the beds. The paths should be of generous proportions, too, as this is high-intensity gardening and you need to be able to get a wheelbarrow to each area. For the same reason, it is best to avoid steps in the cutting garden or plot. Paths of brick, gravel or stone might initially seem an extravagance, but will prove a worthwhile investment in the long run, as grass requires far more maintenance.

Walls, hedges and fences

It is well worth using part of your budget to provide some form of windbreak. Plants will grow better and quicker in a sheltered site. In the long term consider building a wall, or the cheaper alternative of growing a hedge, to protect the whole area. As a temporary measure, hazel hurdles or closely spaced picket fencing are the most attractive alternatives. For areas of particularly high-density annuals you might consider fencing around the beds so that you will not have to worry endlessly about staking and support, both of which are time-consuming.

Choosing a Planting Scheme

Once you have made all the structural decisions, it is time to start planning the planting design. One of the most fundamental questions you must ask yourself is whether you want shrubs, perennials and annuals all mixed together, or whether you would prefer to concentrate on one of these groups? If your site and funds are limited, then consider stocking the whole patch with annuals. They require more work, but with minimal capital outlay. They will provide flowers in summer and autumn only, but you can always extend the picking season with spring bulbs. Remember, though, that if your plot is stocked mainly with annuals it is important to keep picking them, for they will stop flowering if the plants run to seed. So if you are someone who is away for a long spell every summer, then perennials and shrubs would be more suitable, as most continue to flower without deadheading or picking.

Another way to spread the cost of making a productive cutting garden is to invest the majority of your planting budget in shrubs during the first year or two, temporarily filling the area you have allocated to herbaceous plants with annuals. Then add perennial plants as you can afford them. It is always cheaper to grow them yourself from seed if you have the space to do so.

One of the great reasons for growing your own flowers is the range of possibilities it opens to you. My own favourites appear in *Flowers and Foliage through the Seasons*, see pages 94–163. But of course there is no reason for you to be limited by my preferences. If you see a flower that appeals to you, check its soil and sun requirements and if they suit your site, try it.

It is always worth keeping a note of the plants you particularly like and those you dislike whenever you see them in garden centres and other gardens. And if you are especially keen on particular groups of plants, such as those that are scented or those that will give you huge, statuesque arrangements, then note them as you find them. One of the chief joys of having a special cutting garden is that you can grow plants, such as flamboyant raspberry-ripple Parrot tulips, multicoloured cactus-headed zinnias and bright, zingy-coloured dahlias, that are fantastic in a vase but might be considered too gaudy for the general garden.

Plant lots of foliage plants as well as flowers. It is easy to forget the importance of beautiful foliage in completing an arrangement. As well as foliage plants, architectural plants should figure large in any list. They immediately make a group of flowers more dramatic. Acanthus, thistles, teasels, bulrushes, globe artichokes, and – in winter – dogwood stems and branches of catkins and pussy willow all add an extra dimension.

Before you make any final decisions about plants, you must make sure that the plants will survive in your garden. The type of soil, amount of sun, and temperature extremes will all have a bearing on your choice. It is no good expecting, for example, a silver-leaved, sun-loving, drought-tolerant artemisia to thrive in boggy shade. For the same reason, it is useful to list all your chosen plants in their site groups: those that do best in sun or in shade, in damp or dry conditions.

Armed with all this information, you can start to place the plants on the plan of your proposed cutting garden.

Balance of plants and colour

If you have decided to include a full range of colours in your garden, group the colours carefully to work well with each other. Concentrate the stronger colours in the foreground, with the whites and pale colours fading off into the distance. Don't try to have too many effects in one enclosed area. It is worth going on to draw out and roughly colour how this will look for every month of the year. You may find that at certain times there are some large gaps in the planting, or that there is a violent pink flower bang next to a scarlet one in the same month. Check your plan and concentrate on achieving a good balance between foliage and flowers at all times of year.

Go from the plan to the ground and back again, time and time again. If you fail to do this, it is all too easy to exaggerate or underestimate the actual scale of your garden and so be in danger of planting too much or too little.

Placing permanent planting

Except with the largest shrubs, always plant in groups. Aesthetically, this will give a more uniform and less dotted effect. Practically, if there are many flower heads, rather than just two or three, picking won't leave holes. Buy the larger herbaceous plants in threes, and the smaller ones in fives or sevens.

Aim to plant closer than you would in your normal garden. Particularly with shrubs, if you pick regularly and with attention to the shape and overall look of the plant, then you can use species which you may have considered too large for your garden, because the plants will always be well clipped. Even in a small patch you could think of including, for example, both a *Viburnum opulus* 'Roseum' and a smokebush. Look up heights and spreads as you plan what to plant, and simply space the plants slightly closer than their estimated span. Having said all this, a common mistake made by people new to gardening is to underestimate the ultimate size a plant will grow to in a few years. Another mistake is to plant a tall, vigorous plant next to a much smaller, more delicate one, which will be swamped and die in a year or two. So always check sizes and also try to group together those of a similar habit.

Note on nursery-bought plants

Don't be tempted to buy large pot-grown shrubs at enormous expense. You may believe that this will give you an instant garden, enabling you to start harvesting right away. In fact, mature plants tend to resent disturbance and may put on almost no new growth for a year or two. In this time a smaller and much cheaper plant may well have caught up in size. The same is true for herbaceous plants, too; a much more expensive 60cm/2ft plant is often less than a year older than a far smaller, cheaper one and may have just been potted on into a larger pot by the retailer for the new season. For a few months the larger plant will look more imposing, but again the younger one will soon catch up.

The Cutting Garden

If you decide to devote a part of your garden solely to cut flower production, you should ideally think about an area large enough to contain a mix of flowering trees, shrubs, climbers, perennials, annuals and bulbs. This will guarantee that there is something to pick all through the year. My own cutting garden, which is illustrated on the following pages, measures 12 × 24m/40 × 80ft.

The design

The rectangular plot is divided by brick paths into eight planting areas: four central beds and four L-shaped peripheral borders. It is contained by evergreen hedges on two sides, hazel hurdles on another, and, at the sunniest end, by a valuable heat-retaining wall that supports a variety of wall shrubs and climbers. The central beds are generously proportioned; you should allow just enough space between plants to enable you to squeeze through them to pick from the middle. Evergreen planting includes four yews clipped into cones at the crossing, and lavender hedges lining the central paths. The trees also contribute a sense of permanence and vertical structure. Flowering cherries, an apple and a crabapple produce blossom and decorative fruit, an amelanchier brings spring blossom as well as good autumn leaf colour, and a sorbus provides bright, silvery foliage.

The planting

The central beds are used for plants that change through the seasons. Bulbs are followed by annuals and biennials, which are simply planted between the lines of bulbs in hazy-edged blocks. A string line with permanent labels at each line end indicates where the invisible bulbs are when their leaves have died down, so that they are not constantly dug up.

The L-shaped beds contain more permanent plantings of shrubs, climbers and herbaceous perennials. These include winter-flowering shrubs underplanted with bulbs that flower in early spring, and a few evergreen plants to provide winter foliage.

Maintenance

Maintenance is minimized by adding a thick mulch of compost or well-rotted manure as soon as temperatures begin to rise in spring when annual weeds start to germinate (see also page 37). Mulching helps keep down the need for watering, but regular watering and feeding is crucial, with high demands being made on plants and soil. The borders are hoed regularly to keep them weed-free.

The Cutting Garden in Spring

Top and centre: These two Lily-flowered tulips, scarlet Tulipa 'Dyanito' (top), and yellow T. 'West Point' (centre), have the pointed curving petals that give them the typical silhouette characteristic of this group of tulips. Each one is tall, svelte and elegant, like the slimmest 1950s model. It is a shape that always adds flair and is very useful in breaking up a too-neat dome in any spring arrangement (see page 62).

Bottom: The Large-cupped Narcissus 'Professor Einstein' is a good one for arranging on its own or cutting down to mix with blue grape hyacinths.

Opposite: The cutting garden in spring in its first year. The central beds are filling up with colourful rows of tulips, daffodils and anemones, as well as yellow euphorbias, all ready for cutting.

At the centre of each panel, not yet in flower, are tall and stately bulbs such as lilies; they will later provide height. Lining the outer edges of the beds are wallflowers and forget-me-nots to mix with any of the bulbs.

In the shady bed against the back hedge, hellebores, pulmonarias and early-flowering primulas have been planted for winter and spring, while later in the season Solomon's seal and scillas will fill any patches around rose bushes and newly planted perennials.

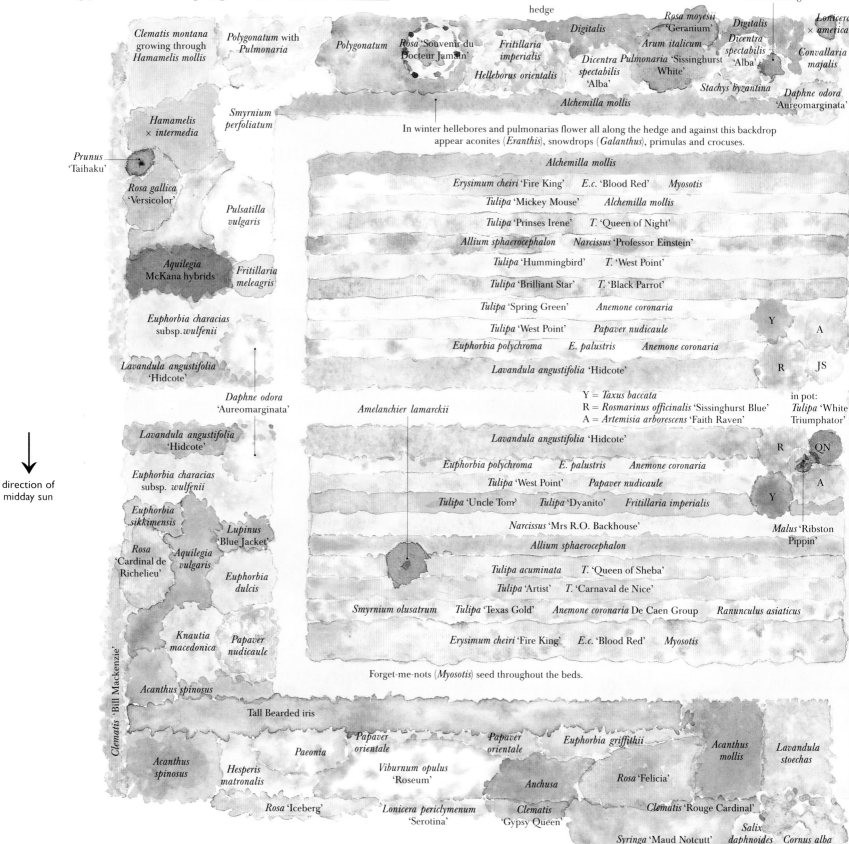

hedge

Rosa 'Iceberg'

Clematis montana growing through *Hamamelis mollis*

Polygonatum with *Pulmonaria*

Polygonatum

Rosa 'Souvenir du Docteur Jamain'

Fritillaria imperialis

Digitalis

Rosa moyesii 'Geranium'

Arum italicum

Digitalis

Dicentra spectabilis 'Alba'

Lonicera × *america*

Helleborus orientalis

Dicentra spectabilis 'Alba'

Pulmonaria 'Sissinghurst White'

Convallaria majalis

Stachys byzantina

Daphne odora 'Aureomarginata'

Alchemilla mollis

Hamamelis × *intermedia*

Smyrnium perfoliatum

In winter hellebores and pulmonarias flower all along the hedge and against this backdrop appear aconites (*Eranthis*), snowdrops (*Galanthus*), primulas and crocuses.

Prunus 'Taihaku'

Alchemilla mollis

Rosa gallica 'Versicolor'

Erysimum cheiri 'Fire King'   *E.c.* 'Blood Red'   *Myosotis*

Tulipa 'Mickey Mouse'   *Alchemilla mollis*

Pulsatilla vulgaris

Tulipa 'Prinses Irene'   *T.* 'Queen of Night'

Allium sphaerocephalon   *Narcissus* 'Professor Einstein'

Tulipa 'Hummingbird'   *T.* 'West Point'

Aquilegia McKana hybrids

Fritillaria meleagris

Tulipa 'Brilliant Star'   *T.* 'Black Parrot'

Tulipa 'Spring Green'   *Anemone coronaria*

Euphorbia characias subsp. *wulfenii*

Tulipa 'West Point'   *Papaver nudicaule*

Y

A

Euphorbia polychroma   *E. palustris*   *Anemone coronaria*

Lavandula angustifolia 'Hidcote'

Lavandula angustifolia 'Hidcote'

R   JS

Y = *Taxus baccata*
R = *Rosmarinus officinalis* 'Sissinghurst Blue'
A = *Artemisia arborescens* 'Faith Raven'

in pot:
Tulipa 'White Triumphator'

Daphne odora 'Aureomarginata'

Amelanchier lamarckii

Lavandula angustifolia 'Hidcote'

R   QN

Lavandula angustifolia 'Hidcote'

Euphorbia polychroma   *E. palustris*   *Anemone coronaria*

Euphorbia characias subsp. *wulfenii*

Tulipa 'West Point'   *Papaver nudicaule*

A

Euphorbia sikkimensis

Lupinus 'Blue Jacket'

Tulipa 'Uncle Tom'   *Tulipa* 'Dyanito'   *Fritillaria imperialis*

Y

Narcissus 'Mrs R.O. Backhouse'

Malus 'Ribston Pippin'

Rosa 'Cardinal de Richelieu'

Aquilegia vulgaris

Allium sphaerocephalon

direction of midday sun

Euphorbia dulcis

Tulipa acuminata   *T.* 'Queen of Sheba'

Tulipa 'Artist'   *T.* 'Carnaval de Nice'

Knautia macedonica

Papaver nudicaule

Smyrnium olusatrum   *Tulipa* 'Texas Gold'   *Anemone coronaria* De Caen Group   *Ranunculus asiaticus*

Erysimum cheiri 'Fire King'   *E.c.* 'Blood Red'   *Myosotis*

Acanthus spinosus

Forget-me-nots (*Myosotis*) seed throughout the beds.

Clematis 'Bill Mackenzie'

Tall Bearded iris

Acanthus spinosus

Hesperis matronalis

Paeonia

Papaver orientale

Viburnum opulus 'Roseum'

Papaver orientale

Euphorbia griffithii

Acanthus mollis

Lavandula stoechas

Anchusa

Rosa 'Felicia'

Rosa 'Iceberg'

Lonicera periclymenum 'Serotina'

Clematis 'Gypsy Queen'

Clematis 'Rouge Cardinal'

Syringa 'Maud Notcutt'

Salix daphnoides

Cornus alba 'Elegantissima'

Rosa 'Iceberg'

Cyclamen

Polygonatum

Muscari azureum 'Album'

Rosa glauca

Sarcococca hookeriana var. *humilis*

Rosa 'New Dawn'

Digitalis emerging

Viburnum tinus 'Eve Price'

Convallaria majalis

Polyanthus

Smyrnium perfoliatum
Arum italicum

Helleborus orientalis hybrids

Daphne odora 'Aureomarginata'

Alchemilla mollis

Euphorbia amygdaloides var. *robbiae*

hedge

In spring scillas, anemones and miniature narcissi form a carpet underplanting pruned roses and shrubs, with violets (*Viola*), cardamine, bluebells (*Hyacinthoides*), Gold-laced polyanthus, forget-me-nots and muscari.

Alchemilla mollis

Malus 'John Downie'

Erysimum cheiri 'Cloth of Gold'   *E.c.* 'White Dame'   *Myosotis*

Hyacinthus 'Ostara'

Narcissus poeticus   *N.* 'Trevithian'   *N.* 'Mrs R.O. Backhouse'   *Tulipa* 'Pimpernel'

Tulipa 'Gudoshnik'

Tulipa clusiana 'Cynthia'   *T.* 'Estella Rijnveld'

Viburnum × *bodnantense*

Myrrhis odorata

Tulipa 'Rococo'   *T.* 'Queen of Night'

Y

Tulipa 'Carnaval de Nice'   *T.* 'Flaming Parrot'

A

Tulipa 'Spring Green'   *T.* 'Pimpernel'

R

Euphorbia cyparissias   *E. polychroma*   *E. schillingii*   *E. seguieriana*   *Eryngium*

QN

Lavandula angustifolia 'Hidcote'

Euphorbia characias subsp. *wulfenii*

Lavandula angustifolia 'Hidcote'

JS = *Tulipa* 'Jewel of Spring'
QN = *Tulipa* 'Queen of Night'
OF = *Tulipa* 'Orange Favourite'

OF

R

Lavandula angustifolia 'Hidcote'

A

Euphorbia cyparissias   *E. polychroma*   *E. schillingii*   *E. seguieriana*   *Eryngium*

Tulipa 'Spring Green'   *T.* 'Hummingbird'

Y

Tulipa 'Mount Tacoma'   *Hyacinthus orientalis* 'L' Innocence'

Euphorbia characias subsp. *wulfenii*

Tulipa acuminata   *T.* 'Angélique'

Tulipa 'Orange Favourite'   *T.* 'Ballerina'

Tulipa 'Queen of Night'   *Narcissus poeticus*

Rosa 'Nuits de Young'

Tulipa turkestanica   *Narcissus* 'Thalia'   *N.* 'Canaliculatus'   *Muscari armeniacum*

Smyrnium olusatrum   *Anemone coronaria* (De Caen Group) 'The Bride'

Helleborus odorata foetidus

Myrrhis

Erysimum cheiri 'Fire King'   *E.c.* 'Blood Red'   *Myosotis*

Leucojum aestivum

Elaeagnus angustifolia

Prunus avium

Sorbus aria 'Lutescens'

hedge

Tall Bearded iris

Lavandula stoechas

Acanthus mollis

Hesperis matronalis

Rosa 'Felicia'

Philadelphus 'Belle Etoile'

Lonicera × *purpusii*

Euphorbia griffithii

Ceanothus

Rosa banksiae var. *banksiae*

Cornus alba 'Elegantissima'

Salix daphnoides

Syringa 'Maud Notcutt'

Planting for Summer and Autumn

Clematis 'Royal Velours' growing through Hamamelis mollis

Delphinium Black Knight Group

Dahlia 'Edinburgh' (LS)

Rosa 'Souvenir du Docteur Jamain'

Anemone × hybrida 'Honorine Joubert' (LS)

Campanula pyramidalis

Rosa 'Iceberg'

Lonicera × america

Digitalis purpurea f. albiflora

Rosa moyesii 'Geranium'

Dahlia 'Mount Noddy' (LS)

Helleborus orientalis

Pulmonaria

Stachys byzantina

Daphne odora 'Aureomarginata'

Hamamelis × intermedia

Crocosmia 'Lucifer' (LS)

Alchemilla mollis

Helleborus argutifolius

Allium cernuum around Prunus 'Taihaku'

Rosa gallica 'Versicolor'

Echinacea purpurea

Papaver rhoeas

Alchemilla mollis

Clematis × durandii

Allium sphaerocephalon

Helianthus annuus 'Velvet Queen'

Centaurea cyanus 'Black Ball'

Eustoma grandiflorum

Nicotiana 'Lime Green'

Cosmos bipinnatus 'Versailles Carmine'

Anethum graveolens

Phlox paniculata 'White Admiral'

Nicotiana 'Lime Green'

Allium varieties

Helianthus annuus 'Velvet Queen'

Amaranthus caudatus (LS)

Allium sphaerocephalon

Bupleurum griffithii 'Dixter'

Rudbeckia

Echium vulgare

Gladiolus commun subsp. byzantinus

Euphorbia characias subsp. wulfenii

Cosmos bipinnatus 'Versailles Carmine'

Moluccella laevis 'Long Spike'

Helianthus annuus 'Valentine'

Tithonia rotundifolia 'Torch' (LS)

Y

A

Verbena bonariensis (LS)

Papaver nudicaule

Euphorbia seguieriana

E. schillingii

Eryngium giganteum

E. × tripartitum

Eryngium alpinum 'Amethyst'

R

Lavandula angustifolia 'Hidcote'

Lavandula angustifolia 'Hidcote'

C

direction of midday sun

Daphne odora 'Aureomarginata'

C = Crinum × powellii
Y = Taxus baccata

in po
Liliu
'Cas
Blanc

Lavandula angustifolia 'Hidcote'

Lavandula angustifolia 'Hidcote'

Malus 'Ribston Pippin'

R

Euphorbia characias subsp. wulfenii

Papaver nudicaule

Euphorbia seguieriana

E. schillingii

Eryngium giganteum

E. × tripartitum

C

E. alpinum 'Amethyst'

A

Euphorbia seguieriana

Verbena bonariensis (LS)

Consolida (Exquisite Series) 'Blue Spire'

Centaurea cyanus 'Black Ball'

Helianthus annuus 'Italian White'

Cosmos bipinnatus 'Purity'

Lupinus

Rudbeckia 'Nutmeg' (LS)

Tithonia rotundifolia 'Torch' (LS)

Allium giganteum

Y

Rosa 'Cardinal de Richelieu'

Salvia × superba S. uliginosa (LS)

Papaver nudicaule 'Matador'

Dianthus barbatus Nigrescens Group

Moluccella laevis

Ammi majus

Nicotiana 'Lime Green'

Amelanchier lamarckii

Allium sphaerocephalum

Matthiola incana 'White Perennial'

Knautia macedonica

Lychnis × arkwrightii 'Vesuvius'

Cosmos bipinnatus 'Purity'

Centaurea cyanus 'Black Ball'

Calendula Art Shades Group

Zinnia Cactus Group (LS)

Antirrhinum majus 'Black Prince'

Gladiolus communis subsp. byzantinus

Physalis alkekengi (LS)

Clematis 'Bill Mackenzie'

Acanthus spinosus

Papaver orientale 'Ladybird'

Anethum graveolens

Bupleurum falcatum

Eryngium × zabelii 'Violetta'

Tall Bearded iris

KEY
LS = plants flowering in late summer

Acanthus spinosus

Alcea rosea 'Nigra'

Paeonia lactiflora

Viburnum opulus 'Roseum'

Euphorbia griffithii

Anchusa azurea 'Royal Blue'

A. capensis

Acanthus spinosus

Lavandula stoechas

Rosa 'Felicia'

Rosa 'Iceberg'

Lonicera periclymenum 'Serotina'

Clematis 'Gypsy Queen'

Clematis 'Rouge Cardinal'

Syringa 'Maud Notcutt'

Salix daphnoides

Cornus alba 'Elegantissima'

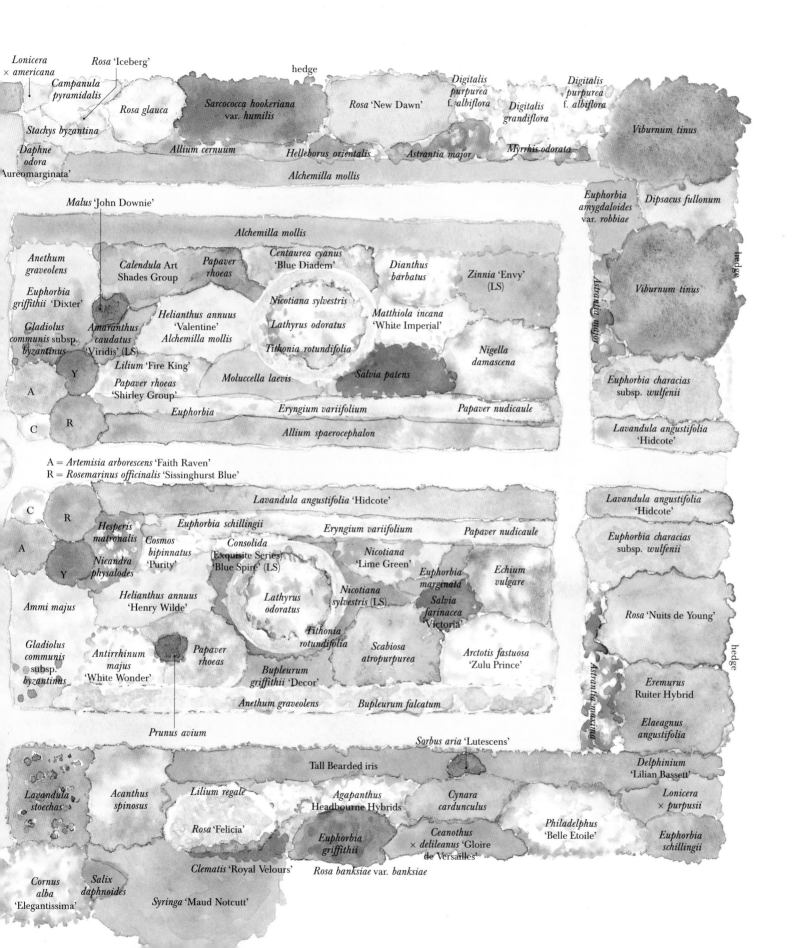

Lonicera
× americana

Rosa 'Iceberg'

Campanula
pyramidalis

hedge

Rosa glauca

Sarcococca hookeriana
var. humilis

Rosa 'New Dawn'

Digitalis
purpurea
f. albiflora

Digitalis
purpurea
f. albiflora

Digitalis
grandiflora

Viburnum tinus

Stachys byzantina

Daphne
odora
'Aureomarginata'

Allium cernuum

Helleborus orientalis

Astrantia major

Myrrhis odorata

Alchemilla mollis

Euphorbia
amygdaloides
var. robbiae

Dipsacus fullonum

Malus 'John Downie'

Alchemilla mollis

Anethum
graveolens

Calendula Art
Shades Group

Papaver
rhoeas

Centaurea cyanus
'Blue Diadem'

Dianthus
barbatus

Zinnia 'Envy'
(LS)

Viburnum tinus

Euphorbia
griffithii 'Dixter'

Nicotiana sylvestris

Matthiola incana
'White Imperial'

Gladiolus
communis subsp.
byzantinus

Amaranthus
caudatus
'Viridis' (LS)

Helianthus annuus
'Valentine'
Alchemilla mollis

Lathyrus odoratus

Tithonia rotundifolia

Nigella
damascena

Lilium 'Fire King'

Euphorbia characias
subsp. wulfenii

Y

Papaver rhoeas
'Shirley Group'

Moluccella laevis

Salvia patens

A

Euphorbia

Eryngium variifolium

Papaver nudicaule

C

R

Allium spaerocephalon

Lavandula angustifolia
'Hidcote'

A = Artemisia arborescens 'Faith Raven'
R = Rosemarinus officinalis 'Sissinghurst Blue'

C

R

Lavandula angustifolia 'Hidcote'

Lavandula angustifolia
'Hidcote'

A

Hesperis
matronalis

Euphorbia schillingii

Eryngium variifolium

Papaver nudicaule

Euphorbia characias
subsp. wulfenii

Cosmos
bipinnatus
'Purity'

Consolida
(Exquisite Series)
'Blue Spire' (LS)

Nicotiana
'Lime Green'

Euphorbia
marginata

Echium
vulgare

Y

Nicandra
physalodes

Nicotiana
sylvestris (LS)

Salvia
farinacea
'Victoria'

Rosa 'Nuits de Young'

Ammi majus

Helianthus annuus
'Henry Wilde'

Lathyrus
odoratus

Gladiolus
communis
subsp.
byzantinus

Antirrhinum
majus
'White Wonder'

Papaver
rhoeas

Tithonia
rotundifolia

Scabiosa
atropurpurea

Arctotis fastuosa
'Zulu Prince'

Eremurus
Ruiter Hybrid

Bupleurum
griffithii 'Decor'

Elaeagnus
angustifolia

Prunus avium

Anethum graveolens

Bupleurum falcatum

Sorbus aria 'Lutescens'

Tall Bearded iris

Delphinium
'Lilian Bassett'

Lavandula
stoechas

Acanthus
spinosus

Lilium regale

Agapanthus
Headbourne Hybrids

Cynara
cardunculus

Lonicera
× purpusii

Rosa 'Felicia'

Euphorbia
griffithii

Ceanothus
× delileanus 'Gloire
de Versailles'

Philadelphus
'Belle Etoile'

Euphorbia
schillingii

Cornus
alba
'Elegantissima'

Salix
daphnoides

Clematis 'Royal Velours'

Rosa banksiae var. banksiae

Syringa 'Maud Notcutt'

Astrantia major

Astrantia maxima

hedge

The Cutting Garden in Summer

A view of the cutting garden showing the planting plan on the previous two pages. In high summer the garden is a mass of flower colour. Banks of herbaceous perennials provide a sumptous summer harvest, supplemented by the centre beds that are now brimming over with annuals. A wealth of foliage – shrubs, perennials and annuals – provides greenery to play a supporting role to the flowers.

Structural foliage

Large shrubs planted for architectural and background foliage during the summer months include the silver-leaved *Elaeagnus angustifolia* and *Sorbus aria* 'Lutescens', the white-and-green-dappled leaves of *Cornus alba* 'Elegantissima' with its striking red branches, and the spiky silver leaves of the artichoke, *Cynara cardunculus*.

Foliage fillers and flowers

The sunny bed in the near fore-ground has a grey-green pompon viburnum tree (*V. opulus* 'Roseum'), that provides glamorous and filling early-summer foliage. Near it are spikes of acanthus (*A. spinosus*). Across the garden, the shadier L-shaped bed has a border of alchemilla (*A. mollis*), while stachys (*S. byzantina*) spreads on either side of the arbour seat.

All over the garden the euphorbias provide a brilliant succession of yellow and green and, in the case of *E. griffithii*, red, for mixing with greens, other orange-reds and blacks. Among the eryngiums are the steely silver Miss Willmott's ghost (*E. giganteum*) and the rich indigo-blue *E. × zabelii* 'Violetta'.

As the season progresses, the annual bells of Ireland (*Moluccella laevis*), dill (*Anethum graveolens*) and a late sowing of bupleurum (*B. griffithii*) supply armfuls of pretty and useful apple-green foliage well into autumn.

direction of midday sun

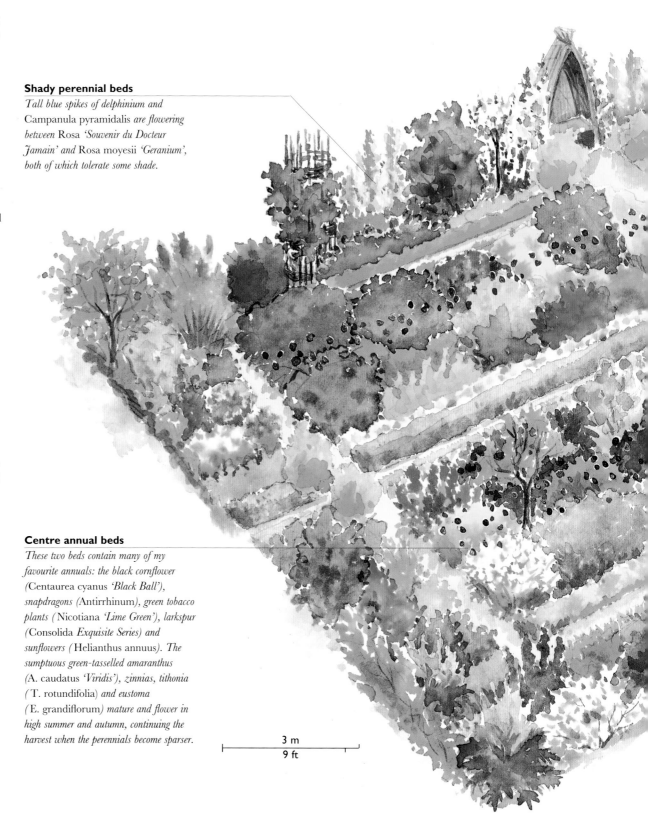

Shady perennial beds

Tall blue spikes of delphinium and Campanula pyramidalis *are flowering between* Rosa *'Souvenir du Docteur Jamain' and* Rosa moyesii *'Geranium', both of which tolerate some shade.*

Centre annual beds

*These two beds contain many of my favourite annuals: the black cornflower (*Centaurea cyanus *'Black Ball'), snapdragons (*Antirrhinum*), green tobacco plants (* Nicotiana *'Lime Green'), larkspur (*Consolida *Exquisite Series) and sunflowers (*Helianthus annuus*). The sumptuous green-tasselled amaranthus (*A. caudatus *'Viridis'), zinnias, tithonia (* T. rotundifolia*) and eustoma (* E. grandiflorum*) mature and flower in high summer and autumn, continuing the harvest when the perennials become sparser.*

3 m
9 ft

Shrub and perennial L-shaped beds
*This end of the garden is planted with subdued greens and quiet silver-greens, a visual device to make the garden appear longer and recede off into the distance. Two large viburnums (*V. tinus*) provide a backdrop to lavender, euphorbias and astrantia.*

Centre annual beds
*In both beds the sweet peas on their tall wigwams go on flowering for many weeks. When the flowers are over, the wigwam is removed and giant tobacco plants (*Nicotiana sylvestris*), mixed with a planting of the tall daisy-like tithonia (*T. rotundifolia*), grow to fill the space and provide dramatic height for the autumn months. Other annuals here are deep blue salvias (*S. patens*), love-in-a-mist (*N. damascena*) and cornflowers (*Centaurea cyanus 'Blue Diadem'*), while poppies (*Papaver rhoeas and *P. nudicaule*) add splashes of red, pink and white.*

Centre
*A fabulous display of 'Casa Blanca' lilies is surrounded by pots of entrancing crinum lilies (*Crinum × powellii*), rosemary (*R. officinalis 'Sissinghurst Blue'*), yew cones and artemisias (*A. aborescens 'Faith Raven'*).*

Sunny perennial beds
*In early summer, Bearded irises and *Viburnum opulus 'Roseum' *pompons provide plenty to pick here, followed by roses (*R. 'Felicia' and *R. 'Iceberg'*), peonies (*Paeonia lactiflora*), ornamental thistles (*Cynara cardunculus*), acanthus (*A. spinosus*), hollyhocks (*Alcea rosea 'Nigra'*) and euphorbias (*E griffithii*) to harvest until the centre beds are in full flower.*

The Cutting Garden in Early Autumn

Left: Though the season is late there are still plenty of flowers to be picked. Orange Lilium 'Fire King' and Allium sphaero-cephalon with its great purple heads go on flowering. Beyond a scattering of white cosmos (C. bipinnatus 'Purity'), late-sown sweet peas (Lathyrus odoratus) still give colour on their hazel wigwam. The tall, rich autumnal-red Tithonia rotundifolia 'Torch' is at its peak.

Above: The sumptuous, velvety rudbeckias and amaranthus, either red-tasselled as shown here or with tassels of green, are a bonus to harvest through the autumn in the cutting garden. The rudbeckia lasts only three or four days in water, but it is such a floriferous annual that you can keep on picking more to replace spent stems.

The Cutting Garden in Winter

*Far left: Dewy snowdrops (*Galanthus*).*
*Left: Frosted aconites (*Eranthis hyemalis*).*

Below: In winter the garden's structure is most clearly seen. Bright blue posts marking rows of bulbs give colour interest when little is in flower. In the outer perennial and shrub borders, aconites and snowdrops appear first.

The Cutting Patch

This small area, 3 × 4.5m/10 × 15ft, stands in a sunny part of the garden. It is stocked with annuals and one or two biennials like the Iceland poppy. The colours and textures of the plants will guarantee a balanced arrangement from almost any combination.

The design

The plan is straightforward: a series of rectangles with a central diamond-shaped bed and a sweet-pea wigwam as the focal point. Woven hurdles, 45cm/18in high, surround the beds and contain and support the plants. Alternatively, the beds could be edged with low wooden picket fences. All parts of the beds are easily reached either from the central paths or from outside.

The plants

As long as they are cut or picked regularly, the plants will provide a continuous supply of foliage and flowers from late spring until the first frosts. They are easily grown from seed, but for those who prefer to buy in plants, most of them are available as seedlings from nurseries and garden centres. All are planted 20-25cm/8-10in apart. Cornflowers and scabious do not transplant well and are sown directly into the ground, and the seedlings thinned.

Preparation and maintenance

Prepare the area in autumn. Seedlings should be planted out as soon as it is safe to do so in spring after the very last frost. Dense planting in blocks gives a lovely mosaic appearance and helps keep the weeds under control. When the plants are still small, fill gaps with a mulch of mushroom compost or well-rotted manure to inhibit weed seedlings and retain moisture. Feed and water regularly. Keep cutting, to stop the plants running to seed.

Extending the picking season

After clearing the cutting patch in autumn, plant it with bulbs for harvesting from early spring through to the beginning of summer, when the annuals take over. Choose hyacinths, scillas, tulips and narcissi from *Spring* and *Winter* in *Flowers and Foliage through the Seasons* (see pages 96–113 and 148–159) and, after picking, lift the bulbs. Also, make effective use of the ground by doubling up the planting of the patch. For example, replace the early flowerers like sweet Williams, which tend to be over by midsummer, with a selection of pot-reared dahlias and penstemons. These will give you rich-coloured flowers right through to the first frosts.

bupleurum and **bells of Ireland** (*B. griffithii* and *Moluccella laevis*)
Plant alternating blocks of bupleurum and bells of Ireland seedlings. These two plants provide essential lime-green foliage to contrast perfectly with brightly coloured flowers or bunches of whites, pinks and blues.

cosmos and **snapdragons**
(*C. bipinnatus* 'Purity' and *Antirrhinum majus* 'White Wonder')
Plant a mixture of cosmos and snapdragon seedlings. This cosmos grows to 90cm-1.2m/3-4ft, an impressive sight in both garden and vase: white flowers are always pretty on their own or useful in mixed colour arrangements.

bishop's flower (*Ammi majus*)
Plant seedlings in rows 25cm/10in apart. Sown as an annual in spring this is a beautiful plant with its filigree flower heads, but if you sow the seed in the autumn you will get bumper-sized plants reaching 90cm-1.2m/3-4ft. The flowers will be over by midsummer, when they can be replaced by a planting of zinnias for autumn picking.

annual scabious
(*Scabiosa atropurpurea*)
Sow seed in rows 25cm/10in apart where they are to flower, and thin them to 20-25cm/8-10in apart. These pink, mauve, deep red, blue and white pompons are good mixed together. Alternatively, separate the colours and combine them with other flowers from the patch. The paler shades mixed with love-in-a-mist, sweet peas, bupleurum and bishop's flower make a fresh-looking bunch.

sweet Williams and **tobacco plants**
(*Dianthus barbatus* and *Nicotiana* 'Lime Green')
Transplant sweet William seedlings in early spring, placing them 20cm/8in apart in a zigzag. After the last frosts fill in around the lines with tobacco plants. These will flower until late autumn, but the sweet Williams can be replaced with Dahlia 'Mount Noddy' or 'Arabian Night' and Penstemon 'Blackbird'.

cosmos and **dill** (*C. bipinnatus* 'Versailles Carmine' and *Anethum graveolens*)
Plant cosmos seedlings 25cm/10in apart in a zigzag or wavy line. Fill in each triangle with plants of dill 20cm/8in apart or grow them here direct from seed and then thin. With strong stems, feathery foliage and vivid lime-green umbels, dill is a good foil to deep carmine-pink cosmos. The cosmos will flower for many months but you may want a repeat-sowing of dill. Fennel (Foeniculum vulgare) is an alternative to dill, but do not grow both as the two can cross-fertilize.

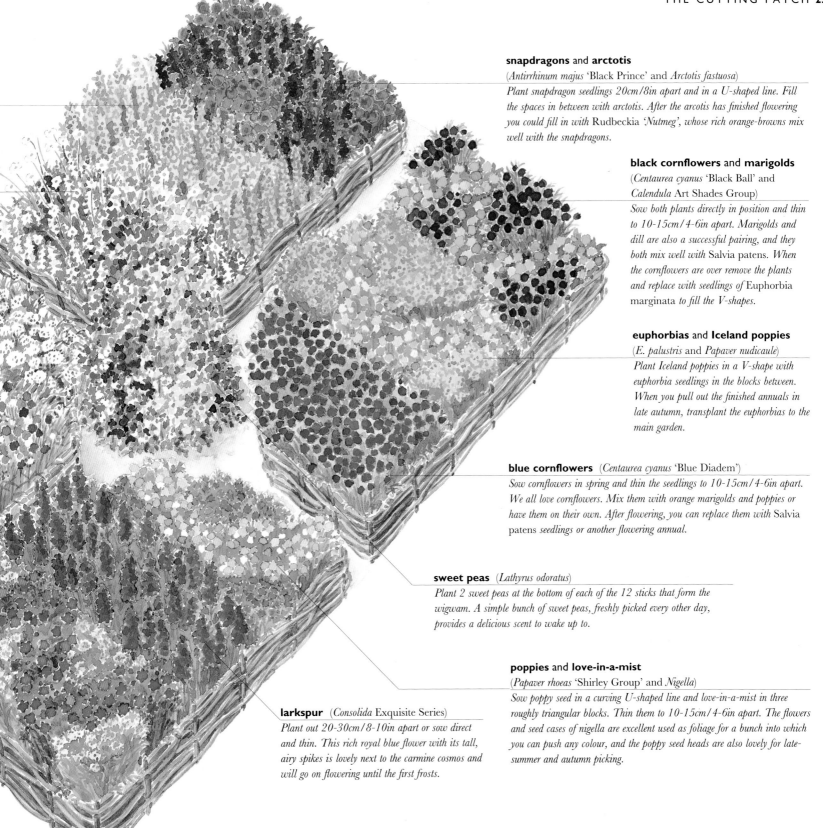

snapdragons and **arctotis**
(*Antirrhinum majus* 'Black Prince' and *Arctotis fastuosa*)
Plant snapdragon seedlings 20cm/8in apart and in a U-shaped line. Fill the spaces in between with arctotis. After the arcotis has finished flowering you could fill in with Rudbeckia *'Nutmeg', whose rich orange-browns mix well with the snapdragons.*

black cornflowers and **marigolds**
(*Centaurea cyanus* 'Black Ball' and
Calendula Art Shades Group)
Sow both plants directly in position and thin to 10-15cm/4-6in apart. Marigolds and dill are also a successful pairing, and they both mix well with Salvia patens. *When the cornflowers are over remove the plants and replace with seedlings of* Euphorbia marginata *to fill the V-shapes.*

euphorbias and **Iceland poppies**
(*E. palustris* and *Papaver nudicaule*)
Plant Iceland poppies in a V-shape with euphorbia seedlings in the blocks between. When you pull out the finished annuals in late autumn, transplant the euphorbias to the main garden.

blue cornflowers (*Centaurea cyanus* 'Blue Diadem')
Sow cornflowers in spring and thin the seedlings to 10-15cm/4-6in apart. We all love cornflowers. Mix them with orange marigolds and poppies or have them on their own. After flowering, you can replace them with Salvia patens *seedlings or another flowering annual.*

sweet peas (*Lathyrus odoratus*)
Plant 2 sweet peas at the bottom of each of the 12 sticks that form the wigwam. A simple bunch of sweet peas, freshly picked every other day, provides a delicious scent to wake up to.

poppies and **love-in-a-mist**
(*Papaver rhoeas* 'Shirley Group' and *Nigella*)
Sow poppy seed in a curving U-shaped line and love-in-a-mist in three roughly triangular blocks. Thin them to 10-15cm/4-6in apart. The flowers and seed cases of nigella are excellent used as foliage for a bunch into which you can push any colour, and the poppy seed heads are also lovely for late-summer and autumn picking.

larkspur (*Consolida* Exquisite Series)
Plant out 20-30cm/8-10in apart or sow direct and thin. This rich royal blue flower with its tall, airy spikes is lovely next to the carmine cosmos and will go on flowering until the first frosts.

The Cutting Patch in Summer

Left: A rich, intense arrangement can be made from Nicotiana *'Lime Green', the deep blue larkspur,* Consolida *(Exquisite Series) 'Blue Spire', and sumptuous* Cosmos bipinnatus *'Versailles Carmine'. This cosmos — one of my favourite plants for cutting — is perfect for the cutting patch as it earns its keep many times over, flowering from late spring until the end of autumn. Mix it too with green dill, both in the cutting patch and in the vase.*

*Opposite, top: When you plant an annual cutting patch, think of arranging the colours as you might in a bunch of flowers. Here, sweet peas, cornflowers and poppies make good partners to pincushion flower (*Scabiosa atropurpurea*), while the black cornflower* Centaurea cyanus *'Black Ball' provides a brilliant contrast to marigolds (*Calendula Art Shades Group*).*

*Opposite, bottom: Nearby, rich crimson snapdragons (*Antirrhinum majus *'Black Prince') are interplanted with burnt-orange* Arctotis fastuosa *(which is nearly over).* Antirrhinum majus *'White Wonder' mixes with anything, in the garden or in an arrangement, and bupleurum,* Euphorbia palustris, *bells of Ireland (*Moluccella laevis*) and globe artichokes (*Cynara cardunculus Scolymus Group*) provide interesting foliage.*

The Mixed Garden

If you have no separate area to devote to cut flowers, think of making some space in different parts of your garden so that you can grow a range of plants for cutting. The least you will need are several spots in full sun, a few in shadier positions, an area for climbers and somewhere to grow tall and small plants. If you are starting from scratch with an average-sized rectangular urban or small suburban garden that is always in view from the house, here is a scheme that is both productive and decorative for much of the year. This garden, measuring 9 × 12m/30 × 40ft, has a brick-paved terrace leading to french windows and the kitchen door. To maximize use, the planting scheme focuses on salads, herbs and a few vegetables, as well as flowers and foliage for the house.

The design

This layout can be adapted to a range of needs. For example, if you wanted to include grass, the central bed could be made into a small lawn. The brick paths are wide enough to allow a wheel-barrow or children's tricycles to pass, and the beds and borders allow easy picking of the plants. The mass of plants is given order and coherence by the low clipped box hedges, the rounded box balls and pairs of mophead bay in pots that punctuate the design.

The plants through the year

Although the garden is seen here in high summer, there are lots of spring flowers planted among the shrub and perennial borders: hyacinths, tulips and anemones grouped in panels down the path, with biennial forget-me-nots and wallflowers, scillas and miniature narcissi under the old apple tree; crown imperials and Solomon's seal combine in the shady border.

The summer annuals – including marigolds, violas, snapdragons and nigella – can be mixed with euphorbias, bupleurum, bells of Ireland and dill for your foliage. There are deep crimson scented roses and pink 'New Dawn' and white 'Iceberg', which will flower until the severe frosts. Among the perennials are lupins, anchusas, peonies and echinops, and white and spotted foxgloves are massed beside the hedge. As long as you pick them, many of the annuals, such as tithonia and sunflowers, will flower through the autumn.

The summer vegetables are selected for dwarf or ornamental characteristics that integrate well with the flowers. As well as miniature broad beans, there are green and crimson lettuces, rocket, aubergines, tomatoes, beans climbing with the sweet peas, and nasturtiums and viola flowers for adding to salads.

Shrub and perennial beds

Scrambling all along the hazel hurdle fence are clematis including the rich-coloured 'Etoile Violette' and 'Royal Velours'. Other climbers include the purple-flowered Akebia quinata, *as backdrop to a group of deep crimson* Rosa 'Tuscany Superb' *while* Lonicera × brownii *and* Solanum crispum 'Glasnevin' *are behind a ceanothus close to the terrace. The highly scented honeysuckle* Lonicera periclymenum 'Serotina' *climbs through* Salix daphnoides *in the corner farthest from the house.*

The sunny terrace beds

The beautiful deep purple-blue flowers of the agapanthus growing all along this bed will later produce elegant seed heads. Deep purple-black aubergines are grown along the low wall and there is a splash of red from cherry tomatoes. The blue-purple colour theme continues into autumn with alliums and various salvias, and in winter with Iris reticulata *and* I. unguicularis. *Green and crimson lettuces flank a large clump of alchemilla along the path, with the alchemilla repeated on both sides of the foreground steps. The small bed here has soft pink* Rosa 'New Dawn' *growing with tall* Allium sphaerocephalon.

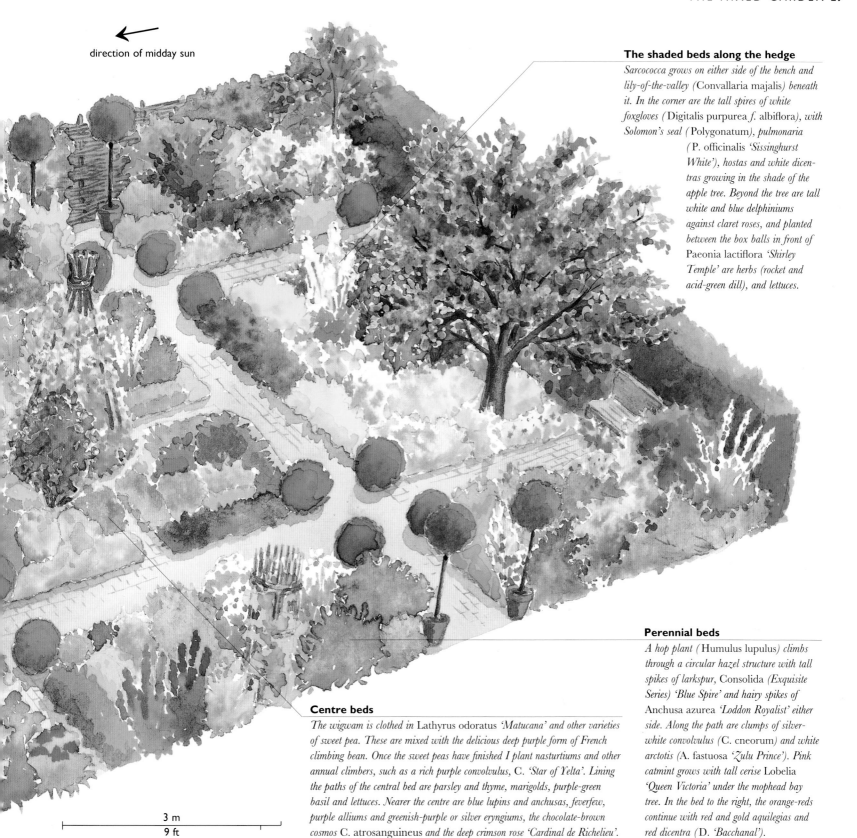

direction of midday sun

The shaded beds along the hedge

*Sarcococca grows on either side of the bench and lily-of-the-valley (*Convallaria majalis*) beneath it. In the corner are the tall spires of white foxgloves (*Digitalis purpurea f. albiflora*), with Solomon's seal (*Polygonatum*), pulmonaria (*P. officinalis 'Sissinghurst White'*), hostas and white dicentras growing in the shade of the apple tree. Beyond the tree are tall white and blue delphiniums against claret roses, and planted between the box balls in front of Paeonia lactiflora 'Shirley Temple' are herbs (rocket and acid-green dill), and lettuces.*

Centre beds

The wigwam is clothed in Lathyrus odoratus *'Matucana' and other varieties of sweet pea. These are mixed with the delicious deep purple form of French climbing bean. Once the sweet peas have finished I plant nasturtiums and other annual climbers, such as a rich purple convolvulus, C. 'Star of Yelta'. Lining the paths of the central bed are parsley and thyme, marigolds, purple-green basil and lettuces. Nearer the centre are blue lupins and anchusas, feverfew, purple alliums and greenish-purple or silver eryngiums, the chocolate-brown cosmos C.* atrosanguineus *and the deep crimson rose 'Cardinal de Richelieu'.*

Perennial beds

*A hop plant (*Humulus lupulus*) climbs through a circular hazel structure with tall spikes of larkspur,* Consolida *(Exquisite Series) 'Blue Spire' and hairy spikes of* Anchusa azurea *'Loddon Royalist' either side. Along the path are clumps of silver-white convolvulus (C. cneorum) and white arctotis (A.* fastuosa *'Zulu Prince'). Pink catmint grows with tall cerise* Lobelia *'Queen Victoria' under the mophead bay tree. In the bed to the right, the orange-reds continue with red and gold aquilegias and red dicentra (D. 'Bacchanal').*

3 m

9 ft

The Mixed Garden in Summer

Far left: The resonant blue Delphinium *Black Knight Group flowers from mid-summer on into autumn. Pick the main stem and the laterals will then develop and flower.*

Left: Annuals good for cutting, like these sunflowers, are sown in any gaps between the perennials and herbs.

Left: Broad clumps of Convolvulus *cneorum with catmint just behind are echoed in the shape of the corner box ball. All around are flowers that are excellent for picking over long flowering seasons:* Arctotis fastuosa *'Zulu Prince',* Antirrhinum majus *'Black Prince' and bronze-claret violas with yellow-dot centres.*

Opposite: This garden integrates vegetables and salad herbs with flowers and foliage for cutting, mixing them throughout the beds. The rectangular beds, the central sweet-pea wigwam, the hazel frames along the boundary fence and pairs of standard bay trees give this productive jungle some order and formality. I do not weed out my bolted oak-leaf lettuces as I love their curvy-leaved acid-green spikes – they make most unusual garden foliage. The foreground pots contain crimson tobacco plants and pink ivy-leaved pelargoniums, with a red-flowered abutilon in the large pot to the right.*

Cultivating Plants: Tips for Success

Stocking and maintaining a cutting garden that is both productive and beautiful involves a little work a lot of the time, with jobs best done for an hour here and there on a regular basis, rather than an occasional manic splurge for a weekend every few months. Try to gear the size of your garden to the amount of time you have to give it. There is nothing more depressing than beds and borders that were full of plants and promise in the spring looking like a wasteland or weed jungle by summer because you did not have the time to do regular watering or weeding. I know, because I've done it.

Growing your own plants from seed or cuttings or from rootstock division is time-consuming, but opens up huge possibilities barred to those who only garden out of a nursery or garden centre. If you grow your own, adding to what you already have from the vast and tantalizing choice of plants in the seed catalogues, it will cost a fraction of the price of nursery plants. You will also get involved in one of the most rewarding of pastimes, and inevitably you will grow plants surplus to your needs, which you can present to your friends.

If you can, buy a propagator, which, in addition to any spare sunny windowsills, will allow you plenty of space for growing seed and cuttings under cover. Better still, invest in a greenhouse and install a propagator bench with heated cables.

Spring

This is the busiest time of year in the cutting garden. On a crisp, clear day you will be out there mulching, pruning and tidying. When it rains or it is freezing cold, you can take refuge in the potting shed or greenhouse and get on with sowing, pricking out and potting on.

As the season continues, picking in earnest will start. It is not compulsory to pick the spring flowers. Unlike the summer annuals, the spring bulbs and herbaceous perennials will be perfectly happy if you leave them where they are. You can either pick to your heart's content or leave your prize blooms to flourish in the garden.

General tips for sowing seed

• Sort your seeds into groups according to whether they are for sowing under cover or direct sowing into the ground, the month of sowing, the temperature needed for germination and any special requirements.

• Always follow directions on the seed packet – for example, some seeds, like lupins and sweet peas, have a hard protective coat and germinate more quickly if they are soaked overnight before sowing. And sow at the recommended time. Overtaken by beginner's enthusiasm the first year I started sowing seed, I began in the depths of winter, and my seeds under cover produced pale leggy plants that never did well, while in open ground many simply rotted before they could germinate. With a few exceptions (see page 43), it is worth waiting for the days to lengthen so the seedlings have more light hours in which to grow.

• Mark all seeds as you sow them with a permanent label giving the name of the plant and the date it was sown.

• Use the finest spray or rose on your hose or watering can to water seeds in. Large drips or dribbles will dislodge soil and seeds, clumping them together or exposing them to the air.

• Don't always sow the whole packet. Just sow what you want for that year and store the rest for next. The germination rate may be slightly lower but will almost certainly be adequate. Fold the inner packet, label it clearly and store in a cool, dry place.

• Remove slugs, snails and caterpillars using pellets, or by hand if you dislike using insecticide. They can munch through your whole crop in a matter of days.

Sowing seeds under cover

• Develop a routine for watering, heating, pricking out and potting on, making it as easy as possible, so that it is all done with regularity. For example, if you have a greenhouse, keep a hosepipe with the finest spray attachment sitting right by the bench.

• Good-quality plastic seed trays are easier to clean than wood and will not twist and snap if you pick them up at one end when they are full of compost. Wash them well at the end of the season and store them in the dark for next year. They soon become brittle if left out in the sun or light.

• For sowing and potting on, use the best seed compost – a good mix of loam, peat, sand and a slow-release fertilizer. You do not want a soggy peat bog forming, so check that the brand you are using is good and friable, or add some grit. Use a coarse metal sieve and a wooden spoon to get rid of any lumps. As a seedling tries to unfurl and grow, a lump may hold it back.

2 *Fill your trays with seed compost to 1cm/½in below the top of the tray. Compress the compost gently with a block of wood the same width as the seed tray.*

3 *To moisten the compost, float your compost-filled trays in water until the air bubbles stop. Leave the trays to drain; the compost should be moist but not dripping.*

Sowing seeds under cover

1 *Gather all your equipment together on a bench at a good working height. You need seeds sorted in batches, seed compost, seed trays, single-cell insets, tall, narrow legume pots, a soil compressor, labels and a soft pencil, a coarse sieve and a wooden spoon, and silver sand.*

4 *Tiny seeds such as poppies are difficult to sow finely so mix them with silver sand in a ratio of about 1 to 6 to give you a better dispersed and more even distribution.*

5 *Sprinkle fine seed evenly over the seed tray. Large seeds like eryngiums are best sown in rows, spaced so they can develop without competition. Sow plants with a long root run, such as sweet peas, in legume pots.*

6 *Cover seeds with a layer of sieved compost to the depth shown on the seed packet. Some seeds, like tobacco plants, do not need covering. Label.*

7 *Place the trays or pots on a windowsill, in a propagator, or on a propagator bench. Water with a fine mist spray and cover with a polystyrene tile, or with glass covered in newspaper, to cut down the light.*

• Before sowing seed, gently compress the compost with a piece of wood to remove any large air pockets. Tiny rootlets are deprived of nutrients and water in air pockets.

• Whether you are using a windowsill, propagator or propagator bench in the greenhouse, you will fit more in a small area if you use square rather than round pots.

• You can use single-cell insets for sowing large seeds such as hollyhocks, or for those that resent root disturbance, such as lupins, *Salvia patens* and cow parsley, as well as for pricking out and potting on. They allow for seedlings to be planted straight out. Peat pots are an alternative.

• Always sow into pre-moistened compost. If you leave watering until after sowing, you may wash seeds to the edges and corners of the trays, where they will clump together and grow less well.

• Never let your trays dry right out or you will destroy the network of delicate rootlets.

• Covering the sown seeds with a polystyrene tile or glass wrapped in newspaper cuts down the light, and so helps many seeds to germinate (an exception is tobacco plant). It also reduces water loss, insulates and conserves any bottom heat from heated cables.

• Check every day for signs of germination. As soon as there is any sign of life, remove the polystyrene tile or piece of glass and move the seed tray to a position of maximum light.

Pricking out

• At first, germinating seeds will grow an atypical pair of leaves. Once there are one or two pairs of true leaves (miniature versions of those on the mature plant), it is time to prick the seedlings out into a richer growing compost in a tray of individual cells. Hold on to the leaves, not the stems, at all times. If you bruise the stem, the seedling will die.

• Have a minimum and maximum thermometer on the wall to check your night-time lows and day-time peaks. You must neither allow the temperature to fall below freezing nor let your plants bake in spring sunshine, although you do need the maximum amount of light. Ideally, avoid extremes in the greenhouse by having a thermostatically controlled heater and temperature-sensitive window vents, which will open and ventilate the greenhouse as soon as temperatures begin to rise. At the very least, keep a soil thermometer in the sand on your bench or do regular checks in your propagator or on your windowsill.

• Acclimatize seedlings gradually to the outdoors. If you are using cold frames, gradually increase the amount of time during the day that the frames are left open, and leave them open on cloudy nights when no frost is predicted. If you do not have cold frames, put the plants outside in a sheltered corner each day, bringing them in at night. Take care not to let the wind batter them – wind burn can be as bad as frost – and beware, too, of the heat of the midday sun. Start leaving them out all night when you are sure there is no risk of frost.

Planting out

• Rake the ground to a fine tilth and feed with a slow-release granular organic feed a few days before you intend to plant the seedlings out.

• When the risk of frost has passed, soak your seed trays in water, remove each plant with its root ball and plant it out with its label.

• Space your plants at slightly less than the recommended planting distance. A little competition for light produces long, straight stems that are perfect for picking, and you can also pick without leaving great gaps in the borders.

Direct sowing of seeds

• Many hardy annuals can be sown directly in the garden. Some, like most poppies and lupins, resent root disturbance, so are best sown in their flowering position. Others, such as dill, bishop's flower, larkspur, marigolds, annual scabious, cornflowers, sunflowers and annual bupleurum, do just as well from direct sowing, which is of course far less time-consuming.

• If possible, start preparing the soil several weeks before sowing. Dig it over, weed and top-dress or add organic fertilizer. Avoid mulching the area or you will then have to clear any mulch to one side to sow straight into the soil. When you are ready to sow, create a fine tilth by breaking up any clods of earth with the back of a strong rake or a hoe.

• Sow seeds in short straight, zigzag or wavy lines. Seedlings in lines are easier to distinguish from weedlings.

• Always keep the area free of weeds, which compete with the seedlings for light, moisture and nutrients.

• Thin seedlings to just less than the distance recommended on the packet. Although the plants will bulk out and compete with their next-door neighbours, with the amount of picking you will do you can afford to plant them slightly closer together.

Taking basal cuttings

• Cutting a young side shoot from a parent plant is a rewarding and easy way to build up stock. Now is the time to take basal cuttings from herbaceous perennials, such as campanulas,

Pricking out

1 *Use a pencil or dibber to ease out a clump of seedlings from the rest. Split the clump carefully by hand into single plants, trying to keep a bit of soil attached to the fragile rootlets. With your pencil, make a hole in the compost in the single cell and place the seedling's root ball in this hole.*

2 *Firm the compost around the seedlings and water them in to dislodge any air pockets. Label. Replace the seedlings on the propagator bench to recover for a week or two. After this disturbance their roots are at a delicate stage.*

3 *The seedlings are now ready to move to a cooler place where there is frost protection but minimal heat. If you have cold frames, put them there. If not, put them in a sheltered corner of the garden each day and bring them in at night.*

Planting out

Dig a generous hole with a hand trowel, mix in some organic matter with the soil at the bottom and place the young plant in this. Then firm the ground around it gently with your hands and water the plants in well.

Direct sowing of seeds

1 *Mark out lines (or areas) where you will sow your seed with sand of a colour that contrasts with your soil. Using a hand trowel, the back of a rake or a hoe, make a shallow seed drill to the depth recommended on the seed packet. Line the base of the shallow drill with sand to maximize drainage. Sow your seed into the base of the drill.*

2 *Replace the soil but do not firm it in, cover with more of the contrasting sand to remind you exactly where the seeds are for watering and weeding, and label with the name and date of sowing. Water the seeds in using your finest rose.*

delphiniums and phlox. Use a clean, sharp blade to remove healthy shoots from the base of the plant. Thereafter, the routine is the same as for semi-ripe cuttings (see page 39).
• Provide a warm, moist atmosphere with light, but not direct sunlight, to ensure that the cutting does not wilt and is given time – two to three weeks – to root properly.

Bringing tubers into growth and taking basal cuttings
• If you are buying tubers, in never leave them in a plastic bag. Even with air holes in the bag the tubers may rot.
• Feel for any soft, diseased areas in the tuber, particularly around the stem, and look closely for mildew and scab. If limited areas are affected, cut them out; otherwise you should discard the tuber.
• For early flowering, start tender tubers, such as dahlias and *Cosmos atrosanguineus,* into growth under cover about six weeks before you expect the last ground frosts. Place the tubers in pots and cover with 10-15cm/4-6in of moist compost. Plant them out when the risk of frost has passed.
• If you want to take basal cuttings, place the tubers in a shallow tray and cover with a thin layer of moist compost so that you can see when the new basal shoots reach 5cm/2in and the leaves start to form. If you put them in deeper compost, the shoots will be too long to be useful for propagating by the time they show.
• Remove the smaller shoots from the tuber – these will root more quickly than larger, more robust shoots. Cut away the lowest leaves and insert each new shoot in a pot of moist compost. Put in a propagator or cover with a plastic bag until roots have formed and the new tuber can be potted on.

Spring planting
• Start planting autumn-flowering bulbs and corms, new herbaceous perennials and tender shrubs.
• Plant gladioli, colchicums and nerines in mid-spring (for the techniques, see page 41). The more time they have in the ground, the better they will form adequate roots to sustain a good crop of flowers for autumn picking.
• Make successive plantings of gladioli corms every two weeks to get a longer summer and autumn flowering season.
• Snowdrops and aconites will establish and spread more quickly if planted after flowering, 'in the green'.
• Plant herbaceous perennials by mid-spring to give them time to form new roots before the rigours of flowering are upon them.
• Plant frost-vulnerable shrubs such as rosemary and camellias in late spring so that they are well established before next winter's

hard frosts. You are likely to lose some if you plant them too early in spring or in the autumn before a hard winter (see also page 40 for tips on planting).

Pruning and care of clematis, shrubs and roses
• Reshape plants that have become wild and unruly, congested in the middle, or insensitively or over-picked, by careful pruning.
• Cut out any dead, damaged or diseased wood that threatens the health of the plant. Taking branches and stems back to about one-third of their length concentrates the energies of the plant, enabling it to produce strong, new growth.
• Use a pruning saw for large branches and sharp secateurs for anything else. Blunt secateurs crush the stems and invite disease.
• Cut back late-flowering clematis at the very beginning of spring. Prune to two buds. If you leave it any later you will delay the flowering.
• Hard-prune shrubs that tend to get woody and bare at the base. Shrubby artemisias and rosemary, for example, benefit from a spring prune. They will almost immediately produce new shoots on the hard, old wood and will make a better-shaped shrub as a result. Many people prune lavender now but it is best to tidy the plant up as you pick, or just after flowering. Do not cut back into the old wood of lavender.
• Cut back the side shoots of winter- and early-spring-flowering shrubs, such as chaenomeles, to two or three buds, after flowering.
• When pruning Floribundas and other bush roses, start by removing any frost-damaged shoots. You may have to remove more at the end of spring if there are any late frosts. Remove suckers at the same time, slicing them off as near the original rootstock as possible.
• Always make cuts on rose branches at an angle. This allows rain to run off immediately rather than sitting on the wound, encouraging disease and rot.
• Make your cut just above an outward-facing bud, so the new branch is encouraged to grow outwards and not create a congested mess at the centre. Choose a bud with two or three buds below it, so that if your chosen bud isn't healthy, there are others below that may be.
• Sadly, for those of us who like to garden organically, it is often necessary to spray roses and other plants prone to aphids, blackspot and mildew, such as dahlias and *Euphorbia characias,* every two to three weeks from late spring onwards.

Dividing herbaceous perennials

After two or three years, most herbaceous perennials have grown enough both above and below ground to make it possible to cut the plant apart into sections, each of which will make a viable whole. Most perennials actually benefit from this. When the clumps get too big, adequate light is prevented from reaching the leaves in the middle, or, in the case of irises, the sun is prevented from baking the central rhizomes (for Bearded irises, see *Planting bulbs and corms*, page 38). Flowering in undivided herbaceous perennials is much less prolific; the old central section may die off, or need discarding.

• Dig up the whole clump, not just the outer sections, using a fork. Lift enough of the surrounding soil to avoid damaging the roots.
• Divide a woody crown with a spade. Take off small healthy pieces from the outside of the clump, each with a few new shoots, and discard the old central part of the crown.
• Insert two forks back-to-back to divide fibrous-rooted clumps, pushing the handles of the forks apart to separate the matted roots.
• Have holes waiting for the new plants so you can replant immediately. Plant them using soil mixed with slow-release fertilizer. Minimize the time they are out of the ground and there will then hardly be a hiccup in growth. (See also *Autumn*, page 41.)

Mulching, staking and tidying

As the weather warms up and you see your plants sprouting from the base, the time has come to give the annual mulch, support any plants that may flop, and generally spring clean the garden.
• Spread an organic mulch as soon as the soil begins to warm up. Do not mulch after a hard frost as you may trap any frost that is still in the ground. You can use forest bark, well-rotted farmyard manure, home-grown compost or redundant compost from a mushroom farm, spreading it to a depth of 5cm/2in. The garden will look immaculate at once! Mulching improves the structure of the soil as well as adding invaluable nutrients. Water evaporation will be reduced – crucial in the heat of the summer to help meet the water demands of fast-growing annuals. Mulching also cuts down on annual weeds. The seeds of weeds from last year will have to push their way through this extra layer and most will peter out. Also, new weed seeds deposited on the coarse mulch will find it harder to germinate.
• Avoid mulching plants that thrive in poor soil, such as dill and Algerian iris, or they will produce lots of lovely healthy-looking leaves and no flowers.
• Stake tall plants, such as delphiniums and eremurus, making a

rough circle of canes or hazel branches around each clump, about half the ultimate height of the clump. As taller flower spikes grow, put in taller stakes to support these too. Tie garden twine or fisherman's nylon from cane to cane, making an almost invisible web of support.
• Heavy-headed plants, such as peonies, alstroemerias and phlox, are better supported with a mesh of hazel pea-sticks. Push these into the ground to leave a structure about half the plant's ultimate height. They will soon grow up through this web to hide it.
• Cut back any seed heads left for winter decoration, or dead growth left for frost protection, once you are sure that there are no more hard frosts coming.

Summer

In the main, you can now sit back and enjoy your garden. Most of the time, the summer jobs in your cutting garden are no more than everyday maintenance. You are demanding a lot from a small area, so you do have to keep on top of the watering, staking, weeding, feeding and picking. Do not allow these jobs to pile up, but do them as you see they are needed.

Watering and feeding

• Regular and generous watering and feeding is a must in an intensively planted and productive cutting garden.
• Water at the beginning or the end of the day, or you will lose a lot of the benefit through evaporation.
• Water plants that are prone to mildew, such as delphiniums, asters, phlox and roses, in the morning. If you water them in the evening, the foliage will remain damp overnight and this will encourage mildew.
• Give your garden a good drenching three times a week, rather than a half-hearted sprinkle every day. With a light watering, much of the water will evaporate. What remains will encourage the development of fine, vulnerable roots near the surface. If you give the garden a good periodic drenching, the water will reach a deeper level and plant roots will grow deep to seek the water out. These longer, stronger roots will sustain the plant through dry times, ultimately producing a bigger and better plant.
• Help your annuals along with regular top-feeding. I keep a hessian sack of manure hanging in my water butt. It makes a rich, smelly, organic top-feed. Give a regular dose of a feed as rich as this and your plants should be happy.

Weeding

• Weed often: in early summer, with everything growing for all it's worth, weeds left for a week or two can easily get the better of a cutting garden.

• Deal with any perennial weeds like couch grass, bindweed and ground elder by spot treatment. Choose a dry, calm, windless day and spray each weed individually with a glyphosate-based weed-killer. Mask plants growing nearby from the weeds to be sprayed using two boards of wood, plastic or metal. Wait six hours before watering so the chemical is properly absorbed. After a week or two, see if there is any new growth. If so, repeat.

• If there is serious colonization by perennial weeds, dig up every plant in the affected area. Wash the plants' roots to remove any weed roots, then spray the entire area. This is a drastic solution for a drastic problem. I've only had to do it once and it is not a pleasant experience. Far better to sort out the perennial weed problem before you plant your cutting garden.

• Remove annuals like groundsel, speedwell, chickweed, fat hen and goose grass as soon as you see them. Don't think you will go back and do it later. They will have flowered, set and distributed seed before you know it. It is worth remembering that one plant of fat hen (*Chenopodium album*) can produce 70,000 seeds in a year.

Staking

• Stake tall-growing annuals and biennials as well as any herbaceous plants that you did not stake in spring. Sunflowers, tithonia, onopordum, dill, moluccella and bishop's flower are among those that will need a hazel pea-stick or cane and string framework. The rule is simple: if it looks floppy or vulnerable, stake it.

Picking and deadheading

• Keep picking, deadheading and removing seed cases to prolong the flowering season. Delphiniums, foxgloves and other perennials will develop lateral flower buds when you remove the leader, and violas will flower for many months if their seed cases are removed. Repeat-flowering roses such as 'New Dawn', 'Felicia' and 'Iceberg' will produce new flowering shoots if you cut stems back to a vigorous shooting bud.

Taking semi-ripe cuttings

If you want to build up a good clump of a favourite plant, or if you are thinking of lining a path in the garden with lavender or rosemary, late summer is the time to take your semi-ripe cuttings.

• Pamper a strong, healthy plant to use for taking cuttings. It is worth giving a chosen plant plenty of food and water so that it is ready, with lots of new growth, when you want to take cuttings.

• Remove the whole shoot from the parent plant by pulling or cutting it off at the junction with the main branch.

• Take more cuttings than you need, and store them immediately in a closed plastic bag to minimize water loss. Pot them up as soon as possible, and take out no more than two at a time.

• Label each pot with the name of the plant and the date.

• You can fit several cuttings in a pot as long as they don't touch.

• Cover each pot with a plastic bag, to retain moisture. But do not let the cuttings come into contact with the plastic. If this happens, mildew may well set in.

• Check cuttings and water regularly. Remove any cuttings that show signs of wilt, disease or mildew. They will infect others.

Sowing and planting out biennials

• Biennials such as sweet rocket, wallflowers and Iceland poppies like to be sown direct into the open ground in summer. Sow as described on pages 34 and 35.

• Plant out spring-sown biennials like sweet Williams and white foxgloves in lines in a prepared bed to mature during the summer.

Planting bulbs and corms and iris rhizomes

• You can still plant autumn-flowering bulbs and corms in early summer.

• Plant spring-flowering bulbs, such as narcissi, cyclamen, erythroniums, scillas and chionodoxas, so they can benefit from an extra two or three months in the ground. They will establish more extensive root systems and flower more prolifically. For the planting technique, see pages 40 and 41.

• Divide and replant Bearded iris. This queen of the cutting garden is unusual in preferring a summer division. After flowering, dig up the rhizomes and discard the leafless centre. Trim the ends, roots and leaves and replant the new rhizome on or just below the surface facing the sun, so that it ripens to flower the following summer (see also page 159).

Planting out late-flowering annuals

• As your wallflowers, Iceland poppies, sweet Williams and sweet peas come to an end, fill the gaps with later flowers nurtured in the cold frame, such as *Nicotiana sylvestris*, rudbeckias, zinnias, tithonia, amaranthus and *Euphorbia marginata*. Remove the spent plants, feed the soil and plant out, as on pages 34 and 35.

Taking semi-ripe cuttings

1 *Set out the equipment you need: labels, 8-10cm/3-4in square plastic pots, hormone rooting powder, a bowl of water, secateurs, a sharp knife, a dibber, plastic bags, short canes or sticks, rubber bands and a watering can. Have one bucket of compost (loam, peat and sand mixed with a slow-release fertilizer) and one of vermiculite or sharp sand. In the third bucket, make a well-draining mix of one-third vermiculite to two-thirds compost. Fill the pots with this mix.*

2 *Cut or pull healthy, non-flowering, 8-10cm/3-4in long side shoots from the parent plant. Gather the cuttings in a plastic bag. At the workbench, remove leaves and side shoots from the lower two-thirds of the stem. Pinch out the soft tip. Make a neat cut at an angle just beneath this year's new wood. Dip the stem end in water, then into the hormone rooting powder, and tap off any excess. Use a dibber to make a hole in the vermiculite/compost mix and push the cutting in to about one-third its length. Firm the compost and water well.*

3 *Place canes in each corner of the pot and stretch a plastic bag over, secured with a rubber band, to make a moisture-retaining tent. Place the cuttings on a propagator bench or on a warm windowsill, but out of bright sunlight. Alternatively, place the pots in a mist propagator.*

4 *After two weeks to a month, turn one pot out to see if good strong roots have formed. If so, it is time to pot the rooted cuttings up individually in fresh, moist vermiculite/compost mix. Make a hole in the fresh compost with your fingers. Plant the rooted cuttings and firm in. Water to dislodge any air pockets.*

5 *Replace the cuttings on the propagator bench or windowsill without plastic bags for another two to three weeks. Then move to a cold frame or a cooler spot until ready to plant up in spring.*

Autumn

Autumn, like spring, is a very busy time of year in the cutting garden. There is plenty of bulb planting and planting out still to be done, the garden must be prepared for the onslaught of winter and there are many other jobs that can be done in a few spare half hours. You can wrap up a tender ceanothus or young abutilon, transplant a patch of biennials or plant a bag of bulbs. Get as much done as you can while it is still a pleasure to be outside.

Autumn planting

For many plants the demands of flowering are over in autumn, but they have not yet reached a dormant stage. This means that newly planted herbaceous perennials, shrubs and trees can put on some root growth before winter cold sets in. Autumn planting is most suited to truly hardy plants such as alchemilla, stachys and astrantia that, even when young, can survive hard frosts.

• Plant well before frost is forecast. Frost endangers the tiny fragile rootlets that are so important for water uptake.

• Give each plant a good soaking before you plant it by immersing the pot in a wheelbarrow filled with water. When the air bubbles stop, all the compost is wet. Water it in very generously once it is in the ground, too.

• Always dig generous holes so that there is plenty of room to spread out the roots of each plant. Never cram the root ball into a confined space, or you will at best delay growth and at worst kill the plant. Mix some organic fertilizer into the bottom of the hole and spread some over the soil you replace around the new plant.

• For a large plant, firm the soil around the plant with your boot, so there are no large air pockets left. For a smaller plant, it is best to use your hands.

• Move biennials that were sown during the summer to their final flowering positions in early autumn. This allows them to settle into their new site and put on some more growth before the cold weather starts in earnest. Dig them up individually, trying to dislodge as little soil as possible from their roots to preserve the smallest fragile rootlets. Water them in and keep moist.

Bulb care and planting

Bulbs provide a sequence of irises, snowdrops, aconites, crocuses, narcissi, scillas, tulips and hyacinths and are the mainstay of the cutting garden from late winter and throughout spring. Some people dig their bulbs up every year and ripen them out of the ground, while others treat them as annuals and throw them away after flowering. Both of these involve what seems to me unnecessary work and expense, so I leave my bulbs in the ground, replenishing them every couple of years by planting new ones on either side of the original line.

• Select and plant your bulbs with their flowering dates in mind. You can then have a continuous flow of bright and brilliant flowers for many months at the beginning of the year.

• Prepare the soil before planting. Bulbs on the whole like humus-rich and very well-drained soil. Add organic matter and grit or coarse sand, according to your soil type. Mine is heavy Wealden clay, so I spread several inches of sharp sand followed by well-rotted manure over the planting area and dig or rotovate them in.

• Knock tall wooden, gloss-painted markers into the ground before planting bulbs in the cutting garden. Put one at each end of the planned row where they will stay from one year to the next, to mark exactly where your bulbs are.

• Try to plant your bulbs as soon as they arrive. With the exception of tulips (see below), the sooner they get in the ground the better. If you cannot plant them immediately, remove them from their bags so they do not get mildewy, and keep them in a cool, dark place. Roll them in a fungicidal powder if you store them for a while.

• Look for signs of old roots on cyclamen corms. This will tell you which way up to plant them.

• Plant anemone corms with their flat axis horizontal, but it does not seem to matter which way you plant them. If you have room, plant them in big blocks, which will make a much more colourful and impressive effect than scattering them about. Dig out a wide trench and place three or four bulbs next to each other.

• Delay planting tulips until the really cold weather starts. This avoids the problem of fire blight, which will rot the bulb. Plant them with the pointed end upright.

• Do not tread the soil in after planting as this may break off the growing point of the bulb; just firm it gently with the flat of your hand. If it is dry or dries out in the next couple of weeks, give it a good soaking.

• To naturalize bulbs in grass, cut and remove a circle of turf and use a bulb planter to remove a core of soil 5-8cm/2-3in deep. Place your bulb in the hole and replace the soil and the turf. If you want the bulbs to flower in a more random and natural pattern, collect a handful of pale stones or use traditional marbles. Cast the whole handful over the area and plant a bulb where each stone or marble lands.

Forcing bulbs

It is a great treat to have lots of bulbs around the house in pots and vases to cheer you in the depths of winter. To do this you need to force them into flower early. Many spring bulbs, such as the sumptuous purple *Iris reticulata* and buttercup-yellow *Iris danfordiae*, the highly scented *Narcissus* 'Paper White' and 'Soleil d'Or', as well as many different hyacinths, tulips, and the delicate, pretty scillas and grape hyacinths, are all suited to this treatment. Start successive plantings in early autumn and you can have flowers throughout the winter and well into spring when the cutting garden gets going again.

• Pot the bulbs up in plastic pots that will fit into a terracotta or ceramic flower pot. When one potful dies you can just remove it and replace it with a fresh one.

• Once potted, store bulbs in moist compost, in a cold, dark place. Traditionally bulbs were buried beneath a sunless wall, but a cold store or darkened cold frame will do. This will encourage strong root growth before the leaves and flowers develop. Narcissi, an exception, need cold, but not dark, for strong growth to start.

• Pot your bulbs up in several different batches, so that the flowering season is extended. You can ask the bulb companies to send them out at different times, or store them in a cool, dark, frost-free place and lay them out, not touching, like apples on a storage rack.

Digging up and dividing herbaceous perennials

• You can divide herbaceous perennials as successfully in autumn as in spring. The hardier perennials can be planted out straight away. With the more delicate plants, it is best to play safe and nurture the new offspring for a while, potting them up and putting them in a cold frame for protection until spring (see *Summer*, page 37, for tips on division).

• Dig up your tender perennials, such as salvias and penstemons, and overwinter them in a frost-free cold frame or greenhouse.

Planting bulbs

1 *You will need: bulbs, wooden markers at each end of the planned row, garden twine tied between the markers as a guide, a trowel or hoe, sharp sand, pelleted organic fertilizer, a watering can and, if planting in grass, a bulb planter.*

2 *Using a trowel or hoe, dig a trench to one side of the garden twine line as wide, and three times as deep, as a bulb. Lay sharp sand to one bulb's depth in the bottom of the trench to maximize drainage and scatter pelleted slow-release organic fertilizer on top.*

3 *Place your bulbs slightly closer than usually recommended, to give you a good density of flowers for cutting without leaving the area looking too empty. Replace the soil and firm it gently with the flat of your hand. If the soil is dry, or dries out in the next few weeks, give it a good soaking.*

• The ground may be drier in autumn so, to make the root ball and soil stick together in one big clod, give the clump a good soaking before digging it up. With more soil sticking to the roots, you damage the tiny delicate rootlets less and so give the transplanted offspring a better start.

Collecting and planting seeds and seedlings

• Seed collecting starts in summer, but most is done in autumn. To save the expense of buying annuals every year it is well worth collecting seeds from all but the F_1 hybrids, which do not come true from seed.

• Catch the seed cases when they are turning brown and drying up. Pick the seed case whole and store it in a labelled paper envelope. By the time you come to sort these through in the winter, they will be thoroughly dried and you can easily separate out the valuable seeds and discard the rest. Return them to the envelope and record what you have and in what quantities. Store them in a cool, dry place until you are ready to plant them in seed trays or in the open (see pages 33 and 35).

• Dig up any hardy annual self-sown seedlings and plant them in blocks or lines. Perennial self-sown seedlings from plants like alchemilla, lupins, euphorbias, astrantia, *Eryngium giganteum*, anchusas and violas can be replanted in the same way or left to grow where they are.

• Put some of your hardy annual seeds, especially cornflowers and nigella, straight into the ground. Some may not germinate, but enough will to make it worthwhile. These plants mature earlier and will extend your season of flowering.

Layering shrubs

• Propagate plants such as hamamelis and philadelphus that have low-lying branches by layering. Simply bend down a healthy, vigorous lower branch so that it can touch the ground. Dig out a 5cm/2in trench about 25cm/10in from the tip of the branch. Strip the leaves and side shoots except at the tip and pin the branch into the trench with a hairpin-shaped piece of wire. Cover it with soil and wait for roots to form. The following spring, sever the branch from the parent and you will have an independent offspring. After a month, dig it up and replant it.

Taking cuttings

• As you dig up your tender perennials for overwintering, take cuttings too. Treat them as for any semi-ripe cuttings (see pages 38 and 39). You should then have lots of strong plants for planting out at the end of spring the following year.

• Take heeled cuttings from perennial pinks by gently tearing off a side shoot, taking a small heel of the central stem with it. Dip this in hormone rooting powder, then insert it into a pot of very sandy compost. Store the cuttings over the winter in a light, frost-proof frame and pot them on in the spring before planting out.

Preparing the garden for winter

• Tidy dead foliage, prune, and mulch, wrap or even dig up to bring inside frost-tender plants.

• As some plants brown and die, cut them back to the ground so they can emerge green and fresh without having to push through their decaying leaves the following spring. Plants such as *Stachys byzantina* and most of the euphorbias will become a soggy mess as soon as a hard frost hits them. These are the ones to cut right down. There is something beautiful about a garden reduced to its skeletal bones in this way.

• Leave some plants whose dead foliage and flower or seed heads are an asset to the winter garden. Thistles, acanthus and alliums look good through the winter.

• Trim back bush roses to prevent wind rock, following the instructions for pruning on page 36.

• Provide protection from the hardest frosts. Semi-tender shrubs, herbaceous perennials, bulbs and tubers need to be covered with a carpet of leaves, straw or even a good layer of compost to protect their crowns. This applies mostly to plants of Mediterranean or Californian climates, such as artichokes, agapanthus, young *Arum italicum* and *Helleborus argutifolius*, and shrubs such as evergreen ceanothus, abutilons and young magnolias; these are safest if protected by netting or fleece. Aim to have them snugly wrapped by mid-autumn.

• Dig up your tender tubers such as *Cosmos atrosanguineus*, dahlias and the tender agapanthus, and overwinter in a cool, dry place, not touching one another. Dig up tender perennial penstemons and salvias, and cut them right back before overwintering in a light, cool, frost-free place.

• Spread a layer of manure or home-made compost over the whole garden and dig it in. If your soil is heavy, leave any large clods – they will be better broken up by the winter weather than by your struggling with them now. Lighten your soil by spreading some horticultural grit or sharp sand. Never walk over newly dug ground or you will undo all the good soil structuring you have done. Lay a plank down and stand on this if you need to go over the ground again.

Winter

In winter there is less to do in the garden, greenhouse and potting shed. One of the main delights of winter is selecting what you want from the seed catalogues. Try and order early so none of your choices is sold out. The only thing to be careful about, as you are seduced by the excitement of having all these lovely plants in your garden, is not to order too many. Remember the time you have to spend on them, as well as the space they require in the greenhouse or on your windowsills.

Taking hardwood cuttings

• You can propagate from many trees and shrubs by taking hard-wood cuttings. Start with ivies and willows that reward you every time by forming roots on every cutting you prepare. Then move on to the more difficult cornus and camellias which are likely to have a smaller strike rate. Remove a woody branch, which in the case of willow can be up to 1.2-1.5m/4-5 ft tall, and insert it in soil lightened with sand in a prepared bed. For ivies, cut one trailing branch into sections with three or four leaves each. Insert these cuttings into a good sandy mix of compost and put them in a cold frame for the winter. If no roots have formed by spring, place them on a heated propagator bench to give them a boost – do this, too, for any trickier plants.

Taking root cuttings

• Take root cuttings when plants are dormant in winter so that parent and offspring both have time to recover and flourish by the next growing season. This is the best way to propagate the autumn-flowering anemones (*A.* × *hybrida* and *A. hupehensis*), the pasque flower, most of the eryngiums, acanthus and Oriental poppies. Mark the position of the parent plant in autumn, for the leaves will have disappeared by winter and, unless marked, you will have no idea where it is. Dig up the whole plant carefully, and, using a sharp knife, slice some of the root into 8cm/3in sections. Angle one end at 45 degrees to tell you which is the top and which the bottom.

• Have your pots of compost waiting. The cut sections of root must not be left to dry out. Tie a bundle together and put them into the compost, making sure you have kept each root facing the right way up. Cover them with 2.5cm/1in of soil and place them in a cold frame or a light, frost-free place. Replant the parent plant.

• By spring, shoots will have appeared on the cuttings. Check they have good roots and then plant them up individually in pots. Leave them where they are until autumn, when you can plant them out into the garden.

Sowing seed

• Sow seeds that are slow to germinate. The superb deep purple lisianthus, for example, should be sown from fresh seed in mid-winter if it is to put on adequate growth to flower that year.

• If you forgot to sow your sweet Williams, lupins and hollyhocks, do so now. You will not have such strong plants as those planted in late summer or autumn, but they will flower in the same year.

• If you did not sow your sweet peas during the autumn for storing in a cold frame over the winter, sow them now so they are ready for planting out in the spring. Pinch out their growing tips so you will have strong, bushy plants.

Pruning

• Now is the time to prune, trim and tidy deciduous shrubs and climbing and large shrub roses, while the framework of the plant is most apparent. Most of the big shrubs, *Elaeagnus angustifolia*, philadelphus and the statuesque *Rosa moyesii* will benefit from pruning in winter, as will any large rampant climbers.

• Start by removing dead, diseased or damaged wood right from the base, then concentrate on weak and spindly branches. Also, remove any suckers, as these will divert energy from the main plant.

• Always stand back and assess the overall shape. In general, aim for a balanced, even silhouette. Be careful not to destroy the graceful arching habit of shrubs such as the species roses by removing more than a third of their stems, although some vigorous shrubs, such as lilac, can safely be cut back hard.

Flower Arranging

Don't feel intimidated – this school of flower arranging is accessible to everyone. There is no need for elaborate equipment or complicated techniques such as intricate wiring. All you need is a love of colour and a sense of drama. Keep in mind a few basic ideas on structure, scale and colour, follow the advice for cutting and conditioning, and you will be away.

Aim to create a heightened version of what is in the garden, with a similar feeling of natural ease and beauty: avoid strict symmetry and dominating vertical or horizontal lines. Remember that a flower arrangement doesn't have to be in a conventional vase. Create romantic globes with billowing flowers and branches of foliage; or construct enormous swags and medallions to hang inside or out. Keep the image of growing plants in mind, and have fun.

As well as creating average-sized bunches of flowers, think of making arrangements for both giants and pygmies. A huge vase of pussy willow, foxgloves or cow parsley is an impressive sight. At the other extreme, one velvety auricula, with a face like a mime artist, is almost guaranteed to lift the spirits. Don't rule anything out.

Blues, greens, whites and yellows make beautiful and peaceful combinations, but think, too, of mixing rich and powerful colours – oranges, purples and near-blacks, or crimsons, golds and royal blues. Balance their strength with calming acid-green or silver. Don't stop here either. Raise eyebrows by using colourful containers to make zinging combinations such as fluorescent pink and turquoise or orange and lime-green. Above all, be brave and let rip.

When you restrict the flower species in an arrangement, you can run riot with colour. Don't be cautious: mix red, yellow, carmine, purple, blue and green to create a show-stopping display.

Cutting

The best part of having a cutting garden is harvesting your own produce from your own garden. I fill my buckets with endless possibilities for colour combinations, gathering a bounty of all shapes and sizes. You can wander around surrounded by luscious scents, textures and colours all of your own making, and any of which can be brought into the house – the choice is yours. And, as you pick, all the anxiety and diligence that have gone into making your cutting garden will, I am sure, be metamorphosed into pride and pleasure.

If you obey a few rules based on common sense when you are picking, everything you cut from the garden will benefit and will have a longer vase life.

Cut when it is cool

You should always try to cut in the early morning or in the evening. These are the most beautiful times of the day, before the dew has fully evaporated, or when the last of the sun enriches the colours of the garden as a whole. During the day, particularly in the summer months with the increased heat, plants will transpire more. They will therefore probably be moisture-deficient and so more likely to droop as soon as they have been cut. Plants that have had the opportunity to restore their moisture balance overnight will be more able to withstand the trauma of cutting. To some extent the same applies when the plants have had some time to recover in the cool of the evening.

Invest in the right equipment

Good-quality secateurs and scissors will repay their price in years of service. They must be really sharp. If they are blunt you will crush the stem end and block it, and could damage the parent plant. If you are picking lots of flowers, invest in a trolley so you can push your buckets round the garden with you.

Don't hack away at your plants

Treat your garden with care. If you cut sensibly it is easy to pick enormous amounts from a garden without it being apparent that you have taken much, or even anything at all. Always try to pick from the back of shrubs and large perennials so that no obvious gaping holes are left near the path. Think of the overall shape of the plant as you pick from it and try to improve, not destroy, it. With smaller plants take one or two stems from several, rather than all the flowers from one and none from the rest.

Cut flowers in loose bud

Most flowers are best cut in loose bud. Ideally they should be showing some colour, but they should not yet be fully open. Find the stems on the plant with the most flowers at this stage. There will often be a flower or two which is more advanced, but this can be removed during conditioning if it has passed its best.

The few exceptions to this rule include dahlias, zinnias and roses, where the flower will not develop fully from a tight bud. These must be picked when already fully out (see the information given for each plant, pages 96–163). At the other extreme some flowers – camellias for instance – will come out from even the very tightest buds.

Cut your stems long

On the whole, the longer the stems, the easier the flowers will be to arrange. Cut each stem right down to the ground, or back to a main stem, so that you can make the most of the natural height of the plant. For a more three-dimensional arrangement, choose some twisting and turning stems as well as some of the more obvious straight ones.

Leave bulbs with some of their foliage

Bulbs are the exception to the rule about cutting stems as long as possible, as they need some leaves left for photosynthesis to store energy in the bulb to carry it through the dormant season. If you cut lilies and crown imperials to the ground you will cut off almost all the leaves. So try to cut the stems leaving about a third of the main bulk of the foliage. Only once the leaves have browned can you cut them off and tidy them up.

Don't leave cut flowers out of water

Once a plant has been picked, it should not be left out of water for a moment longer than necessary. This is most important in the heat of summer. Some plants, like peonies, will never fully recover if they are left out of water, and their heads will droop. Others come to no apparent harm, but their cut life will be much curtailed. Keep one or more buckets one-third filled with water near you as you pick.

Keep your sizes separate

If you are picking both short and tall plants, keep them in separate buckets, or the taller, heavier plants will crush the flowers of the shorter, delicate ones. If their petals are broken or end up in the water, they won't be much use for arranging.

Strip the bottom leaves as you go

Strip the bottom leaves and side branches of each stem into an empty container as you go. If you remove them now, you will decrease the surface area that is transpiring and hence decrease the demands and stress on the newly cut flower. These leaves would need to be removed before conditioning anyway.

Think of arrangements as you go

As you pick in the garden, try to bunch plants loosely together, creating a balance of flowers and foliage, colours and textures. Particularly if you have a lot of arrangements to do, this could save enormous amounts of time, and it will avoid repetition.

Don't just pick the obvious

Use your imagination in what you pick. There will of course be flowers and foliage for picking that are obviously pretty to arrange. But look around for the less obvious, too. Check hedges, or any scrubby wild parts of your garden that you hardly ever go into. Keep an eye out for interesting buds, seed cases, twisting or unusual coloured stems, berries and hips as well as flowers and foliage for your bunches. Just because something is not in this book, it does not mean it will not do. Experiment with your picking. If a plant flops the first time, try searing the stem the next (see page 48). Making your own discoveries will give you far more satisfaction.

Equipment for cutting

Deep bucket, filled to one-third with water for long stems

Shallow bucket, filled to one-third with water for short stems

Empty bucket for the stripped leaves and side stems

Trug or basket to carry flowers from the middle of a border to the buckets

Thorn-proof gloves, for picking roses and blackberries

Rubber gloves for picking euphorbias and rue

Secateurs for cutting woody stems

Florist's scissors for cutting fleshy stems

Folding knife for slitting stems and removing thorns

Stripping and cutting stems

Strip the bottom third of your cut stems, taking off all leaves, side branches or thorns. Put the waste into a bucket and then on the compost heap. Divide your flowers into tall and short and keep them in separate buckets, so the larger and more robust ones do not crush the smaller, more delicate ones.

Dealing with rose stems

Strip the thorns from the bottom third of your rose stems so you do not prick yourself when conditioning and arranging. Cut the stem end again at a sharp angle and then make a 2.5cm/1in slit up the middle of the stem to increase the surface area for water absorption and prevent a seal forming on the newly cut end. This is ideally done under water so no air locks can form.

Conditioning

Once you have gathered in your harvest, you need to put the flowers in a cool place out of direct sunlight, with a sink and a flat surface to condition them. After conditioning, leave everything here overnight or through the day in deep water, so that the newly cut flowers have time for a good drink. Tepid water is absorbed better than water that is ice-cold and it is a good idea to add some commercial cut-flower food containing nutrients and anti-bacterial agents. This sets the flowers up to withstand excess heat and bright sunlight much better. If you cut, arrange and put the vases straight into the house, the life of your flowers will be shortened by several days.

For all plants there are some basic rules of conditioning.

Remove any leaves below the water line

The water line should always be kept just below the top of the vase and no leaves that will be below this should be left on the stem. If you have not removed enough while outside in the garden, you should do this first. Any leaf that touches the water will quickly decay and produce a bacterial soup, which will stink and clog up the stems and shorten the life of the other flowers. Too much leaf also puts great demands on the flower stem of the cut plant, so aim for the minimum that looks nice. Don't go over the top though and leave a collection of bald, top-heavy beauties – except with lilac and moluccella, which should have all their leaves stripped.

All stems should be recut

Before you give your flowers their long drink you must recut the stems with really sharp secateurs, scissors or a knife. This is best done under water to avoid the risk of air locks forming in the capillary network of the stem. Cut them at an appropriate angle: for soft stems, cut at a slight angle so they don't sit flat at the bottom of the bucket; for woody stems cut at a 45-degree angle, thereby exposing more of the pithy centre for water uptake.

Sear sappy and soft stems

If you find that a plant you particularly like always seems to droop, even if you put it straight into water in the garden, it is worth trying searing the stem ends in boiling water. This technique is the saviour of many a wilting cut flower. It is particularly useful for sappy, soft-stemmed plants (for example, euphorbias, smyrnium, acanthus, artemisia, poppies, hellebores, viper's

Searing sappy or soft stems
The vase life of flowers with soft stems or stems that 'bleed' can be prolonged by searing them in boiling water. Keeping their heads well clear of the steam, dip the newly cut stems in boiling water for 20 seconds before plunging them in tepid water.

bugloss, hollyhocks). In the case of euphorbias it also stops the leaking of the very allergenic white milk from the stem end (see page 96). Make sure that the flower heads are well away from the heat, either by angling the flowers away from the steam, or by wrapping the flowers in stiff brown paper. Dip the stems into 2.5cm/1in of boiling water for about 20 seconds. During this time you will often see bubbles emerging as the stem seals off. Then place the flowers immediately in tepid water.

Even flowers with tough but non-woody stems such as roses seem to benefit from this treatment. First cut their stems, preferably with a sharp knife, at a 45-degree angle. If the head has already flopped, which happens so often with bought roses, try searing the stems as soon as possible and they almost always miraculously pick up again over the next few hours.

Hammer woody stems

The ends of woody stems of trees and shrubs (for example, lilac, viburnum, cotinus, philadelphus) should be crushed. Hammering the last 2.5-5cm/1-2in of each stem increases the surface area for water absorption and prevents a skin or seal forming over the stem end, blocking the plant's water uptake. Once the stems have been crushed they should be plunged immediately into a deep vase of tepid water.

Hammering woody stems

To prevent a seal forming and to increase the surface area for water absorption, crush the end 2.5–5cm/1–2in of each stem with a hammer or mallet on a hard surface. Then plunge them into tepid water.

Binding long thin stems such as tulips

If you want straight stems, they must be supported during the conditioning process. Wind string or florist's tape along the complete length of the stems and wrap them in stiff paper before leaving them in water overnight.

Bind long thin stems

Heavy-headed flowers with long thin stems (such as tulips and dill) and greenhouse plants (such as gerberas) tend to bend after picking. If you leave them untreated as they suck up water in the conditioning process, the stems will become set in this bent position. Prevent this by binding the stems to hold them straight.

Support hollow stems

Hollow-stemmed plants with heavy heads (for example, amaryllis, lupins or delphiniums) may break under the weight of the flower head. To avoid this, gently insert a thin cane as far as you can up the stem. Fill the stem with water, then plug the end with cotton wool secured with a tight rubber band.

Aftercare

Once you have gone to the trouble to pick, condition and arrange your flowers, it is worth doing all you can to prolong their vase life. Just as cut flowers need a cool place for conditioning, so they will last longer away from heat or direct sunlight. Research has shown that carnations held at 10°C/50°F age eight times faster than those held at 1°C/34°F. So avoid placing arrangements near a radiator in the winter or in direct sunlight in the summer.

Add nutrients and preservatives to the water

What cut flowers need is a balance of sugars that can be utilized for metabolism, a substance to raise the acidity of the water and an anti-bacterial agent. Commercial sachets of cut-flower food contain agents for all three. It is worth going to a commercial market and buying them in quantity. Otherwise, add a few drops of bleach and a teaspoon of sugar to the vase and stir.

Make sure the flowers have clean water

Cut flowers last longer in clean water. Make sure you start with a pristine vase. Bacteria otherwise build up in the dirty water, as we all know from the stench you get when throwing away flowers that have not had their water changed for a week. The bacteria act on the cut ends of the stems, creating a slime which blocks the capillaries by which water is drawn up to the leaves and the flowers, so causing the plant to wilt. Check the water level every other day, as flowers will die quickly with only a tiny bit of water in the bottom of the vase. In hot weather you should try to change the water every other day. To do this, you do not have to destroy your arrangement: just leave the vase under a running tap for a couple of minutes and then replenish the cut-flower food. At the same time, you can remove any dead or dying flowers with your scissors to give the arrangement a face-lift.

Choosing a Vase

If you marry your flowers to a vase that is sympathetic in shape and colour, you are halfway to creating a beautiful arrangement. So it is important that when you begin to grow flowers for cutting, you should also invest in at least a basic variety of vases and containers (see opposite). I recommend the following: a simple clear glass vase, full-bellied with a neck, about 20-30cm/8-12in high (see page 72); a similar-shaped vase or a jug which is about 45cm/18in high, for generous larger arrangements (see page 71); a tall straight or slightly shaped vase between 20cm/8in and 30cm/12in high (see page 53); a tall narrow vase for a single rose or giant tobacco flower (see page 82); at least one or two shallow ceramic or glass bowls for table centres (see page 62); a few coloured glasses for smaller posies and single flower heads for putting beside a bed or on your desk, as well as one or two 2.5-5cm/1-2in vases for a single crocus or auricula (see pages 56–7, 79). As you grow more and varied flowers, and become more adventurous in your arrangements, you will find that you want to add to your vase collection all the time. Try jumble sales and junk and antique shops as well as more unusual china and glass stores.

Height of vase

For any arrangement to be in harmonious proportion, the height of the vase you choose should be one-third to one-half the height of the tallest flowers and foliage you have picked. If the vase is more than this, it will make the flowers appear as if they are straining to peep out of the top. If it is less, then the whole arrangement will look as if it is about to topple over.

Colour and style of vase

I love bright, contrasting colours and so my favourite arrangements are often those with zingy pink flowers in turquoise or apple-green ceramic or glass containers. A few stems of the crimson hyacinth 'Jan Bos', for example, will combine with a container of an equally strong but contrasting colour to produce a powerful attention-seeker. A subtle mixture of more delicate flowers, such as nigella with cornflowers, delphiniums and alchemilla, needs a lighter, less dominant vase.

Similarly, great bosomy peonies and roses can look good in an elaborate vase, while simple wild-style flowers on the whole look better in unpatterned, unfussy containers. It is important that the vase never overwhelms the flowers.

Acquire a good collection of vases *(right) Choose plain glass or a neutral-coloured material like pewter to get the most use out of your vases to begin with, but don't neglect other colours. You will soon learn which sizes, shapes and colours suit your favourite flowers and arrangements.*

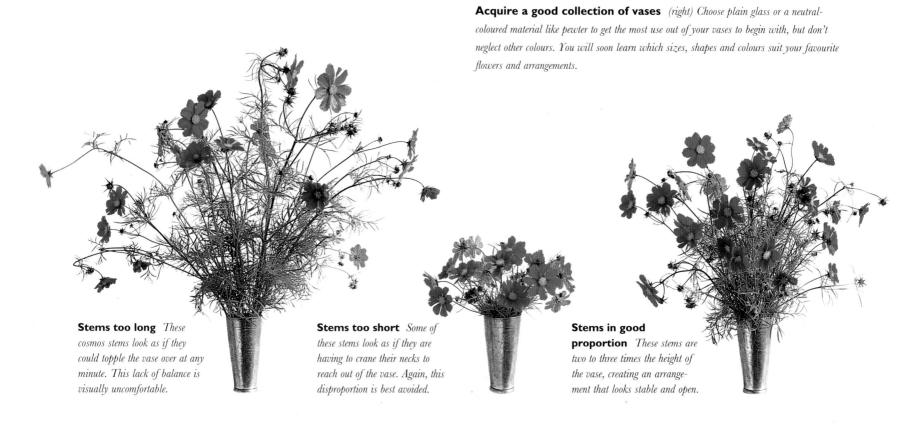

Stems too long *These cosmos stems look as if they could topple the vase over at any minute. This lack of balance is visually uncomfortable.*

Stems too short *Some of these stems look as if they are having to crane their necks to reach out of the vase. Again, this disproportion is best avoided.*

Stems in good proportion *These stems are two to three times the height of the vase, creating an arrangement that looks stable and open.*

Equipment for arrangements

1 cone or funnel for extending stems

To lengthen stems in especially large arrangements. Push each stem into a cone, secure the join with florist's tape and fill the cone with water before pushing the cone spike into oasis. To lengthen stems even further, attach each cone to a cane with strong tape and then push the cane into oasis.

2 23 x 11 x 8cm/9 x 4¼ x 3in block of oasis

Foam used by florists to hold stems in place. Easily cut to size and water-retaining once it has been soaked, it is especially useful for arrangements in shallow bowls.

3 water vial

To hold stem ends in medallions, wreaths and globes. Once they have been placed, the water-filled vials can be hidden by the foliage. Most plants will survive for one to two days with this amount of water.

4 heavyweight pin-holders in 3 sizes 2.5cm/1in, 5cm/2in, 8cm/3in

To hold firm, average-sized stems, such as those of roses and euphorbias, in place. (Use marbles for finer stems and use oasis wrapped in chicken wire for very large or robust stems.) Secure the pin-holder to the bottom of the vase with florist's fix before adding water.

5 glass marbles

To hold delicate stems in place, especially in glass vases. You need enough to fill about one-third of a vase.

6 glass stem-holder

To hold firm stems in place in arrangements in large shallow bowls. Secure to the bottom of the vase with florist's fix before adding water.

7 florist's fix (strong waterproof glue-tack)

To attach florist's frogs, pin-holders, and so on, to bowls and vases.

8 candle-holder (shown inverted)

To insert into a block of oasis to hold a candle upright.

9 florist's frog or spike

To hold blocks of oasis in place. Attach to the bottom of a bowl or vase with florist's fix and push the oasis on to the four plastic teeth.

10 gardener's twine

To make wreaths and tie bunches.

11 fine-gauge florist's wire

To tie in and bind stems in swags, wreaths, globes and medallions.

12 florist's scissors

To trim leaves, stem ends, etc.

13 plastic sheeting

To protect the floor where you are working. If lifted by the four corners it can be emptied into a dustbin when you have finished.

14 chicken wire, 30cm/12in wide

To wrap around oasis in the construction of swags and globes, and also to hold stems in place in huge arrangements.

15 watering can

To fill vases, water vials, etc.

16 20cm/8in globe of oasis

To create globes for special occasions.

17 moss

To line a hanging basket, especially to pad the areas not filled by oasis. Also to hide any unsightly oasis in large arrangements.

18 a pair of hanging baskets

To construct large globes. Fill with soaked oasis and wire together.

19 heavy twine

To tie larger bunches and wreaths; hop-bine (Humulus lupulus) can be used instead.

20 strong binding wire

To secure large, heavy swags and hanging globes.

21 strong hold-all

To carry all your equipment.

Creating Arrangements

Making beautiful and impressive flower arrangements is not that difficult. There are no hard and fast rules that must be slavishly obeyed. However, there are a few basic guidelines that work for me, although I sometimes disregard them deliberately when the occasion or plant demands it. Even when you bear the following advice in mind, it is important to use your imagination and follow your own inclinations.

Avoid strict symmetry at all costs

Neat domes of flowers usually look boringly restrained and predictable. Create a livelier arrangement by allowing branches to burst out in different directions, balancing an upward spike here with a downward bough of berries there. To emphasize this, use odd numbers of the dominanting flowers and spikes of foliage. Work in threes, fives and sevens, not squarely placed fours, sixes and eights. Use, for example, three of your most glamorous flower, five of your middle-sized flower and nine or eleven of a more abundant 'padding' flower.

Create a broken silhouette and a billowy effect

Don't cut everything with equal length stems. As you place your flowers, push some right into the heart of the arrangement, leaving others standing proud.

It is painful to see beautiful plants poked into a vase with no room for their natural lines, twists and turns. In general, try to allow each stem to stand or hang as it would on the parent plant in the garden. Avoid creating any vertical and horizontal lines with the dominant flower, because this will segment the vase into zones and destroy the overall effect.

Arrange in three dimensions

Even if you are making an arrangement that is to sit against a wall or window, always aim to construct it 'in the round'. Don't fall into the short-at-the-front-and-tall-in-the-back trap. It is tempting to put all your best flowers where they will be most obviously seen. But doing this will not only give your arrangement an unnatural two-dimensional look, but also cause it to become unbalanced in weight, making it all too easy for it to topple over. If you arrange a vase that could be viewed at any angle, it will immediately look much livelier. And you will be surprised to find that you will be able to see all your flowers. Glimpsing them from varying view points will make the arrangment far more dynamic.

Emphasizing the effect of strong flowers
When yellow and brick-red sunflowers are mixed with substantial, bursting artichoke buds the arrangement becomes even more commanding, the focal point of a room.

Diffusing the effect of strong flowers
The impact of the same yellow and red sunflowers is softened by the feathery heads of dill, making a less powerful arrangement, one that can blend into the background.

Teaming flowers and foliage

It is usually best to team strong foliage with strong flowers and light, fluffy foliage with more delicate flowers. Each enhances the other. Robust, architectural foliage, such as acanthus, green artichokes or horse chestnut buds, will reinforce the flamboyant effect of flowers like Parrot tulips, sunflowers and dahlias. If you want to soften the effect of flowers with strongly defined shapes, use feathery foliage such as dill.

Choosing foliage

Your selection of foliage or 'greenery' is as important as your choice of flowers. Even when it is used as a background, it can dictate the basic overall flavour of an arrangement. I tend to avoid the heavy dark evergreen forms of privet, box, and laurel. I think that their ramrod stems can be limiting and that their glossy texture and dark tone weigh down an arrangement and tend to swamp the colour and light produced by the flowers. I choose enlivening acid-green at any opportunity and rarely make an arrangement without euphorbia or smyrnium in spring, and alchemilla, bupleurum or dill in summer and autumn.

In addition to foliage, try and forage something – pussy willow, hazel catkins, emerging spring leaves, ears of wheat, bulrushes, clematis seed heads, sprays of blackberries or crabapples – from the wilder parts of the garden. Often one of these less obvious plants can be the making of an arrangement.

Colour contrast

An arrangement is always more interesting for using at least two contrasting colours. Think of this when choosing foliage as well as flowers. If you cut some sumptuous carmine snapdragons and cosmos they could look sombre on their own, being so closely matched in colour, especially when they are teamed with one type of foliage. Adding a few deep blue salvias and gentians would immediately make the arrangement come alive. Adding acid-green and deep crimson foliage, such as dill, bupleurum and cotinus, brings richer colours and greater interest. Don't be tempted to overegg the mixture. If you go on and add two or three more flower shapes and colours, the style and grace of the arrangement may collapse.

I feel that you can successfully have either limitless colour or infinite flower variety, but not both at once. When a colour jamboree is what's wanted, it is probably better to restrict the number of types of flowers. When the flower types are limited, anything goes.

Subdued colour *The colour match between cosmos and snapdragons is almost too perfect and, with only privet foliage, there is not enough going on to arrest the eye.*

Balanced colour *With blue (salvia and gentian), acid-green (dill and bupleurum) and deep purple foliage (cotinus), the arrangement immediately becomes livelier.*

Chaotic colour *With yet more colours and types of flowers (here, purple lisianthus, yellow rudbeckia and white cosmos) an arrangement can become so busy that it loses its presence.*

Creating a mixed arrangement

1 Start with the background

foliage *Use your leafiest, bulkiest foliage to create the overall basic structure.*
Failure *(left) These branches of acorns have not been thinned and the stems have been cut to equal lengths and placed neatly and too symmetrically, making the arrangement look dense and boring.*
Success *(right) Lots of leaves have been removed to emphasize the acorns and lighten the overall effect of the dark foliage. The stems are arranged so that one leans over the vase on one side, and another curves into the air on the other. The result is asymmetrical and more natural.*

2 Add more background greenery

Choose something that will contrast with the fairly dark, solid shapes of the oak leaves. Fill out the arrangement to the point when you feel it could almost be left without the flowers.
Failure *(left) The usually pretty bupleurum is lost in the dense green sea of leaves. The silhouette remains too solid, adding little interest to the arrangement.*
Success *(right) Strong foliage with boughs of crabapples and green love-lies-bleeding with its long, lime-green, dangly tassels contribute subtle colour contrast, as well as different shapes and textures.*

3 Add the most dominant flowers

Place flowers at very different levels, some cut quite short for the heart of the arrangement, and others standing right out, left long to break up the silhouette. Avoid overpacking, so the plants can follow their natural lines and are not held too upright and alert.
Failure *(left) An even number of flowers has been placed symmetrically in the vase. Each one is forced too far into the foliage. The result looks cramped and suffocated.*
Success *(right) An odd number of sunflowers has been added, all at different levels in the arrangement. The effect is open and relaxed.*

A Spring Tapestry

Illustrated on pages 56–57.

This array of mid-spring flowers and elegant glassware is inspired by the idea of Pointillism, that dashes of colour create an overall image of richness and depth. Cut the plants to suit the heights of your vases.

Equipment

glass bowls and plates, scent bottles, mini decanters and modern glasses
2 pliable twigs (e.g. hazel), 30cm/12in long
8–10 glass marbles
2.5-7cm/1-3in pin-holder, held in place by florist's fix

Plants

25 sweet violets (*Viola odorata*)
15 wood anemones (*A. nemorosa*)
9 flame-coloured wallflowers (*Erysimum* 'Fire King')
5 stems of *Euphorbia amygdaloides* var. *robbiae*
3 heads of *Daphne odora* 'Aureo-marginata'
9 auriculas (*Primula auricula*)
1 plum snakeshead fritillary (*Fritillaria meleagris*)
3 heads of *Magnolia denudata*
7 young globe artichoke leaves (*Cynara cardunculus* Scolymus Group)
15 Lenten rose flowers and seed heads (*Helleborus orientalis*)

Method

Pick a selection of delicate flowers that look good close to. Some, like the snakeshead fritillary, are so perfect that one stem is best on its own. Others look balanced when several flowers are combined. Add one or two vases of more robust flowers, like the wallflowers and the hellebores, to enhance the delicacy of the rest. Here I have kept the flower stems quite short and all at a similar level to intensify the image.

Mix the violet stems with a few leaves in your hand and put them into the water all together. For the wood anemones, first bend the pliable twigs into a zigzag, so that they form a web in the shallow bowl to hold the fine anemone stems upright. Use the strong stems of the wallflowers to provide a structure and then place the euphorbias in between. Cut the daphne sprigs short and make sure their stem ends stay in the shallow water. For the auriculas, fill the glass to about a third with eight to ten marbles and poke in the flower stems, one by one. Simply place the fritillary and magnolias in their narrow-necked decanters. For the hellebore arrangement, use the pin-holder to place the artichoke leaves fairly evenly in the bowl, followed by the flowers.

From a Spring Hedge

The classic splendour of the silver bowl provides a good contrast to the simplicity of these wild flowers, all cut at full height.

Equipment

raised shallow bowl, 30cm/12in wide
soaked oasis block, cut to reach 2.5cm/1in above the bowl's rim
florist's frog and florist's fix

Plants

9–11 each of:
Solomon's seal (*Polygonatum* × *hybridum*)
Arum italicum 'Marmoratum' leaves
sweet cicely (*Myrrhis odorata*)
15–20 cuckoo flowers (*Cardamine pratensis*)
25 mixed blue and white bluebells (*Hyacinthoides non-scripta*)
15–20 cowslips (*Primula veris*)

Method

Fix the frog in the bowl and place the oasis on top. Use the Solomon's seal and arum to make an asymmetrical structure, about 1½ times the bowl's height. Let the sweet cicely foliage curve to one side. Place the flowers evenly, but put some cowslips at the centre, some to give height, and some to accentuate the asymmetry.

Woodland with Parrots

These huge-headed, flamboyant Parrot tulips are best mixed with equally stylish and strong, or structural, foliage. Alexanders is perfect for this. To give height and lift to this robust arrangement, also use some maple branches, with newly emerged claret foliage and acid-yellow flowers to echo the colour in the tulips.

Equipment
waisted glass vase, 30cm/12in tall

Plants
9 maple branches (*Acer platanoides* 'Crimson King'), 60-75cm/ 24-30in long

7 alexanders (*Smyrnium olusatrum*), 45-60cm/18-24in long

15 tulips (*Tulipa* 'Flaming Parrot'), at full height, about 45cm/18in long

Method
Arranging these ingredients could not be easier. The waisted vase holds the first few maple branches in place. The maples then provide both support and structure to hold the floppier stems and flowers of the alexanders and tulips.

So simply create a good overall structure and height with the maples, leaving the tallest branches standing about 1½ times the height of the vase. Do not make it too symmetrical, but it should look balanced at this stage. Next, poke in the alexanders, placing them fairly evenly throughout the arrangement. Finally, add the tulips, making sure there are no blank holes; with only one flower species used – and a powerful one at that – you need to give these tulips an even, but not linear, distribution.

A Vivid Globe of Venetian Colours

This is a combination of many of my favourite colours and plants. These fiery oranges, resonant black-purples, and pale and acid-greens recall the vivid colour schemes used in Titian's paintings. Imagine a line of these globes hanging above your head at a party overlooking the Grand Canal in Venice, and they should not feel too out of place. Hung en masse or singly, they will enhance any party, inside or, as here, in a romantic garden setting.

Equipment

soaked oasis globe, about 20cm/8in
    diameter
90cm/36in length of 5cm/2in gauge
    chicken wire
strong 3mm/⅛in binding wire
fine-gauge florist's wire
wire cutters and florist's scissors
length of chain for hanging globe

Plants

20 stems each of the following,
    30-35cm/12-14in long:
alexanders (*Smyrnium perfoliatum*)
Euphorbia cornigera
Euphorbia polychroma
guelder roses (*Viburnum opulus*
    'Roseum')
Euphorbia griffithii 'Fireglow'
Aquilegia vulgaris
40 black tulips (*Tulipa* 'Queen of
    Night' and *T.* 'Black Parrot') also
    30-35cm/12-14in long
5 trails of *Clematis montana*, taking as
    much length as you can

Method

Follow steps 1–6.

1 Assemble all the necessary pieces of equipment, tools, foliage and flowers. Cut a piece of chicken wire so that it will encircle your oasis globe, with a generous overlap. Cut a piece of the strong wire so that it is long enough to encircle fully the globe with the chicken wire wrapped around it, and add on an extra 30cm/12in length to make a loop to which you will attach the length of chain.

2 Bind the chicken wire carefully with the fine-gauge wire and string the piece of strong wire through the chicken wire right round the globe. Twist the wire ends several times; the weight of the globe will hang from this twist of wire, so it must be secure.

3 Attach the chain with another couple of twists of the strong wire. Hang the globe at easy working height, so you can poke the flowers into the oasis without having to tire yourself by reaching up. Gradually cover the globe lightly with your first foliage plant, *Smyrnium perfoliatum*, spacing the stems evenly.

4 In the same way add the *Euphorbia cornigera* and *E. polychroma* and the guelder rose stems.

Remember to check that the green oasis is well hidden at the bottom of the globe, too, as the view from underneath is most important.

5 Add the orange *Euphorbia griffithii* 'Fireglow', the aquilegias and the black tulips, distributing them evenly.

6 (*right*) Add a few twists and turns of *Clematis montana*, breaking any neat symmetry. Move the globe into position, hauling it up by attaching the chain to a piece of rope flung over a branch or beam or through a hook in the ceiling.

The Painter's Palette

This bold, brassy arrangement abandons all rules of colour association. Instead of just one or two contrasting colours, oranges, yellows, purples, pinks, blues and greens all clash in glorious disharmony to make a brilliant eye-catcher for a special occasion.

Equipment

shallow glass bowl, 36cm/14in wide and 8cm/3in deep
soaked oasis block, cut to reach 2.5-5cm/1-2in above the bowl's rim
florist's frog and florist's fix

Plants

the following stems, 20-25cm/8-10in long:
10–15 each *Euphorbia palustris* and *E. amygdaloides* var. *robbiae*
10 ceanothus (C. *arboreus* 'Trewithen Blue')
the following stems, 25cm/10in long:
10–15 each red, picotee yellow and plain yellow *Ranunculus asiaticus*
10–15 each purple and deep pink *Anemone coronaria* De Caen Group
10–15 orange, yellow and bicoloured tulips (e.g. 'Apricot Parrot', 'Mickey Mouse', 'Orange Favourite', 'Texas Gold')
about 30-40cm/12-16in long:
10–15 Lily-flowered tulips (e.g. 'Aladdin')

Method

Sear the euphorbia stems by plunging the ends into boiling water. Use florist's fix to secure the frog in the bowl. Place the oasis on the frog. Distribute the euphorbias and ceanothus evenly over the oasis, remembering to place some down the sides so that almost all the oasis is covered. Add the ranunculus and anemones, the yellow, orange and bicoloured tulips, and finally the Lily-flowered tulips to stand proud and slightly to one side. Water the oasis daily to leave a little spare water standing at the bottom of the bowl.

The Height of Spring

A lush arrangement of spring cherry blossom looks unfussy, simple and stylish. Spikes of acid-green euphorbia and sticky chestnut buds make the arrangement more substantial. If you prefer a lighter, silhouetted effect, you can leave them out.

For maximum impact, position the arrangement in the middle of a large table. Choose a site that has back or side light, so the sun can flood through the petals and highlight their simple beauty.

Equipment

glass vase, 45cm/18in tall with a wide mouth and narrow waist, which
 will hold the stems securely but
 allow the blossoms to splay out
 informally
75–100 glass marbles

Plants

the following branches or stems,
 about 90-120cm/3-4ft long:
15 *Euphorbia characias*
15 white cherry blossom (*Prunus*
 'Taihaku')
15 wild cherry blossom (*Prunus avium*)
10–15 horse chestnut (*Aesculus hippo-
 castanum*), with sticky buds and
 newly emerging leaves

Method

Carefully place the marbles in the vase. Position the euphorbia spikes evenly, in a not too tidy dome, poking the stems right into the marbles. This mesh of stems will then hold the other branches where you want to position them.

Add the heads of white cherry and then the wild cherry blossom, allowing some to flop out over the sides of the vase, with the blossom hanging as it might on the tree.

Finally, add the branches of sticky chestnut buds, some cut taller, some shorter, to break up any symmetry that remains, with an upward emphasis on one side, to balance the hanging cherry branches on the other.

A Midsummer Feast

Illustrated on pages 64–65.

The vibrant flowers and seed-laden foliage plants from cornfield, garden and hedgerow combine beautifully to make swags and sheaves to decorate a marquee and a long table for a great outdoor summer feast.

The Swag

It's much more interesting and colourful to create swags of brilliant flowers to dress up a plain white marquee rather than hire a more elaborate one with a fancy ruched blue or pink lining.

Equipment

surveyor's tape
blocks of oasis
kitchen knife and wire cutters
2.5-5cm/1-2in gauge chicken wire
strong 3mm/⅛in binding wire
fine-gauge florist's wire

Plants

approximate plant quantities for each
90cm/3ft of swag, all stems
10-15cm/4-6in long:
30–40 stems of hornbeam (*Carpinus betulus*), with seed cases
30–40 stems of alchemilla (*A. mollis*)
15–20 bunches each of 3–5 sprigs of cornflowers (*Centaurea cyanus*)
15–20 bunches each of 3 sprigs of lavender (*Lavandula stoechas* subsp. *pedunculata*)
15–20 mixed poppies and poppy seed heads

Method

Measure the front of the tent, or where you want to hang your swags, and divide the distance into manageable sections, not more than 1.8m/6ft long. Loop the tape by as much as you want the swags to curve.
Follow steps **1**–**5**.

1 After soaking the blocks of oasis, cut them with a sharp knife to make them square in section; the swag needs to be kept as light as possible, and it will then hold its shape better.

Cut the chicken wire to the length of each swag, adding 10-15cm/4-6in at either end to bend inwards to secure the blocks of oasis.

Cut a length of strong binding wire twice the length of the swag, plus an extra 1.2m/4ft for securing the swag ends to the marquee. Bend the wire in two.

2 Thread the double length of strong binding wire through the chicken wire from one end to the other, securing it with fine-gauge wire at 45cm/18in intervals. Place the blocks of oasis on the double wire, along the length of the chicken wire.

3 Wrap the chicken wire around the oasis, overlap the two edges, and use the fine-gauge wire to join them securely. Bend the chicken wire ends in and secure them, leaving a 30cm/12in loop of binding wire to protrude at one end and two wire ends 30cm/12in long at the other.

4 Hang the structure in place, twisting the strong binding wire loop or ends round and round your tent poles or the eyelets in the canvas. Ensure that the double run of binding wire is on the bottom, supporting the weight of the swag.

Now begin adding the plants. Distribute the hornbeam seed cases evenly along the swag. Don't forget to put as many above and below as at the sides. If you don't think about this now, you may find large bare areas that you had forgotten about and have nothing to cover them with.

5 (*right*) Add the alchemilla until the oasis is almost covered. Add the made-up bunches of cornflower and lavender sprigs, then distribute the poppies, concentrating on the most conspicuous areas.

Finally, give the whole swag a good spray with a water atomizer.

The Corn Sheaf

For the main table decoration, I can't think of anything nicer than the colourful, simple and fresh sheaf of bright poppies, grasses, oats and wheat tied simply with hop-bine.

Equipment
hop-bine (*Humulus lupulus*) or twine

Plants
mixed wild grasses, wheat and wild
    oats, 45-60cm/18-24in long
10–15 alchemilla (*A. mollis*), 30-45cm/
    12-18in long
20 cornflowers (*Centaurea cyanus*),
    45cm/18in long
10–15 nigella (*N. damascena*),
    30-45cm/12-18in long
30–40 corn poppies (*Papaver rhoeas*)
    and Iceland poppies (*P. nudicaule*),
    cut slightly shorter and to different
    lengths

Method
The sheaf is too big to hold in your hand all at once, so I make up four bunches and tie them together.

Sear the stem ends of the poppies and do not recut them. For each bunch, take a handful of the mixed grasses, hold them halfway along their stems and tie together loosely with hop-bine or twine. Holding the bunch in one hand, poke in the flowers, all facing more or less the same way: the alchemilla, cornflowers and nigella, and lastly the poppies. Place some poppies high and some low – but their stems should not reach to the bottom of the sheaf.

Tie the bunches together securely with the hop-bine or twine. Trim the stem ends (except for the poppies) so that they reach a common level.

Stand the sheaf on the table with the stems splayed slightly so that it stays upright. You can keep the flowers fresh by standing the sheaf in a little water; take it out and dry the stem ends when the table is laid. Scatter poppy petals among the plates.

Globe of Hedgerow Honeysuckle and Rose

Create your own sweet-smelling mixture of wild hedgerow flowers and foliage at the height of summer. Twine scented roses and honeysuckle around a globe, allowing the stems to bend and twist, just as they would if they were growing in a country lane. For maximum enjoyment, raise the globe to head height. Resist any urge to over-tidy the beautiful natural chaos of the plants.

Equipment

wire globe, about 80cm/32in
    diameter
stainless steel bucket
a few half-bricks or large pebbles, to
    weight the bucket
florist's fix, to stick on the rim of the
    bucket to hold the globe in place
pedestal or small decorative stand
    or table
30–40 florist's water vials in two sizes,
    8cm/3in and 13cm/5in
fine-gauge florist's wire
florist's scissors
wire cutters
rope to hang globe as you work

Plants

the following stems, cut as long as
    possible:
30–40 alchemilla (*A. mollis*)
30–40 mixed oats, grasses and corn
the following stems, 60-90cm/
    2-3ft long:
10–15 honeysuckle (*Lonicera*)
10 15 briar rose, or a single Rambler
    rose such as *Rosa mulliganii*

Method

Follow steps **1**–**6**.

1 Before you arrange the plants, check the position of the pedestal with the bucket and globe in place. When you are happy, remove the globe, weight the bucket and fill it with water.

2 All the stems, except the corn, need to be in water. Place those that won't reach the bucket in florist's vials. Put a mixed spray of alchemilla, oats and grasses in each of the shorter vials.

3 Hang the globe at the right height for working on. Start at the top, winding the honeysuckle stems in and out, and allowing the stem ends to hang down to sit in the water.

4 Tie in the honeysuckle stems with the florist's wire at roughly regular intervals. Weave in the rose stems and tie them in.

5 (*above*) Place any stem that will not reach the water in one of the larger vials. Tuck the vials inside the globe.

6 (*right*) Fill all gaps with the alchemilla sprays and corn. Take the globe down and place it on the bucket, pushing it firmly on to the florist's fix. Make sure all the hanging stems stay in the water. (If you just want to hang the globe, put all stem ends into vials.)

Posy in Crimson, Carmine and Gold

This posy is the most luscious combination of the richest colour, scent and texture. Mix deep crimson-black sweet Williams, sweet peas and Rosa *'Souvenir du Docteur Jamain' with carmine stocks, cosmos and* Rosa *'Nuits de Young', and add gold marigolds with crimson centres. For a real treat, place the vase beside your bed so you can wake up to this exotic mixture of highly scented flowers.*

Equipment
silver cup, 13cm/5in tall

Plants
5–7 each of the following stems,
     20-25cm/8-10in long:
roses (*Rosa* 'Nuits de Young' and
     R. 'Souvenir du Docteur Jamain')
carmine stocks (*Matthiola incana*)
cosmos (*C. bipinnatus* 'Versailles
     Carmine')
sweet Williams (*Dianthus barbatus*
     Nigrescens Group)
sweet peas (*Lathyrus odoratus*
     'Matucana' and *L.o.* 'Pageantry')
euphorbia (*E. cyparissias*)
perennial bupleurum (*B. falcatum*)
yellow marigolds (*Calendula* Art
     Shades Group)
stachys (*S. byzantina*)

Method
This arrangement starts with flowers rather than foliage because it is the flowers that are dominant here. Make a structure 1½ times the height of the vase, using all the crimson and carmine flowers and letting them spread out from the cup. Start with the roses, and add the stocks, cosmos, sweet Williams and sweet peas. Then place the acid-green euphorbia and bupleurum, distributing them evenly. Add the marigolds and finally the stems of stachys, letting them curve out from under the flowers as if to contain and support them in their luxurious, velvety folds.

Summer Abundance

This sumptuous celebration of summer is worthy of a still-life painting. Here for the picking are flowers of unsurpassed stature and opulence. Go over the top in creating this one, with huge alliums and agapanthus, great wands of eremurus and delphiniums and heavy-headed, heady-scented lilies.

Equipment
china urn, 45-60cm/18in-24in tall

Plants
5–9 each of the following stems, using
     as much height as possible:
eremurus (*E. stenophyllus*)
delphiniums (*D.* 'Cristella' or
     D. 'Nobility')
eryngiums (*E. alpinum* 'Amethyst')
dill (*Anethum graveolens*)
bells of Ireland (*Moluccella laevis*)
alliums (*A. giganteum*)
lupins (*Lupinus* 'The Governor')
lilies (*Lilium* 'Casa Blanca')
orange marigolds (*Calendula* Art
     Shades Group)
agapanthus (*A. campanulatus*
     var. *albidus*)

Method
First position the dominant structural flowers, the eremurus and the delphiniums, to give the arrangement its height and architecture. Make sure they are placed asymmetrically.

Add the eryngiums, green dill and bells of Ireland. Put in the alliums, the lupins and the lilies next, placing them some high and some lower, and giving emphasis to the centre rather than the silhouette. Use the bright, contrasting marigolds to punctuate the centre.

Finally, position the towering stems of agapanthus, using them to break up any neat lines and unbalance any symmetry that may have crept in as you placed the other flowers.

Vase of Pure White, Cream and Green

When it is hot it is tempting to pick the freshest of flowers and the lightest of foliage in pure white and green. Mix great bunches of scented roses, acanthus and teasel spikes with glowing white foxgloves and epilobium. Combine them with alchemilla, bishop's flower, astrantia and the caper spurge to make a stylish, yet un-grand arrangement.

Equipment

glass waisted vase, 30cm/12in tall

Plants

the following stems, 45-90cm/
   18-36in long:
10 teasels (*Dipsacus fullonum*)
10 bishop's flower (*Ammi majus*)
10–15 alchemilla (*A. mollis*)
7 astrantia (*A. major*)
5 caper spurge (*Euphorbia lathyris*)
5 white foxgloves (*Digitalis purpurea*
   f. *albiflora*)
5 epilobium (*E. angustifolium album*)
7 acanthus (*A. spinosus*)
7 *Rosa* 'Iceberg'

Method

Use the teasels and bishop's flower to make a structure 2½ to 3 times the height of the vase. Place a few teasel heads high to mark the height and cut the rest shorter to put at the heart of the arrangement.

Add the bright, fluffy alchemilla, astrantia and spurge, distributing them evenly. Next, add the foxgloves and epilobium, some to catch the light and create a radiant outline.

Then add the dominant acanthus and roses, making sure there is no symmetry but a balance between them. Let the acanthus create height to one side. Put the roses at the heart and slightly to the other side, curving out from the neck of the vase.

Collection of Scarlets and Blues

The velvety textures and rich colours of the scarlet lychnis, green tobacco plants and purple-blue anchusas and alliums contrast well with the clear simplicity of the blue and grey striped jug. The single zinnia in its blue glass continues the theme. Flowers often look more beautiful grouped in a collection of vases, decanters and jugs like this than they would if simply standing on their own.

Equipment

blue glassware
jug, 30cm/12in tall

Plants

5–7 each of the following stems,
    45-60cm/18-24in long:
anchusas (*A. azurea*)
salvias (*S. patens* and *S. × superba*)
tobacco plants (*Nicotiana* 'Lime
    Green')
alliums (*A. cernuum, A. neapolitanum*
    Cowanii Group, *A. sphaerocephalon*)
triteleia (*T. laxa* 'Koningin Fabiola')
lychnis (*L. chalcedonica* and
    L. × arkwrightii 'Vesuvius')
orange alstroemerias (*A. ligtu* hybrid)
globe artichokes (*Cynara cardunculus*
    Scolymus Group)
plus: a single zinnia (*Z.* 'Envy')

Method

For this arrangement, place the flowers first and the artichoke foliage last. Using the robust anchusas and salvias, make a structure about 1½ times the height of the jug. Their stems make a network into which you can add the tobacco plants, the alliums and the triteleia, to create an up and down rhythm in the bunch.

Add the contrasting bright lychnis and alstroemerias before placing the artichokes. Put some artichoke foliage at the heart of the arrangement and some right on the edge.

Place the single green zinnia in the blue glass to highlight the acid-green colour scattered among the flowers.

A Party Pompon

This vivid and dashing bauble is spectacular for a summer party. If you are eating outside, hang it from a tree or close to the table. It looks equally striking hanging from a beam in an outdoor arbour or marquee, or above the table in your dining room. Don't aim for a tight, neat affair, but make an extravagant statement: a dramatic globe some 90cm/3ft across of rich-coloured late-summer flowers and foliage.

Equipment

2 wire hanging baskets with chains, 30cm/12in diameter
moss, to line the baskets
4 blocks of soaked oasis
strong 3mm/$\frac{1}{8}$in binding wire
wire cutters and kitchen knife
rope or twine
tent peg (optional)

Plants

15–20 each of the following foliage stems, 40cm/16in long:
golden privet (*Ligustrum ovalifolium* 'Aureum')
smokebush (*Cotinus coggygria* 'Royal Purple')
silver-leaved elaeagnus (*E. angustifolia*)
the following stems of background flowers, 50cm/20in long:
10 bear's breeches (*Acanthus mollis*)
15 bells of Ireland (*Moluccella laevis*)
20 bupleurum (*B. griffithii* 'Decor')
15 dill (*Anethum graveolens*)
10 eryngiums (*E. giganteum*)
5 Scotch thistles (*Onopordum acanthium*)
15 each of the following rich-coloured flowers, 45cm/18in long:
claret-red gladioli (*G.* 'Black Lash')
claret-red dahlias (*D.* 'Black Fire')
large sunflowers (*Helianthus annuus* 'Henry Wilde' or 'Valentine')

Method

Strip off the bottom 8-10cm/3-4in of leaves and cut the stems at an angle so they are easy to poke through the moss and into the oasis blocks.
Follow steps **1**–**5**.

1 Remove the chain of one basket and leave the chain from the other basket free, so you can use it to hang the arrangement. Line the baskets with moss.

3 Place the two baskets rim to rim and bind them together securely with the strong binding wire.

2 Cut one of the blocks of oasis into quarters. Place a whole block of oasis in one of the baskets and wedge it in with a quarter block at either side. In the other basket put two blocks on top of each other in the centre and a quarter at either side.

4 *(above)* Hang the globe at a height where it is easy to work on. Secure the end of the rope and, if necessary, attach some rope or twine to the bottom of the globe and pin it to the ground with a tent peg to prevent it from swinging. Start with the golden privet, pushing the stems well into the oasis and covering the globe evenly.

5 *(right)* Add the smokebush and elaeagnus so the grey and purple leaves are evenly distributed. Insert the background flowers, one type at a time, all around the globe. Don't let it get too symmetrical. Next push in the gladioli and dahlias. Finally, add the sunflowers, placing them randomly.

Autumn Arrangements

An Autumn Gift

Illustrated on pages 76–77.

This rich, bright, multicoloured bunch of flowers and leaves wrapped in clear cellophane will impress and cheer any friend or relation. With the carmine-pink, claret-red, clear turquoise and deep orange, all set against the silver and green of cyperus, artemisia and elaeagnus, it would be hard to beat this mixture for rich colour.

The cellophane looks good and protects the flowers for a journey. Never transport cut flowers in a hot car without water – they will wilt in a few minutes. Wrap the stem ends in soaked kitchen paper, place in a plastic bag and secure with a rubber band.

Equipment
twine
clear cellophane
florist's scissors

Plants
5–7 of each of the following,
    45cm/18in long:
elaeagnus (*E. angustifolia* or
    E. 'Quicksilver')
artemisia (*A. arborescens* 'Faith Raven'
    or *A. pontica*)
bupleurum (*B. fruticosum*)
iris seed heads (*I. foetidissima*)
salvia (*S. uliginosa*)
pennisetum (*P. villosum*)
5–7 of each of the following,
    30cm/12in long:
dahlia (*D.* 'Glow' and 'Natal', 'Queen
    Fabiola' or 'Arabian Night')
Michaelmas daisy (*Aster novi-belgii*
    'Carnival')
cyperus (*C. albostriatus* or *C. eragrostis*)

Method
Strip all the bottom leaves of the flowers that you would expect to be below the water line in the vase.
Follow steps **1**–**4**.

1 Make a structure in your hand from the elaeagnus and add the artemisia and bupleurum, leaving some elaeagnus stems standing proud. The foliage should be balanced yet not too symmetrical, with some stems curving down at the front.

2 Still holding the bunch in your hand, add the dahlias and Michaelmas daisies, distributing them evenly, and then poke in the iris seed heads.

3 Add the final touches of the contrasting sky-blue salvias, the bright green cyperus and feathery pennisetum, putting some at the heart and some at the edges of the bunch, so the arrangement is balanced and yet not neat. It will now be difficult to hold together so many stems.

4 Either get someone to help you by tying the stems as you hold them, or lay the bunch carefully on a table, hold it with one hand and tie it with the other and your teeth. Trim the stems to the same length. If you cut any woody stems, slit them again to about 2.5cm/1in so that they can still readily absorb water.

An Autumn Collection

By autumn there is no longer the summer abundance to choose from, so collect a few stems of many different things – whatever is still around – and arrange them by colour. None of the vases here would make an impact on its own but, combined, each one becomes part of a sumptuous and handsome group. The hop medallion and a scattering of hop seeds on the table serve to link the different elements of the display.

Equipment
glasses and vases of varying heights,
    including a thin-necked vase, e.g.
    a traditional hyacinth glass
15–20 marbles for the small vases, to
    hold fragile stems in place
strong binding wire, for the base of
    the hop medallion

Plants
hop-bine (*Humulus lupulus*)
the following flowers and foliage, cut
    to 1½ to 2 times vase heights:
5–7 ampelopsis (*A. glandulosa* var.
    brevipedunculata)
3–5 euonymus (*E. europaeus*)
3–5 abutilons (*A.* 'Ashford Red')
7–9 cosmos (*C. atrosanguineus*)
3–5 deep red violas (*Viola* variety)
7–9 dahlias (*D.* 'Bishop of Llandaff')
3–5 purple violas (*Viola* variety)
3–5 large-flowered nicandras
    (*N. physalodes*)
3 anchusas (*A. azurea* 'Royal Blue')
7–9 gentian heads (*Gentiana triflora*)

Method
Make the hop-bine medallion first (see page 88). Entwine one end of hop-bine into the other and it will stay put. Arrange the ampelopsis, euonymus and abutilons in separate vases. Put the cosmos and red violas in the thin-necked vase, and the dahlias in a vase on their own. Place the violas, nicandras and anchusas in one small vase with the marbles and the gentian flowers in the other.

Autumn Table Centrepiece

The yellows, oranges and greens of this arrangement could be echoed in a sea of ornamental and edible fruits and vegetables harvested from the garden, such as the pumpkins and gourds included here.

Equipment

shallow fruit bowl, about 30cm/12in
    wide and 10cm/4in deep
soaked oasis block
florist's frog and florist's fix

Plants

7–10 each of the following,
    30-45cm/12-18in long:
blackthorn stems (*Prunus spinosa*)
viburnum stems with orange berries
    (*V. opulus*)
Chinese lanterns (*Physalis alkekengi*)
gloriosa daisies (*Rudbeckia*)
tithonias (*T. rotundifolia* 'Torch')
zinnias (*Z.* Scabious-flowered Group)
penstemons (*P.* 'Blackbird')
15 red hot pokers (*Kniphofia* 'Yellow
    Hammer')

Method

Use florist's fix to stick the frog to the bowl. Place the oasis on the frog, so that the block stands 2.5-5cm/1-2in above the rim. Make a balanced but not too symmetrical structure from the blackthorn and viburnum stems, spreading out over the table in each direction, but with the emphasis more to one side than the other. Let the foliage of the Chinese lanterns curve over the edge of the bowl, where they will be highlighted.

Add the gloriosa daisies, tithonias and zinnias, mainly to emphasize the heart of the arrangement.

Finally, place the penstemons and (yellow) red hot pokers, twisting and turning all around the outside, giving height to one side to counterbalance the downward curve of blackthorn and Chinese lanterns on the other.

Venetian Glass

This is proof that you need only one stem of a dramatic and beautiful flower to make an arrangement. Given enough space and in the right vase, a solitary stem silhouetted like this can have more impact than a vast elaborate vase of ten or twenty different types of flowers and foliage. In spring try this with a single frilly, flamboyant Parrot tulip. In summer choose one perfect sunflower, or a stem of a huge-headed Oriental poppy.

Equipment
Venetian glass chemist's jar,
   50cm/20in tall

Plant
single 1.2-1.5m/4-5ft stem of
   giant tobacco plant
   (*Nicotiana sylvestris*)

Method
Remove enough of the bottom leaves to allow the stem to be safely anchored in the base of the tall vase. Then simply place the tobacco plant so that it does not stand bolt upright, but continues a line from the vase, curving gently upwards to its full and magnificent height.

Red Hot Leaves

A late harvest of sprays of leaves, berries, hips turning colour, and bulrushes, with just a few dahlia, delphinium, salvia and leonotis flowers. Let the foliage go in all directions, with no careful harmony of colour or texture – a mound of dazzling red leaves and remaining splashes of flower colour contrasting with the white snowberries.

Equipment
pewter jug, 30cm/12in tall
glass fisherman's floats
large Christmas baubles

Plants
5 each of the following stems,
   60-90cm/24-36in long:
smokebush (*Cotinus obovatus*)
oak (*Quercus rubra*)
bulrushes (*Typha*)
7–11 each of the following stems,
   45-75cm/18-30in long:
euphorbia (*E. griffithii* 'Fireglow' or
   'Dixter')
rose hips (*Rosa moyesii* 'Geranium' or
   Rugosa rose)
snowberry berries (*Symphoricarpos albus*)
5–7 each of the following flowers,
   60-90cm/24-36in long:
delphinium (*D.* Black Knight Group)
leonotis (*L. ocymifolia*)
dahlias (*D.* 'Edinburgh')
blue salvias (*S. guaranitica* or *S. farinacea*
   'Victoria')
red salvias (*S. elegans* or *S. fulgens*)

Method
Using the smokebush and oak stems, make a framework about twice the height of the jug. Add the euphorbias to fill in any gaping holes. Place the vertical emphasis next, using the bulrushes, delphiniums and leonotis, so that the arrangement does not become too round and ordered. Then arrange the hips and berries fairly symmetrically, so no area is left out. Use the heavy hips to curve over the lip of the jug. Finally, add the dahlias and salvias at the centre.

A Winter Feast

Illustrated on pages 84–85.

A relaxed three-part table arrangement centred on large, festive candles uses foliage mixed with fresh yellow and white winter flowers. The combination of the raised classical vase, complemented by glazed terracotta side bowls, and the bright bursts of informal flowers among waving spikes of old man's beard, clematis and violet willow, appears both simple and yet grand.

For a clear, unclichéd country look, aim to combine plants that associate well in nature – many of these delicate flowers might be found growing wild under a hazel stool on a sheltered bank at the edge of a wood.

Equipment

raised classical or formal vase, preferably on a plinth, about 38cm/15in tall

2 side bowls, preferably raised and matching the colour of the formal vase

3 ivory church candles, 40cm/16in long, for the raised vase

2 ivory candles, 30cm/12in long, for the side bowls

5 candle holders

3 florist's frogs

3 blocks of oasis

florist's fix and florist's scissors

Plants for each side bowl

10 stems of hazel catkins (*Corylus avellana*), 30cm/12in long

5 arum leaves (*A. italicum* 'Marmoratum'), stems 15-20cm/6-8in long

5–10 cyclamen leaves (*C. hederifolium*), stems 10-15cm/4-6in long

3 clematis stems (*C. cirrhosa*), 50cm/20in long

5 honeysuckle stems (*Lonicera × purpusii*), 30cm/12in long

5–10 hellebore stems (*Helleborus orientalis*, green and white forms), 20-25cm/8-10in long

10–15 narcissi (*N.* 'Cheerfulness'), 20-25cm/8-10in long

3–5 white Fairy hyacinths (*Hyacinthus orientalis* 'Sneeuwwitje'), stems at full length

Method for side bowls

Cut the oasis to fit the bowls so that the block projects about 2.5cm/1in above the rim.

For each bowl, follow steps **1–3**.

Plants for the centre vase

5–10 stems each of the following, 60-90cm/2-3ft long:

violet willow (*Salix daphnoides*)

hazel catkins (*Corylus avellana*)

old man's beard (*Clematis vitalba*)

bird's foot ivy (*Hedera helix* 'Pedata')

clematis (*C. cirrhosa*)

15–20 cyclamen leaves (*C. hederifolium*), stems 5-20cm/6-8in long

10–15 stems each of the following, 20-30cm/8-12in long:

arum leaves (*A. italicum* 'Marmoratum')

hellebores (*Helleborus orientalis* and *H. foetidus*)

daphne (*D. laureola*)

narcissi (*N.* 'Cheerfulness')

15–20 snowdrops (*Galanthus nivalis* and *G.n.* 'Flore Pleno')

5–7 white Fairy hyacinths or *Hyacinthus orientalis* 'L'Innocence'

Method for the centre vase

Use florist's fix to secure the frog in the bottom of the vase. Cut the remaining block of oasis to fill the vase as much as possible and so that it sits at least 2.5cm/1in above the rim. Place it on the frog and insert the 3 long candles in holders into the oasis.

Make the arrangement in a similar way to that shown in steps **1–3** for the side bowls. Start with the willow and hazel stems, making a relaxed but even arrangement around the candles. Insert the old man's beard, ivy, clematis, cyclamen and arum leaves, and then add the flowers, spacing them evenly to keep the arrangement open and light.

Once you have placed the finished vase and bowls on the table, scatter a few ivy leaves between them and, if you like, add some extra candlelight to the display by including a few small nightlight candles.

1 Use florist's fix to secure the frog in the bowl. Position the block of oasis on the frog. Place the candle in a holder and push firmly down into the oasis. Place the hazel stems around it, spacing them evenly in the oasis.

2 Insert the arum and cyclamen leaves. Let the clematis stems trail out to one side and balance them with the honeysuckle, leaving the stems long to keep the arrangement light, flowing and relaxed.

3 Infill with the flowers, distributing them evenly but avoiding any rigid symmetry. The final effect should not be too dense.

Remember to light the candles just before your guests are seated.

Winter Branches

This arrangement of winter branches looks beautiful in a well-lit corner of the room or on a large central table in an entrance hall. You can use willow and hazel as your base, as I have here, or a mixture of yellow and red dogwoods and any of the brightly coloured willows. The large amaryllis (Hippeastrum) flowers add a touch of glamour and bold colour and, like the branches, last two to three weeks in water in a coolish room if well-conditioned.

Equipment

glass vase with a neck, 30cm/12in tall

fine canes and rubber bands for the amaryllis stems

a little cotton wool

Plants

10–12 violet willow stems (*Salix daphnoides*), 75-90cm/30-36in long

6 hazel stems (*Corylus avellana*) 75-90cm/30-36in long

a mix of 9–12 red and white amaryllis stems (*Hippeastrum*), some 50cm/20in and some 60-75cm/24-30in long

Method

Cut the canes to the right lengths for inserting in the hollow amaryllis stems, right up to the flower head. This prevents their huge, heavy heads breaking their stems. Block the canes in with small pieces of cotton wool. Rubber bands secured around the stem ends prevent them splitting after a few days in water.

Arrange the violet willow into a balanced and yet not too symmetrical structure, standing about 1½ times the height of the vase. Let the hazel stand naturally, with the catkins hanging as they would on the tree.

Finally, place the amaryllis, using the shorter stems to form a heart to the arrangement and raising those left longer to highlight their bright, sumptuous silhouettes.

A Winter Medallion

This dramatic yet simple wall hanging is easy to make. You can leave it hanging for many months, decorating it with fresh flowers whenever you have some. I have chosen hellebores, but Narcissus *'Paper White' or* Iris unguicularis *will look equally lovely.*

Before you construct the medallion, decide where you are going to hang it and put a hook in the wall. Work out how large you want the finished medallion to be, according to the expanse of wall.

Equipment

strong 3mm/⅛ in binding wire
fine-gauge florist's wire
florist's scissors
wire cutters
odourless hair spray, for holding
  clematis seed heads in place
10–15 small florist's water vials
  (optional)
a tack or picture hook for hanging the
  medallion

Plants

10–15 freshly cut stems, 90cm/36in
  long, of each of the following:
pliable willow, e.g. weeping willow
  (*Salix babylonica*); red or yellow
  dogwood (*Cornus*) makes a good
  alternative
violet willow (*Salix daphnoides*) or
  pussy willow (*S. caprea*)
10–15 stems of each of the following,
  about 45–60cm/1½–2ft long:
hazel (*Corylus*) or other catkins; alder
  (*Alnus*) makes a good alternative
old man's beard (*Clematis vitalba*)
  seed heads; any fluffy clematis
  seed heads, such as *C. tangutica* or
  C. 'Bill Mackenzie', are fine
10–15 stems of hellebores (*Helleborus
  orientalis*), 30cm/12in long

Method

Follow steps **1–7**.

1 Form a wire circle from the binding wire and fasten the ends with fine-gauge wire. Bend three pliable willow or dogwood stems around the wire hoop, weaving them in and out. These willow stems will hold themselves in place once you have wired their thicker ends on to the circle; you can then tuck in their whippier ends.

2 Starting at a different spot, add more stems, poking the cut ends into the willow framework. Always weave the willow around the wire in the same direction to create a regular shape. Add further branches until you have constructed a substantial base. Bind the branches together firmly with the fine-gauge wire.

3 Add all the violet or pussy willow stems, one at a time, winding them around the base and poking in the ends. Again, make sure you weave them in the same direction as the first willow or dogwood stems. With the fine-gauge wire, secure the main stems of violet or pussy willow.

4 Add the catkins, poking them in randomly and at different angles, so that the medallion doesn't look too stiff and formal.

5 Hang the medallion on the wall. If the circle looks at all asymmetrical or out of shape, carefully bend it back into a circle.

6 Insert branches of old man's beard at random intervals, taking care not to knock off its fragile seed heads.

7 (*right*) If you want the flowers to last longer than a few hours, insert their stems into the florist's water vials before adding them to the medallion. The vials can be hidden among the willow branches.

A Winter Desk

Many of the small winter flowers are particularly lovely when seen close to– decorating a desk or a bedside table, for example. Only then can you really enjoy the delicate veining of their petals, their subtle scents and their intricate structures.

Equipment

glass bowl, 10cm/4in wide
2 metal goblets, 8-10cm/3-4in tall
tiny coloured glass holder, such as a
  scent bottle
drinking glass, about 8cm/3in tall
8–10 glass marbles
2.5cm/1in pin-holder
florist's fix

Plants

10–15 dried copper beech leaves
  (*Betulus purpurea*)
10–15 winter aconites (*Eranthis*)
3–5 *Iris danfordiae*
5 *Narcissus* 'Tête-à-Tête'
1 *Narcissus* 'Topolino'
3 stems of witch hazel (*Hamamelis*)
7–9 *Iris reticulata*
1 stem of sweet box (*Sarcococca*)
1 *Crocus tommasinianus*

Method

For the bowl of aconites and beech leaves, fill the bowl with water, float the dried leaves on top and push the short aconite stems in between them.

Fill one of the metal goblets about a third full with glass marbles and push the stems of the *Iris danfordiae* and the *Narcissus* 'Tête-à-Tête' between them. Use the florist's fix to secure the pin-holder in the bottom of the other goblet. Push the witch hazel stems into the pin-holder and add the *Narcissus* 'Topolino'. Place the *Iris reticulata* in a little glass about a third to half of their height and add the sprig of sweet box. Simply put the single crocus in the scent bottle.

Finally, arrange the vases so that they make a balanced group.

Flower Curtain for a Winter Party

This light muslin curtain embroidered with fresh flowers and foliage makes an elegant and romantic party decoration. The cool green hellebore petals take on a glowing luminosity as sunlight streams through them; at night, by candlelight, their angular flowers and seed heads are thrown into sculptural relief. For best effect, place a double row of flowers down one edge; massed, the flowers create shadows that conceal the wires.

Begin by hanging lengths of muslin at the windows. Simply turn over the tops and, making gentle gathers, pin them at regular intervals along the top of the curtain pole with drawing pins.

For a swagged effect, loosely tie back the floral border side of the curtain using a curtain tie of the same material.

Equipment

2 lengths of cotton muslin
curtain pole and drawing pins
fine-gauge florist's wire
florist's scissors and superglue

Plants

Quantities will depend on the curtain size and how many flowers you can spare from the winter cutting garden. Choose from the following, cutting the stems to 8-10cm/3-4in long:
green hellebore heads (*H. argutifolius*, *H. foetidus* and *H. orientalis*)
snowdrops (*Galanthus nivalis* and *G.n.* 'Flore Pleno')
cyclamen leaves (*C. hederifolium*)
Fairy hyacinths (*Hyacinthus orientalis* 'Sneeuwwitje')

Method

Follow steps **1**–**5**.

1 Cut the wire into as many 4cm/1½in lengths as you have flowers, and bend each to form a U-shaped staple.

2 Carefully push one end of the staple and then the other just through the stem. Then push both staple ends right through together.

3 Attach the flowers to the curtain by pushing the staples gently through to the other side of the fabric.

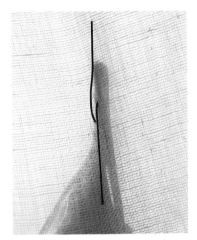

4 Bend the staple ends in opposite directions to lie flat behind the stem and flower head, holding them securely in place.

5 According to your quantities, arrange a double border of wired flowers down one or both vertical edges of the curtain. Dab superglue 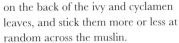 on the back of the ivy and cyclamen leaves, and stick them more or less at random across the muslin.

Harbinger of Spring

This little vase of miniature flowers, one of my favourite types of arrangement, could not be easier to assemble. Each flower can be seen individually and, viewed close to, you can appreciate fully the different textures, colours, structures and scents.

Towards the end of winter the earliest bulbs, such as grape hyacinths, scillas, chionodoxas and miniature narcissi, begin to bloom in the more sheltered, sunny spots of the garden. Mix these with late-winter flowers such as pulmonarias, cyclamen, crocuses and polyanthus to create a brilliant, gem-like collection for your bedside table.

Equipment
coloured-glass container, 8-10cm/
    3-4in tall

Plants
5–10 stems, cut as long as possible, of
    each of the following:
crocuses, e.g. *C. chrysanthus* 'Brass
    Band' (yellow) and *C. vernus*
    'Remembrance' (purple)
pulmonarias (*P. officinalis* 'Sissinghurst
    White' and 'Blue Ensign')
polyanthus varieties
scillas or chionodoxas
narcissi (*N. cyclamineus* or
    N. 'Canaliculatus')
cyclamen (*C. coum*)
grape hyacinths (*Muscari*)
snowdrops (*Galanthus nivalis* varieties)

Method
Start with the more robust and fuller flowers, such as the crocuses, pulmonarias and polyanthus, to create your structure. Poke the finer ones, like the scillas, narcissi, cyclamen and grape hyacinths, in between these stems, making sure no single type of flower is too clumped together. Lastly, add the snowdrops.

Flowers and Foliage through the Seasons

The flower and foliage plants included here are all personal favourites. They may exist in particularly rich and exotic colours, they may have an irresistible scent, or they may be extremely good 'doers' with long and productive flowering seasons. Almost all are easy to grow, without too many special requirements. With so many annuals you are guaranteed to have a good number of quick-growing plants that are harvestable in a matter of months.

So, for one reason or another, each and every plant in this catalogue is a bonus to the cutting garden. When you make your choice, try to include varieties of plants that look good at more than one time of year. Look out for the plants that have beautiful flowers as well as colourful hips, leaves or fruits. With agapanthus the umbels of blue and white flowers on their long stalks are invaluable in summer, but their green seed heads are equally good for autumn foliage. With peonies the same is true. Their spring emerging leaves, their spring and summer flowers and then their seed cases in autumn are all excellent for cutting.

Large quantities of flowers in the house are a treat at any time of the year, but don't forget to make choices for the colder, bleaker months, when the weather brings you inside and there is less to divert you in the garden.

In making your choice from my selection, you will have a beautiful and productive all-seasons cutting garden.

A riot of spring colour from a giant globe containing acid-green and bright red euphorbias (E. cornigera, E. polychroma and E. griffithii 'Fireglow'), the deep purple tulip 'Black Parrot' and white Clematis montana.

Spring

In the wild, spring is the flowering of the year. It is the first great burst of life, and for the gardener, brings an embarrassment of riches in filling out and frothing borders. For the small arrangement there are snakeshead fritillaries, pasque flowers, auriculas and species tulips. For bigger, more dramatic displays there are armfuls of fruit blossom, basketfuls of elaborate, punchy Parrot tulips, and boughs of emerging chartreuse-green leaves.

Green and Silver

CYNARA
Cardoon, globe artichoke,
Main entry: Summer Blue and Purple, page 132. *The grey-green young leaves of the cynaras are a dramatic foil to hellebores or velvet polyanthus (see pages 56–8).*

EUPHORBIA
Spurge, milkweed
Evergreen and deciduous sub-shrub, annual, biennial and perennial Zones: E. charactas *cultivars 7–10; E.* amyg- daloides *var.* robbiae, E. lathyris, E. marginata, E. seguieriana *8–9; E.* amygdaloides, E. schillingii *7–9; E.* cornigera, E. sikkimensis *6–9; E.* cyparissias, E. dulcis, E. polychroma, E. griffithii *cultivars 4–9; E.* palustris *5–8 Height: E.* cyparissias, E. dulcis *30cm/ 12in; E.* amygdaloides, E. polychroma, E. seguieriana *45cm/18in; E.* amygdal- oides *var.* robbiae, E. marginata *60cm/ 2ft; E.* cornigera, E. griffithii *cultivars, E.* palustris, E. schillingii *90cm/3ft; E.* characias *cultivars, E.* lathyris, E. sikkimensis *1.2m/4ft*
Varieties good for cutting *This plant genus is certainly in my top ten – I use them with anything and everything. Their upright habit and vivid, acid-green flower bracts provide the perfect contrast in the flowerbed and flower arrangement to all colours from pastels to richest ecclesiastical*

tones. For a succession lasting throughout the year, start with the shrubby evergreen E. characias *varieties. E. subsp.* wulfenii *'John Tomlinson' and 'Lambrook Gold' are two of the best cultivars; both combine well with large bunches of fruit blossom (see page 63). In early spring, too, there is the smaller E.* amygdaloides *and E.a. var.* robbiae *that mix well with any bright tulips or a colourful bunch of* Anemone coronaria *(see page 62). They are followed by the flat-topped E.* polychroma *and the taller E.* palustris *(see page 109). One of the best mixtures is these two and the orange E.* griffithii *'Fireglow' contrasted with black aquilegias and* Tulipa *'Queen of Night' (see page 60). In late spring I use E.* cyparis- sias *with its delicate little acid-green flowers and bracts in smaller bunches and posies.*

During summer and on into autumn euphorbias continue to be a mainstay of my cutting garden (see pages 116 and 137) and even in winter acid-green E. cornigera *goes on flowering – I have picked some to mix with* Anemone × hybrida *at Christmas.*

I used to scoff slightly when I read that you should never cut euphorbias without gloves on because it has a highly allergenic milky sap. But this is a plant to which you can gradually develop a sensitivity and I certainly have. If I fail to put on gloves or rigorously wash my hands after picking, my face swells up like a football. The reaction seems to be most violent on a hot day.

Conditioning *Euphorbias should last about 10 days if you soak them overnight or sear the stem ends for 20 seconds, to stop the sticky sap leaking out (see page 48). If you don't, it will cover your hands as you arrange them and turn the water cloudy. The leaking sap also blocks the capillary action of the stems, and prevents them drinking.*
Cultivation *When buying euphorbias from a nursery, I recommend choosing smaller plants and paying less. They are all quick growing, and you will have a good-sized plant in one growing season. I have*

different varieties either side of the central path in my cutting garden, so there are always one or two within easy reach to pick through most of the year. Depending on the space available, and how many varieties you decide to have, I suggest planting in clumps of three, except for E. characias, *which makes a good single specimen.*

Most euphorbias prefer full sun (but tol- erate partial shade) and reasonably drained, fertile soil. They will benefit from a mulch of compost or well-rotted manure in spring. Wood spurge, E. amygdaloides, *and its variants, which are woodland-edge perenni- als, will tolerate a poor, dry soil, and even spread beneath a shady wall or hedge.*

E. characias *produces biennial stems of leaves one year, and flower spikes the next. You should cut these back as they brown to allow room for the new growth, perhaps leaving one or two spikes for self-seeding.*

The deciduous perennials, like E. poly- chroma, *should be cut to the ground in autumn when the garden is tidied.*

❶ *Cynara cardunculus* (leaf)
❷ *Euphorbia cyparissias*
❸ *Euphorbia characias*
❹ *Euphorbia amygdaloides*
❺ *Euphorbia amygdaloides* var. *robbiae*
❻ *Helleborus argutifolius* (seed heads)
❼ *Smyrnium olusatrum*
❽ *Smyrnium perfoliatum*

5 cm/2 in

5 cm/2 in

6

5 cm/2 in

7

8

5 cm/2 in

Grow euphorbias from seed, by division or from cuttings. The annual E. marginata should be sown early in the greenhouse, and then planted out in full sun for the best results. E. palustris grown from seed will flower in the same year, if sown early enough. E. characias is another easily germinated from seed, although you may get variable-looking offspring. E. cornigera and E. schillingii will also germinate well if sown in the greenhouse in the spring.

Some euphorbias are free self-seeders. E. characias, E. lathyris, E. dulcis and E. amygdaloides will all produce volunteers, which should be collected from beneath the parent plant and potted up while they are still young.

E. cyparissias, E. dulcis, E. amygdaloides var. robbiae and E.a. cultivars, E. schillingii, E. sikkimensis, and E. griffithii cultivars all have rapidly spreading roots. Allow new plants to become established and then divide. They will take off readily from even the smallest clump. E. cyparissias is so rampant, you will want to choose its planting site quite carefully, as it does tend to take over. E. seguieriana, E. polychroma, E. cornigera and E. palustris form large root balls, which can also be readily divided. Many euphorbias can also be propagated successfully from cuttings.

HELLEBORUS ARGUTIFOLIUS
Corsican hellebore
Main entry: Winter Green and Silver, page 149. The chiselled, sculptural seed heads of the Corsican hellebore are best combined with the black Tulipa 'Queen of Night' or, for a somewhat weird 'Cruella de Vil' look, Fritillaria persica.

SMYRNIUM
Alexanders
Biennial Zones: 7–9
Height: 60-90cm/2-3ft
Varieties for cutting S. perfoliatum is an elegant plant with its lime-green bracts arranged like tutus up the stem, surrounding chandeliers of tiny yellowish-green flowers. I like it best of all mixed with the fine Dicentra 'Bacchanal' and the plum Fritillaria meleagris, on a brightly lit windowsill. The larger S. olusatrum is also good value cut. With a chunkier, more robust feel, it combines well with the flamboyant Parrot tulips and crown imperials. Its one drawback is its quite unpleasant smell, so I use only a few stems at a time and would not put it in an enclosed room.
Conditioning Strip the bottom leaves and then give it a good soak overnight. It will otherwise have a tendency to droop.
Cultivation S. olusatrum prefers a sunny, open site, with a fertile, well-drained soil. S. perfoliatum likes some shade, and in the garden mixes well with other deciduous woodland plants, such as hellebores and

Solomon's seal. Smyrniums are rarely found in nurseries, but S. olusatrum can be grown from seed, treated as a biennial.

S. perfoliatum can be a tricky plant to establish from seed but, once established, it will freely self-seed. The best thing is to dig some up from a good-sized patch, which will most likely contain some young seedlings. In midsummer it goes dormant, so the best time to dig up the plants is when the leaves reappear in winter. Though widely described as a biennial, it often does not flower, seed and die until the third year.

TULIPA
Tulip
Main entry: Spring Orange and Red, page 108. I am very keen on T. 'Spring Green', the freshest of the Viridiflora Group in its simple cream and green. It mixes well with whites: Prunus 'Taihaku', lilac, peonies and Dicentra spectabilis 'Alba', and it looks dramatic combined simply with the black Parrot tulip. T. 'Hummingbird' is elegant in its pale green contrasted to grapefruit yellow, while the smaller T. 'Pimpernel' is a drama queen, with its grey-green-edged white flowers and foliage, best arranged on its own in a small brightly coloured glass. As the flowers age, the white streaks turn a deep red.

9 Tulipa 'Hummingbird'
10 Tulipa 'Pimpernel'
11 Tulipa 'Spring Green'

11

9

10

5 cm/2 in

White

AMELANCHIER
Canadian shadbush, juneberry, serviceberry, snowy mespilus

Deciduous shrub and tree Zones: 5–9
Height and spread: to 6m/20ft × 3m/10ft
Varieties good for cutting *There is widespread confusion between the commonly available amelanchiers, A. canadensis, A. laevis and A. lamarckii, which are in fact very similar – even botanists argue about which is which. So never mind its label in the nursery, just look out for the shrub or small tree that has fine, oval leaves and an overall delicate structure and form. I love the combination in mid-spring of newly emerging copper-coloured foliage with white blossom: a chalky-white cloud of fine flowers, until the wind blows them away. I use it as the main structure in a huge spring mixture of white lilac, Viridiflora tulips, white pompon peonies and the white bleeding heart, Dicentra spectabilis 'Alba'. It proves its worth again in autumn, with its small leaves turning an irridescent mix of reds, oranges and ochres.*

Conditioning *It is worth hammering the cut stem ends, and giving them a cool, deep overnight drink before arranging.*

Cultivation *This is a good tree for the smaller garden, as it will never get too big. Plant just one of them, unless you have plenty of space and then you could have three to five in a shrubbery or wooded area.*

In keeping with other trees, amelanchier is best planted in late autumn, when the leaves have been shed, but when it is not too frosty and cold for the tender roots to settle. Choose a site in sun or semi-shade, with soil that is well drained but not too dry. Mulch with manure or well-rotted compost in early spring. Most amelanchiers cannot tolerate lime, thriving in neutral to acid soils. As with many acid-lovers, the lower the pH, the stronger the autumn colour.

It's unlikely that you will want to propagate amelanchiers as you are best buying in a good-sized specimen for quick picking, but if you do want to increase your stock, do so from division or seed or, if you have a shrubby specimen, by layering.

ANEMONE
Anemone, windflower
Perennial
Zones: 5–9 (A. × hybrida 6–9)
Height: A. blanda and A. nemorosa cultivars 10cm/4in; A. coronaria 20-25cm/8-10in; A. hupehensis 60-75cm/2-2½ft; A. × hybrida 1.5m/5ft
Varieties good for cutting *Anemones are excellent for cutting in spring, summer or autumn, and even during winter. The wild wood anemone, A. nemorosa, with its simple Catherine-wheel flowers, is lovely on its own. Beautiful cultivars include the wisteria-blue form with buttercup-yellow anthers, A.n. 'Robinsoniana', and the double white, green-streaked A.n. 'Bracteata Pleniflora'. A well-illustrated bulb catalogue will help you to choose your own favourites.*

A. blanda has a greater number of finer petals and flowers from late winter until mid-spring. Among many colour variants is the evening-sky-blue A.b. 'Atrocaerulea' (see pages 112 and 113). The A. coronaria cultivars are another spring mainstay for cutting. I like these best as single colours: the rich velvety deep blue-purple, the zany carmine-pink and the pure white 'The Bride', are all good, but they are difficult to find unmixed. You may want to plant them in a trial area for one year, and transplant them into colour blocks in the cutting garden for the next. I always choose the single De Caen Group, not the double St Brigid.

From late summer, and sometimes up until Christmas, you will find flowers of the A. hupehensis and A. × hybrida types (see page 139), which with their tall, straight stems are invaluable for cutting. They all last well for up to two weeks in water.

❶ *Anemone blanda*
❷ *Anemone coronaria*
  (De Caen Group)
  'The Bride'
❸ *Anemone nemorosa*

5 cm/2 in

Cultivation *The A. nemorosa and A. blanda types thrive in dappled shade, with a humus-rich, well-drained soil. They are particularly good for naturalizing in grass or in a wooded area, where they can spread to form a spectacular carpet. If A. coronaria has full sun and a well-drained soil, it will flower for months on end. A. hupehensis and A. × hybrida like an open position but will grow in shade. Their colonizing roots can be invasive, especially in light soils. Despite their height, they do not need staking.*

A. blanda, A. nemorosa and A. coronaria are cheap to buy as corms, so get them in quantity. They grow better if these are soaked for 24 hours before planting. They form leafy clumps that can be divided as the leaves die down in early summer.

With the larger perennial anemones, A. × hybrida and A. hupehensis, buy three to five of your chosen forms so you will have lots for picking. Buy decent-sized plants if you want tall flowers the first year. Within two to three years you will start getting a good harvest.

Propagate by division or root cuttings in winter – even the smallest section of root is likely to grow a plant (see pages 37, 41, 43). Although it is more of a palaver (and so worth it only for the rarities), anemones can also be grown from seed sown in late summer, but the seed has to be fresh. Collect the seed when the heads are still green and unripe or it will scatter before you get there.

A. coronaria St Brigid Group is grown commercially from seed, sown in spring, and then flowers from late summer to the following spring, but the plants have to be kept at a minimum temperature of 8°C/45°F throughout the winter.

ANTHRISCUS SYLVESTRIS
Cow parsley

Biennial Zones: 4–8
Height: 90cm/3ft
Varieties good for cutting *A white cloud of fluffy, delicate cow parsley hovers along the edges of English country lanes in late spring. But, for a rarity, choose the black-leaved cultivar 'Ravenswing'. It has thinner flowers, but its finely cut black foliage is a real asset in any garden. Cut*

tall, the flowers look dramatic on their own in a plain glass vase. Picked shorter, they add a light, rural feel to a mixed arrangement. I use cow parsley, either the species or 'Ravenswing', to make simple all-white hanging pompons for late-spring parties.

Cultivation Both forms grow on any soil, and prefer a well-drained, sunny spot. Seed of the species is available commercially, but if you collect some from a lane in summer, you won't have to buy it. Cow parsley does not like being transplanted, so sow and then thin seedlings to about 30cm/12in apart, where you want them to flower. A.s. 'Ravenswing' seed is not available commercially, so to make a good-sized clump, buy three to five plants and then collect your own seed. Treat as ordinary cow parsley, or if you have fewer seeds, sow in a cold greenhouse. Prick them out when the first, atypical (cotyledon) leaves appear. Don't wait until you see the recognizable feathery leaves, as they will resent disturbance at that stage.

CLEMATIS
Evergreen and deciduous climber and herbaceous perennial
Zones: C. cirrhosa 7–9; C. × durandii, C. montana, C. tangutica 6–9; C. vitalba, C. viticella 5–9
Height: C. × durandii 1.8m/6ft; C. 'Rouge Cardinal', C. cirrhosa, C. viticella 2-3m/6-10ft; C. tangutica 3-3.7m/10-12ft; C. montana 6m/20ft; C. vitalba 9m/30ft

Varieties good for cutting There isn't really a clematis that is not good for picking, but the problem is their short flower stems. You can get round this if you're feeling brave and brutal by cutting one or more boughs of flowers. In spring, the C. montana cultivars are ideal for this treatment. They have strong, woody stems, covered from top to bottom with open, fresh-faced flowers, and are extremely vigorous and quick-growing, so they can take this treatment two or three years after planting. I use them often as the main feature in late-spring and early-summer bridal bunches. You can cut them long and trailing, and then bind them together to give you any length that you want. They will not last all day without water, but if you make up the bunch just before it is needed,

they will look fine for many hours. You can make a pretty and dramatic bouquet simply by mixing C. montana with Viburnum opulus, and using tall, curving Solomon's seal to form the crown. Clouds of white clematis bound one stem to another trail down the church behind the bride.

When making up a bridal bunch, a good tip is to do it in front of a full-length mirror, holding it as the bride will be, and putting in the flowers to be viewed from that angle. Leave the stem ends bare in water until just before the bunch is needed, then dry them as much as you can before wrapping them in clingfilm, followed by the ribbon or tape.

In summer there are lovely rich, velvety, red and purple clematis to choose from such as 'Royal Velours' (see page 126), while in autumn the yellows (C. tangutica and 'Bill Mackenzie'), and in winter the fluffy seed heads of old man's beard (C. vitalba) are mainstays (see pages 88–9, 137, 149).

Cultivation Clematis are best planted in spring. Like most climbers, they thrive with their roots in shade and the stems climbing up a wall or tree, or over trellis in full sun. The montanas take shade and will grow to cover a shady wall. C. × durandii and others that do not cling are best grown in the herbaceous border or tied into a hazel or bamboo wigwam. All clematis like a soil that is retentive of moisture, without getting water-logged. For maximum flowers, feed regularly. Cut dead wood from winter, spring and early-summer flowerers (C. cirrhosa, C. montana, C. tangutica) straight after flowering, shaping them at the same time. C. × durandii and the herbaceous clematis should be cut down close to the ground in autumn. Those that flower later, like the Viticella cultivars, should be cut down to within 30cm/12in of the ground, in late winter or early spring.

To propagate clematis, take softwood or semi-ripe cuttings from the cultivars, or layer them in early summer (see pages 39, 42). For the species, sow seed in autumn. C. viticella self-seeds, although not rampantly.

4 *Amelanchier canadensis*
5 *Anthriscus sylvestris 'Ravenswing'*
6 *Clematis montana*

5 cm/2 in

5 cm / 2 in

CONVALLARIA MAJALIS
Lily-of-the-valley

Deciduous perennial Zones: 4–9
Height: 20-23cm/8-9in

Varieties good for cutting *This plant not only produces the most sweetly scented, white bell-shaped flowers in late spring, but it does so from the dark, uncompromising corners of your garden where little else thrives. I cannot resist picking bunches of them to put by my bed.*

C.m. 'Fortin's Giant' is an excellent cultivar that has larger flowers and broader foliage than most. It flowers two weeks later than the species, so if you plant both, you will prolong the picking season. For lovers of pink, there is a flushed-pink variety, C.m. var. rosea, which looks rather like a mini bluebell. There is also a good variegated form that requires a sunny site, or it reverts to the usual green-leaved type.

Cut flower and leaf together for a fresh-looking and fresh-smelling arrangement. The strong green foliage balances the delicate, pretty flowers. You will find that the scent fades and the flowers brown after four to five days, or sooner in a warm room.

Cultivation *This is a plant which will grow where it wants, and not necessarily where you want it, so plant clumps of 10 to 15 crowns in early autumn in several spots, preferably in semi-shade (although full sun and deep shade will also do) and see where*

they thrive. Also, planting it in different sites in varying degrees of light and sun will prolong your picking season, with those in full sun flowering up to a month earlier.

If bought dry, lily-of-the-valley's long, thong-like roots should be laid out about 2.5cm/1in deep, horizontally, and made as firm as possible. Almost any soil will do, except wringing wet bog or clay. Give your colonies a top-dressing of manure or compost in autumn when the leaves have died down. If lily-of-the-valley is happy it can become invasive, and you may find yourself digging it out to control its spread.

Propagate by division in early spring, every three or four years but not more often. In dividing the clumps, dig up and then plant them as square sods, with earth and creeping rhizome together. They can also be grown from seed sown in autumn.

DICENTRA
Bleeding heart, Dutchman's breeches, lady's locket

Perennial Zones: 3–8
Height : D. 'Bacchanal' 45cm/18in;
D. spectabilis 60cm/24in

Varieties good for cutting *The fine, lime-green leaves, light structure and dangly heart-shaped flowers of D. spectabilis 'Alba' combine beautifully with the Viridi-flora Tulipa 'Spring Green', Solomon's seal and the loveliest white cherry blossom, Prunus 'Taihaku'.*

Another favourite is D. 'Bacchanal', which has delicate velvet-crimson flowers over elegant greyish finely cut foliage. I like this in a small arrangement with the acid-green Smyrnium perfoliatum and Erythronium dens-canis. Its very long flowering season compensates for the lack of flower profusion at any one time, and it will form a good ground-covering clump, the foliage lasting well into autumn.

Conditioning *Give all dicentras a good drink before arranging.*

Cultivation *Buy three to five plants of each variety you like, and they will quickly become established and merge into a good-sized clump. They thrive in part shade in a humus-rich, moist, but well-drained soil, and like a cool position. Shelter the plant*

❶ *Convallaria majalis*
❷ *Iris 'Natascha'*
❸ *Dicentra spectabilis 'Alba'*
❹ *Hesperis matronalis var. albiflora*

5 cm / 2 in

from wind and late frosts, which will damage any new shoots. They will also put up with full sun, provided that the soil does not dry out completely.

The foliage of D. spectabilis yellows and dies back soon after flowering. You can tidy this up as it collapses, but otherwise you should avoid cutting the foliage in its full green, as it weakens the plant. Plant in either autumn or early spring. Propagate by division when the plant is dormant in late winter (see pages 37 and 41); these are, however, plants that hate disturbance, so division should be kept to a minimum.

D. spectabilis 'Alba' can also be grown from seed, germinating more easily after cooling for a time in the refrigerator, but D. formosa is more difficult from seed.

FRITILLARIA MELEAGRIS
Meadow or snakeshead fritillary
Main entry: Spring Yellow, page 109. *The delicate F.m. subvar. alba is best on its own or with the plum-coloured form.*

HESPERIS MATRONALIS
Sweet rocket, dame's violet
Main entry: Spring Pink, page 104. *The white sweet rocket, H.m. var. albiflora, is ideal for mixed arrangements, or combine in a heady bunch with the mauve-pink form.*

HYACINTHOIDES
Bluebell
Main entry: Spring Blue and Purple, page 112. *A white form of the bluebell H. non-scripta is lovely arranged with*

Tulipa '*Spring Green*' and Anemone coronaria '*The Bride*'; or simply combine blue and white bluebells (see page 58).

HYACINTHUS
Hyacinth

Bulb Zones: 4–9
Height: 17-20cm / 7-8in

Varieties for cutting The best of the hyacinths for cutting are the old-fashioned Fairy or Roman hyacinths (see page 152). I find the usual garden hyacinths rather chunky as cut flowers, with their short, thick stems, and heavy drumstick heads, although I do enjoy the lurid, almost fluorescent pink H. orientalis '*Jan Bos*' (see page 154). A few stems of these, even if not exactly beautiful, should certainly make you smile. Another freak form that I am very keen on is H. '*Distinction*' in an extraordinary, intense, velvet carmine-purple-pink. The white, tinged-green H.o. '*L'Innocence*' and the very deep blue H.o. '*King of the Blues*' are both

worth growing for their scent. Place a single stem beside a bed or in a bathroom.

Cultivation Hyacinths like a sunny, open site. They thrive in any ordinary well-drained soil, preferably enriched with manure the previous autumn. For bumper flowers, give them a liquid feed after the flower spikes have appeared. They are cheap to buy in 20s or 50s from bulb wholesalers. Plant 8-10cm / 3-4in deep, and about 20cm / 8in apart, in autumn. I also force a lot of hyacinths to cheer up the house during the winter, both for cutting (Fairy hyacinth) and pots (ordinary hyacinth). (See page 41.)

You can propagate them by removing the bulb offsets, if you lift them in late summer. These will flower when about three years old, but will not be full size until they are seven years old. I am too impatient for this and so buy more bulbs every autumn.

IRIS

Main entry: Winter Blue and Purple, page 158. *The delicate, ghostly white miniature Reticulata iris '*Natascha*' is best arranged simply, a few stems in a small glass. Put beneath a table light, so the orange flash and violet veins are individually lit.*

MAGNOLIA

Evergreen and deciduous shrub and tree
Zones: M. grandiflora 7–9; M. stellata 5–9; M. denudata 6–8
Height and spread: M. stellata 2.5-3m/8-10ft × 3-6m/10-20ft; M. denudata both 9m/30ft; M. grandiflora both 9-12m/30-40ft (it can grow to 30m/100ft high)

Varieties good for cutting I always feel magnolias are particularly suited to urban gardens, which are, on the whole, more sheltered and less prone to ruinous late frosts. The luxurious, waxen flowers are all spectacular for cutting. Pick a simple spray of M. stellata to admire close to. This is a good one to grow because, although like many magnolias it is slow-growing, it is unusual in starting to flower when still young. It is also very free-flowering, and has a perfect combination of texture and form with its soft, velvet buds and calyx surrounding whorls of cream, curving petals with darkened centres. The flowers are often damaged by frost, but with so many buds on each branch, there are always more to come.

M. denudata is another beauty. Once established it will be densely covered in the fragrant, pure white, shapely saucer-like

flowers, which feature in so many Japanese and Chinese paintings. Again, pick just a sprig of this to enjoy at close quarters.

Those who garden on a grander scale, and who have a spare expanse of south-facing wall, should consider the huge evergreen, summer-flowering M. grandiflora (see page 121), although it takes several years to flower. Or plant instead the cultivar M.g. '*Goliath*', with its large rich green leaves and extra-big lemon flowers.

Conditioning The loose stamens of M. grandiflora will fall and cover the table they are standing on, so you would do best to remove these before arranging.

Cultivation Magnolias thrive best in rich, deep soil that is retentive of moisture, but not boggy. They need sun or part shade, and shelter from strong winds. Most species prefer neutral to acid soil. When planting, dig a large hole that will allow plenty of room for the root ball plus lots of organic material. The fleshy roots are easily damaged, so plant in late spring when the risk of hard ground frosts has passed. You may need to protect the evergreen species with netting in severe winters. Mulch annually with rich compost until established.

❺ *Fritillaria meleagris subvar. alba*
❻ *Hyacinthoides non-scripta*
❼ *Hyacinthus orientalis '*L*' Innocence*
❽ *Magnolia denudata*
❾ *Magnolia stellata*

5 cm/2 in

❶ *Myrrhis odorata*
❷ *Rosa banksiae var. banksiae*
❸ *Viburnum × burkwoodii 'Park Farm Hybrid'*

5 cm/2 in

MYRRHIS ODORATA
Sweet cicely
Perennial Zones: 4–8
Height: 60-90cm/2-3ft

Varieties good for cutting *Sweet cicely is an old-fashioned herb, now often naturalized as a garden escape. Its finely cut, fern-like foliage is a real asset in the garden, where it will grow in shady positions under a tree, or beside a hedge. It looks lovely next to the strong heart-shaped leaves of Brunnera macrophylla. I grow it for its light, feathery flowers, which start about a month before cow parsley or bishop's flower. From the middle of spring, I use it together with its foliage to lighten up any wild flower bunch (see page 58).*

Conditioning *Give the leaves and flowers a good soak at least overnight before arranging, or they may droop.*

Cultivation *It thrives in shade or sun, in well-drained soil. If you keep cutting the flowers, the plants will preserve energy, and will soon form good established clumps. Plant three to five plants in autumn or early spring. It will then self-seed freely.*

This is an easy plant to grow from seed in spring. Sow in a seed bed, thinning the seedlings to 30cm/12in as needed, or
propagate by division in summer or autumn.(see pages 37 and 41)

NARCISSUS
Daffodil, narcissus
Main entry: Spring Yellow, page 109.
Favourite narcissi of mine are the delicate and highly scented N. poeticus var. recurvus and the pure white, multiheaded Triandrus, such as N. 'Ice Wings' and N. 'Thalia', with their smaller heads and long, thin flower shape and reflexed petals.

PAEONIA
Peony
Main entry: Spring Pink, page 105.
The double white peony P. lactiflora 'Shirley Temple' has a delicious scent and outside petals of pinkish-white with the middle pompon brushed with cream.

POLYGONATUM
Solomon's seal, David's harp
Rhizomatous perennial Zones: 4–10
Height: P. odoratum 60cm/24in;
P. falcatum 50-90cm/20-36in;
P. multiflorum 1m/40in; P. × hybridum 1.2m/4ft; P. biflorum (syn. P. commuta-tum) 1.5m/5ft

Varieties good for cutting
Solomon's seal is invaluable as a background flower for spring. If an arrangement is boring me or just does not seem to gell, I often find that Solomon's seal saves the day. With its tall, arching stems, silver-green foliage and dangly bellflowers, it can be used standing tall in a huge vase, or cut down to mix with more delicate plants.

As well as the stately P. × hybridum (P. multiflorum × P. odoratum), there are other more exotic varieties. Try the double form P.o. 'Flore Pleno', which looks like a raised row of frou-frou dresses, or the variegated form of P. falcatum, with its reddish stems and white-edged leaves. The smaller P. odoratum is a good dwarf and, as its name suggests, is strongly scented. If you have room for a giant, grow P. biflorum to mix with white lilac, peonies and cow parsley in a huge spring bunch.

Cultivation *Solomon's seal thrives in a cool, shady situation, with a humus-laden, retentive soil. It will in fact grow almost anywhere that is not hot and dry. Plant five to seven in a good clump and leave them to spread. Top-dress annually with well-decayed manure, and otherwise leave well alone – this plant resents disturbance.*

Propagate by division of the near-surface rhizomes in spring or autumn. Plant them again immediately, or store them, but only for a short time, in moist compost.

ROSA BANKSIAE var. BANKSIAE
Banksian rose
Main entry: Summer Pink, page 124.
The early-flowering, powder-puff R. banksiae var. banksiae is one of the most delicate roses. It needs a sunny, sheltered wall to climb over. It is ideally suited to arranging: try just three sprigs on their own, perhaps on a dressing table.

SYRINGA
Lilac
Deciduous shrub and tree Zones: S. vulgaris 4–8; S. microphylla 5–8
Height and spread: S. vulgaris cultivars 5m/16ft × 2.5m/8ft; S. microphylla 1.8m/6ft × 1.8m/6ft

Varieties good for cutting *Many people refuse to have lilac in the house as it once meant bad luck. It would be a real pity to miss out on that delicious wafting scent, so rid yourself of superstition and pick vast bunches of it. The most robust for cutting are the straightforward S. vulgaris varieties. I am not keen on the mauve forms, which look tinged with grey. I also tend to choose the single-flowered forms rather than the double, which can sometimes remind me of curly poodles. I like the pure whites, S.v. var. alba 'Maud Notcutt', which has larger individual flowers, and a smaller-flowered, dense variety, S.v. 'Mme Felix', which is famously good for picking and forcing. The small-flowered cream S.v. 'Primrose' is pretty mixed with early yellow roses. I grow too the reddish-purple S.v. 'Andenken an Ludwig Späth' (see pages 112 and113).*

Other species varieties, while also very pretty, tend to have no scent. S. microphylla 'Superba' is an exception, with its deep pink buds and smaller, paler fragrant flowers in early summer. You can produce a second crop of flowers in autumn by thinning out the spent flower twigs.

Conditioning *Hammer the woody stem ends. The flowers will last longer if you strip the leaves, but if I am arranging lilac* on its own, I keep some of the leaves for a more natural look.

Cultivation Lilac will grow in most fertile, well-drained soil in sun, though they will not tolerate very acid conditions. They thrive on chalk. Plant in late autumn or winter. They do not like being transplanted and will take a couple of years to settle down before flowering well, so don't despair before that. No regular pruning is needed, but it is a good idea to take your plant back to an attractive shape and structure after flowering, and to remove any weak shoots in winter. Always rid the plant of suckers, which divert energy and hence flowering potential

from the main stems. Young plants benefit from deadheading or regular picking. For really showy dense flower heads the plant can be coppiced; that is, cut right back after flowering in early summer. You are unlikely to want more than one of each variety, but you can propagate from softwood (semi-ripe) cuttings or layers in late summer (see pages 38, 39 and 42).

TULIPA
Tulip
Main entry: Spring Orange and Red, page 108. I love the Lily-flowered tulip 'White Triumphator' for its look of purity

and haughtiness. Arrange several on their own, in a tall narrow vase to keep the heads held high. The sumptuous, blowzy, peony-flowered white tulips are ideal for the sentimental bunch, for weddings or for when friends have a baby. Combine them with deep purple anemones, and some emerging hornbeam, oak or beech leaves, with the twigs just rising above a tightly tied bunch. More my type for cutting are the raspberry-ripple 'Carnaval de Nice', and the ripple-edged Parrot 'Estella Rijnveld', both too flamboyant for most gardens. This same flamboyance makes them the very thing for picking. Arrange them on their own or mixed

with another pure white double late, T. 'Mount Tacoma', or tumbling out of a simple white jug in the middle of your dining room. When the flowers open right out and their petals begin to drop, they look more and more like spectacular tropical birds.

VIBURNUM × BURKWOODII
Main entry: Winter Pink, page 154. The wonderfully fragrant, late-spring-flowering V. × burkwoodii has white flowers with buds flushed with pink, and lasts for up to a week in water. Unlike many of the leggy members of this family, it is a handsome bush when not in flower.

④ *Paeonia lactiflora* 'Shirley Temple'
⑤ *Polygonatum × hybridum*
⑥ *Narcissus poeticus* var. *recurvus*
⑦ *Syringa vulgaris* var. *alba*
⑧ *Tulipa* 'Carnaval de Nice'
⑨ *Tulipa* 'Estella Rijnveld'
⑩ *Tulipa* 'Mount Tacoma'
⑪ *Tulipa* 'White Triumphator'

5 cm/2 in

Pink

ANEMONE CORONARIA
Windflower

Main entry: Spring White, page 98. *The radiant carmine-pink De Caen Group anemone has an almost unrivalled intensity of colour. I use these pink anemones in zingy multicoloured arrangements, mixed with tulips and euphorbias (see page 62). They also look good on their own, in a bright green vase for a bedroom or bathroom.*

CARDAMINE
Cuckoo flower, lady's smock

Annual and perennial Zones: 3–9
Height: 45cm/18in

Varieties good for picking *From the very beginning of spring C. pratensis, the lilac-pink cuckoo flower, covers the banks of our lane, and has crept in around the damp edges of the garden. Its delicate colour and form mix beautifully with the bluebells and wood anemones that also grow wild on the banks. For the garden there is an improved form, with slightly bigger flowers, C.p. 'Flore Pleno'.*

Arrange them simply in a blue glass vase on their own, or mix them with other spring wood and meadow wild flowers – cowslips,

bluebells and Solomon's seal (see page 58). I may sound sanctimonious, but I think it is always better to grow your own wild flowers in the garden, and leave the ones in the lane to lift someone else's spirits after you.

Flowering earlier than C. pratensis is its big brother, C. quinquefolia (see page 153). You can often start picking this from mid- to late winter, for fresh informal bunches by the bedside.

Cultivation *Cardamines thrive in sun or semi-shade, and moist or wet soil. Plant five to seven in a group in a damp corner of your cutting garden, in autumn or spring. They will gradually spread. Propagate from seed sown in pots in a cold frame in spring, or by division in autumn (see pages 32–4, 41).*

CLEMATIS MONTANA

Main entry: Spring White, page 99.
C.m. 'Elizabeth' is a vigorous pale pink climbing clematis that is ideal for bridal bouquets, or for table decorations, where it can weave its way across the table top. Combine it with white lilac and green guelder rose pompons for a fresh, pretty look.

DAPHNE × BURKWOODII

Main entry: Winter Pink, page 153.
D. × b. 'Somerset', one of the latest daphnes to flower in late spring or early summer, has a sensational scent, like all of this family. I put three to five stems in a green glass decanter for a bathroom or bedroom.

ERYTHRONIUM
Dog's-tooth violet

Tuberous perennial Zones: 3–9
Height: E. dens-canis 13cm/5in;
E. 'Pagoda', E. californicum 30cm/12in

Varieties good for picking *The dog's-tooth violet is a wild woodland flower in Italy, and you often come across clumps of its beautiful dappled leaves standing out*

against the coppery tones of the wood floor. You would never find this delicate, intense plant in a florist's shop, and yet it is a beauty. Just put three to five stems, with their leaves, in a shallow glass, and have them on your desk or by your bed for close inspection. With their bending and twisting reflexed petals, they also form an elegant silhouette against the light on any window-sill. There are now many colour varieties available, so look through a good bulb catalogue to make your choice. I am keen on the rich purple E. dens-canis 'Frans Hals'.

The more robust cousins E. 'Pagoda' (see page 109) and E. californicum do not have the striking leaf markings, but their larger flowers last better in water. Arrange these on their own too, or mix them with the species tulip T. tarda.

Cultivation *These tubers are expensive, so invest in just a few and wait for them to spread. You must not allow the tubers to dry right out, so plant them immediately on arrival or store them in moist bark or compost until you are ready. These plants*

can be propagated from bulb offsets in summer, but I am impatient for the flowers, which will not be produced until the bulb is at least three to four years old. Plant them 8-10cm/3-4in deep and about 5-8cm/2-3in apart, in humus-rich, well-drained soil, in shade. They hate disturbance.

HESPERIS MATRONALIS
Sweet rocket, dame's violet

Perennial Zones: 4–9
Height: 90cm-2.2m/3-7ft

Varieties good for cutting *The tall, pale lilac, honesty-like sweet rocket is better for cutting than the rich cardinal-purple Lunaria annua. It has a sweet scent, particularly at night, and a more densely flowery habit. It will flower from the end of spring through to midsummer, and the more you pick the longer it will go on producing flower spikes. Grow both the pinkish-purple and the white forms (see page 100), mix them together in a bunch, and arrange them in a huge jug for the kitchen table, or mix them with the wild cherry, Prunus avium.*

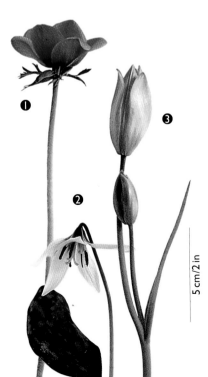

❶ Anemone coronaria De Caen Group
❷ Erythronium dens-canis
❸ Tulipa saxatilis
❹ Cardamine pratensis
❺ Clematis montana 'Elizabeth'
❻ Daphne x burkwoodii 'Somerset'

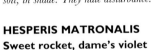

⑦ Hesperis matronalis
⑧ Paeonia lactiflora
   'Sarah Bernhardt'
⑨ Paeonia officinalis
⑩ Tulipa 'China Pink'

5 cm / 2 in

P. lactiflora *are also lovely for picking.*
Take them sparingly as they may be flower-
producing stems. I also pick handsome,
sculptural peony seed heads in late summer
and autumn (see page 117).
Conditioning *Peonies can be tempera-*
mental. Do not leave them out of water at
all after picking, since once they have
drooped it will be difficult to perk them up
again. Pick them in bud or full flower, and
if the water is kept clean and fresh, they may
last for up to two weeks.
Cultivation *Peonies thrive in rich, well-*
drained soil that does not dry out in summer.
Plant them in full sun. You may need to
stake them, for the flower heads, particularly
in the double forms, are often heavy enough
to bend over in the mud and dirty their faces,
or even break the stem. Give them a dressing
of bonemeal forked in every autumn, and a
mulch of compost or well-rotted manure in
spring. When you cut them, it is important
to take only one or two stems from each
plant, since the leaves grow on the same
stems as the flower. This will leave enough
foliage for photosynthesis, and hence food
storage for root development.

You need to plant clumps of three to five
of each variety to give you enough for cutting.
The crowns should be planted just below the
surface, with the resting buds not more than
3cm / 1¼in below the soil. If you plant
them too deep, they will flower less freely.

Propagate peonies by division in autumn
(see pages 37 and 41–2).

TULIPA
Tulip
Main entry: Spring Orange and Red,
page 108. *After a long journey and several*
days of searching, I found the wild species
T. saxatilis *on a rocky hillside at the*
western end of Crete. This, by far the most
brazen species tulip with its bright pink
petals and deep egg-yolk-yellow base and
centre, should not be mixed with anything
else, but valued as a real empress on its own.

The strong and strident pinks, such as
Lily-flowered T. 'China Pink', *I mix only*
with bright green Smyrnium perfoliatum
or euphorbias, which contrast with their
colour, and also cool them down.

Cultivation *Sweet rocket will do well in*
shade as well as full sun, and the white
variety can form a lovely luminous haze at
dusk beneath trees in a garden, with the
scent wafting over you as you walk. Plant
five to seven plants, and you will have plenty
for cutting. This biennial could not be easier
to grow from seed. Sow it in drills in a seed
bed, at the beginning of summer, and thin to
20-30cm / 8-12in. Either leave it where it
was sown and pick it from there, or
transplant it to its flowering position in
autumn. Mulch with manure in late spring.

PAEONIA
Peony
Shrubby and herbaceous deciduous
perennial Zones: 3–9
Height: P. lactiflora *and* P. officinalis
cultivars 60-75cm / 2-2½ft
Varieties good for cutting *Peonies,*
like bearded iris, lilies and great swags of
roses, always seem luxurious and extrava-
gant to pick. As you chop them off with the
secateurs, they make you feel slightly wicked

and, at the same time, excitingly indulgent. I
almost find myself looking over my shoulder,
waiting to be told off. My favourites are the
deep crimson and carmine double forms, such
as P. officinalis 'Crimson Globe', P.
lactiflora 'Inspecteur Lavergne' *and, the*
darkest of all, P.l. 'Monsieur Martin
Cahuzac'. *I also like white* P.l. 'Shirley
Temple' (see pages 102 and 103).

The blowzy pink peonies you see at late-
spring and early-summer weddings are not
my style. The colour and form remind me of
both candyfloss and ballroom dance dresses,
with their layer upon layer of pink material.
But P.l. 'Sarah Bernhardt' *is one of the best,*
as it does also have a faint scent.

The single peonies, with their purer looks
and great cup faces, look similar to waxen
magnolias, and are also good cut. Try P.l.
'Whitleyi Major', *which has white petals*
and a bright yellow centre.

Sadly, the flowers of the shrubby tree
peonies do not last more than a day or two,
so I tend to leave them on the bush.

The young reddish-tinged leaves of

Orange and Red

AQUILEGIA
Columbine, granny's bonnet
Perennial Zones 5–9
Height: 50-75cm/20-30in
Varieties good for cutting *These beautiful and elaborate flowers remind me of a nun's headdress. Although they last only three to four days in water, they make elegant and delicate cut flowers that are well worth growing.*

Grow a mix of fine long-spurred varieties, such as the McKana Hybrids in red, pink, white, blue, single and bicoloured forms, and display them in a jumble of colour for informal table centres. Or grow generous blocks of the bicoloured, long-spurred aquilegia varieties in red and gold or blue and white, and single-coloured varieties like the short-spurred, almost black A. vulgaris *(see page 112). Arrange these simply in a glass on their own or combine them with other flowers that highlight their colouring.*

Conditioning *Stand them in deep water for several hours before arranging.*
Cultivation *The McKana Hybrids like a sunny position with well-drained, but not dry, soil. Other aquilegias thrive in light shade and can even be planted by a sunless wall. In the main, aquilegias are short-lived perennials and you will need to restock regularly. They are grown easily from seed in spring. Sow under cover and line them out into a fertile seed bed for the summer. Move to their flowering positions in autumn. Or sow fresh seed in late summer, prick out and pot on in the autumn, storing the young plants in a cold frame through the winter. They will self-seed, hybridizing madly, so to keep your colours true, keep them well apart.*

ERYSIMUM CHEIRI
Wallflower
Perennial and biennial Zones: 3–9
Height: 30-50cm/12-20in
Varieties good for cutting *The sweet, old-fashioned smell of wallflowers, mixed with snapdragons and forget-me-nots, is reminiscent of old ladies' cottage gardens. They come in all the best colours, from deep rich black-crimson E.c. 'Blood Red', burnt-marmalade-orange E.c. 'Fire King' and bright vibrant yellow E.c. 'Cloth of Gold' to white and cream E.c. 'White Dame'.*

*Planted, they are best in colour blocks in the garden, rather than in multicoloured mixtures. I use them as a broad scalloped edging to my annual cutting patches, underplanted with forget-me-nots, and backed by clumps of alexanders (*Smyrnium olusatrum*). The unmixed rule does not apply when they are cut: there is nothing nicer than a wonderfully smelly jug of mixed wallflowers for the centre of your kitchen table, or in a large container for the sitting room. They last well even in a hot room, which brings out their scent more intensely. They look good arranged with Euphorbia amygdaloides var. robbiae, cut short for a small vase (see pages 56–8). Being all-round robust plants, wallflowers will last up to 10 days in clean water.*

Cultivation *Wallflowers are widely available in the autumn as bare roots in garden centres, but take care not to buy assorted colours or dwarf varieties, which are less use for cutting. They like a sunny position in fertile, well-drained soil and are easy to grow from seed, treated as biennials. Sow in colour lines 20-30cm/8-12in apart, directly in a seed bed in early summer. Thin the plants to 30cm/12in apart (save and transplant the thinnings if you wish) and then in mid-autumn transplant to their flowering positions. Try to keep a good sod of earth around the root when you transplant, for the tiny spider's web of rootlets gives the plant a good start before the depths of winter.*

❶ *Aquilegia olympica* (long-spurred hybrid)
❷ *Erysimum cheiri* 'Fire King'
❸ *Erysimum cheiri* 'Blood Red'
❹ *Euphorbia griffithii*
❺ *Euphorbia sikkimensis* (spring leaves)
❻ *Fritillaria meleagris*

5 cm/2 in

– the violet-purples of Anemone coronaria and the warm burnt-oranges and reds of the wallflowers. Cool this mixture with the contrasting acid-green of new hornbeam leaves or the ever-useful smyrniums and euphorbias. Or you can display red peonies with other flamboyant flowers, like Tulipa 'Carnaval de Nice' and the Parrot tulips, using the handsome peony leaves as your main foliage. The reddish-stained new leaves of P. lactiflora and P. mlokosewitschii are also lovely cut, mixed with hellebores and young artichoke leaves.

PRIMULA
Auricula, polyanthus
Main entry: Spring Yellow, page 110.
The red polyanthus are great favourites of mine – they look so velvety and inviting. Arrange them on their own from late winter through to the end of spring in an array of coloured glasses. They also look lovely mixed with other small spring flowers, such as scillas and violas.

Auriculas, with their thick felt petals, are the flowers the Victorians and Edwardians were so fond of putting in their still-life paintings. They should be cut a few stems at a time, and arranged on their own to be admired under a table lamp or bedside light (see pages 56–8).

RANUNCULUS ASIATICUS
Ranunculus, Persian buttercup
Main entry: Spring Yellow, page 111.
Looking like an elegant anemone, this bulb is showing off its richest Burgundy-red tones here. Mix it with pink, yellow and orange ranunculus, or the red Anemone coronaria and bupleurum.

EUPHORBIA
Spurge, milkweed
Main entry: Spring Green and Silver, page 96. The vibrant orange-brick-red of E. griffithii varieties is a must in any cutting garden. They last well when cut and mix beautifully with other lime-green-flowered euphorbias, and almost any of the tulips (see pages 60–61). I also pick them endlessly in the autumn, when the foliage has turned a tomato-soup red, to mix with bright and browning cotinus and oak leaves (see pages 82–3). The young emerging E. sikkimensis leaves, with their vibrant red veining, are also intense and bright mixed with ranunculus and tulips in the spring.

FRITILLARIA MELEAGRIS
Meadow or snakeshead fritillary
Main entry: Spring Yellow, page 109.
This delicately beautiful flower still grows wild in meadowland. Show off its plum-coloured snakeskinned bells on their own or with the white form (see pages 100 and 101).

PAEONIA
Peony
Main entry: Spring Pink, page 105.
The rich crimson of the pompon peony P. officinalis 'Rubra Plena' is irresistible when mixed with other deep, opulent colours

7 Primula auricula
8 Primula Cowichan Garnet Group
9 Primula Cowichan Garnet Group
10 Primula variety
11 Paeonia officinalis 'Rubra Plena'
12 Paeonia mlokosewitschii
(spring leaves)
13 Ranunculus asiaticus

5 cm/2 in

TULIPA
Tulip

Bulb Zones: 3–9
Height: Greigii 15-30cm/6-12in;
Fosteriana, Single and Double Early 30-
40cm/12-16in; Darwin, Lily-flowered,
Parrot, Viridifloras, Single and Double Late
45-60cm/18-24in

Varieties good for cutting *Tulips make supreme cut flowers. So much so, that there is not a month in the year when they are unavailable in the commercial cut flower markets. In the garden, you can plan to have one tulip or another to cut at least throughout the whole of spring. I have no real favourites among the early Fosteriana or Greigii varieties, but the Single Early 'Prinses Irene' with its strong, vibrant orange base colour and violet-purple marking at the bottom of each petal, and the bicoloured red and yellow 'Mickey Mouse' (see pages 110 and 111), can hardly be beaten. Another good one is the rich red 'Brilliant Star'. Coming after these are the Darwin Hybrids, the Single Lates, the Viridifloras and the Lily-flowered forms. An excellent Darwin Hybrid is 'Gudoshnik' with its red-on-yellow marbling, and you must grow the dramatically beautiful, deep purple-black Single Late 'Queen of Night' (see pages 112 and 113). Of the Viridifloras, cream and green 'Spring Green' (see page 97) and green and orange 'Artist' are both unusual and stylish. The Lily-flowered varieties are also elegant, with curving stems and pointed silhouettes. I particularly like the vibrant orange 'Ballerina', which has the added bonus of a freesia-like scent. Try also 'Queen of Sheba' or 'Aladdin', both red with yellow margins.*

Next come the Double Late forms. 'Uncle Tom' is a rich deep claret, but it is hard to beat the theatrical 'Carnaval de Nice' for style and panache (see page 103).

❶ *Tulipa acuminata*
❷ *Tulipa 'Artist'*
❸ *Tulipa 'Ballerina'*
❹ *Tulipa 'Gudoshnik'*
❺ *Tulipa 'Orange Favourite'*
❻ *Tulipa 'Prinses Irene'*
❼ *Tulipa 'Uncle Tom'*

In a class of its own, too, is the spidery T. acuminata. I often put a single stem alone in a tall glass. With the fantastic Parrot tulips we reach a climax. They look like a procession in a Guatemalan festival, their orange mixed with green ('Orange Favourite'), yellow veined with red ('Flaming Parrot', page 111), white dappled red and green ('Estella Rijnveld', page 103), crimson and green tipped with scarlet ('Rococo') and deep purple-black upon black ('Black Parrot', pages 112 and 113). Nothing else in the garden can beat these in the glamour stakes.

Conditioning *Tulips last well in water. Strip the bottom leaves and tie the stems up in paper (see page 49) before soaking them for about eight hours. This is to keep their stems bolt upright: if floppy stems absorb water, they will stay bent, hiding their faces.*

Cultivation *Tulip bulbs are cheap to buy from bulb wholesalers. Buy them by the 25, or, if you have room, 50 to 100. For easy picking, plant them in rows or blocks in your vegetable patch or cutting garden. Like most bulbs, tulips enjoy a good baking in the sun in summer and a well-drained soil. Position them about 10cm/4in deep, and 10-15cm/ 4-6in apart, in mid-autumn. Left in the ground, they form bulb offsets that will eventually flower, but if, like me, you are too impatient to wait, buy more in each year. If you cut tulips very heavily, you may find that you exhaust all the bulbs, and few will flower the following year. So it is always worth putting in more tulips than you think you will want to cut, and then there will still be some flower heads to look at in the garden, and you will have more of a chance for a decent show the following year.*

You can lift the bulbs to store until planting time once the leaves have died down by midsummer, when photosynthesis will have provided energy to carry them through the dormant season. For ease I usually leave the bulbs in the ground, only lifting and dividing them every three to five years.

5 cm/2 in

Yellow

ERYTHRONIUM
Dog's-tooth violet
Main entry: Spring Pink, page 104.
The beauty of the erythroniums is in their minutely detailed flowers and the elegant outline of their swept-back petals. Arrange the yellow-flowered E. 'Pagoda' on its own, or mixed with the species tulip, Tulipa turkestanica or the perfect T. clusiana 'Cynthia' (see pages 110 and 111).

EUPHORBIA
Spurge, milkweed
Main entry: Spring Green and Silver, page 96. *The yellow-green euphorbias provide some of the best spring foliage. Mix E. polychroma and the taller E. palustris with each and every colour.*

FRITILLARIA
Fritillary
Bulb Zones: 4–9
Height: F. meleagris 25-30cm / 10-12in; F. persica, F. imperialis to 1.5m / 5 ft.
Varieties good for cutting *A prima-donna among spring flowers, the statuesque crown imperial, F. imperialis 'Lutea', has tall, curving stems below a circle of huge*

yellow hanging bells. It is spectacular on its own or even better mixed with the 'Flaming Parrot' tulip and boughs of the horse chest-nut's sticky buds. I also love the burnt toffee orange form F.i. 'Rubra Maxima' in a fiercely exotic mix with the other queen of fritillaries, F. persica, Euphorbia chara-cias and the shaggy 'Black Parrot' tulips. Pick the lantern-like seed heads hanging below the whorl of leaves that top the stem. The only drawback to these fritillaries is their faint foxy smell, but I hardly notice it.

At the other end of the scale are the perfect chequerboard white or plum-coloured bells of the snakeshead or meadow fritillary (see pages 100, 101, 106 and 107).
Cultivation *Fritillaries like a deep, rich soil and prefer full sun, though F. imperi-alis tolerates some shade. Grow F. persica in a well-drained site with the protection of a sunny wall. Avoid disturbing these plants and never cut them right to the ground because they may stop flowering. Top-dress annually with well-decayed manure.*

The snakeshead fritillaries, cheap to buy from wholesalers, can be planted by the hundred in an area of unmown grass. Or, plant them in a large clump by a path, but put in a conspicuous label so you don't dig them up later on. Put them in 10cm / 4in deep, and about 15cm / 6in apart.

The larger, more expensive fritillaries do not flower until they are four to six years old so buy them from a good wholesaler, who will supply mature bulbs. If you buy cheaply you are likely to be buying a younger bulb. Plant several bulbs 15cm / 6in deep and 20-30cm / 8-12in apart. You can propagate fritillaries from seed or offsets, but again you will have to wait for them to flower.

NARCISSUS
Daffodil, narcissus
Bulb Zones: 3–9
Height: miniatures 15cm / 6in; full-size 30-45cm / 12-18in
Varieties good for cutting *I used to have reservations about the huge yellow, or orange and yellow, trumpeted varieties of daffodils. I now love them, especially in grass, and they look fantastic all jumbled up together in a tall white jug. I much prefer*

these unsophisticated flowers to the appar-ently overbred Split-corona and double forms.

Of the miniature narcissi, the tiny Tazetta N. 'Canaliculatus' is lovely mixed with other small-flowered bulbs like scillas, muscari and polyanthus. Another good Tazetta is the lightly scented pale cream N. 'Geranium'. Other narcissi I pick for their scent are N. 'Soleil d'Or' and the elegant and delicate pheasant's-eye narcissi, which have a particularly swoony scent in the evening. N. 'Paper White' (see page 152) is also especially fragrant, and it is easy to force indoors for winter.
Cultivation *Narcissi can be grown in any well-drained soil, in sun or even in quite shady borders. They are inexpensive bulbs if you buy them by the 50 or 100 from a good*

1. *Erythronium 'Pagoda'*
2. *Narcissus 'Canaliculatus'*
3. *Euphorbia polychroma*
4. *Euphorbia palustris*
5. *Fritillaria imperialis 'Lutea'*
6. *Narcissus 'Geranium'*

5 cm / 2 in

5 cm/2 in

PRIMULA
Auricula, cowslip, polyanthus, primrose

Perennial Zones: 4–9 (auriculas 3–8)
Height: 15-30cm/6-12in

Varieties good for cutting *By the end of winter, the primulas and polyanthus start to flower, beginning with the luscious, rich Venetian colours of the Cowichan polyanthus (see page 107). Arranged in separate, coloured glasses they will look as rich as a church procession. The Gold-laced polyanthus, cowslips and primroses come after them. The wild primrose, P. vulgaris, looks lovely in a shallow glass on its own, while the cowslip, P. veris, with its longer stems, looks good either on its own or as the star of a wild flower display (see page 58).*

In mid-spring the auriculas come into flower. Their texture is so rich and plush that they seem almost made-up. A creamy fluff (farina) covers the stem and buds. The petals often have a border in another colour as if wearing eye-liner (see page 107).

One of the main problems with growing polyanthus of any kind is that birds often get to the flower buds before you do. Avoid this by constructing a simple web of black cotton tied on short twigs pushed into the ground to stand about 8cm/3in above the flowers.

Cultivation *Gold-laced polyanthus, P. vulgaris and P. veris all need moist but well-drained non-acid soil, in sun or partial shade. Originating from a woodland plant, most will grow in full shade, too. Auriculas need a grittier, alkaline soil and sun.*

All primulas and polyanthus can be grown from seed, sown at the beginning of the year. If this is done early enough, you may have flowers the same year. If not, visit a good nursery and choose a selection yourself. Pick them out when they are in flower to be sure to get the best colour forms. Buy at least five of any one type, so you can make up a decent clump, which will provide you with more flowers the more you pick them. Plant them 30cm/12in apart, and the gap between them will quickly close. They will self-seed and you can build up a good stock by dividing the clumps the first autumn.

wholesaler. You will get bigger and better flowers if you plant them by the end of summer, as unlike tulips they benefit from being longer in the ground. Planted later they will do well enough, and even better the following year. They benefit from picking and deadheading, so the bulb does not deplete its food store trying to produce seed. After flowering, don't cut the leaves, or mow over them if in grass, until they have turned yellow. This allows the leaves time to feed the bulb to sustain it until the next season.

Plant the large forms 8-10cm/3-4in deep, and 10-15cm/4-6in apart; the miniature varieties should be 5-8cm/2-3in deep and the same apart. If you are planting in grass, use a tubular bulb planter or trowel to make a hole for each bulb (see page 40). If you are planting them indoors for forcing (see page 41), use a potting compost mixed 2:1 with sharp sand or horticultural grit.

Propagate by division, no sooner than six weeks after flowering; the clumps will benefit from being broken up every three to five years.

❶ *Primula auricula 'Blairside Yellow'*
❷ *Primula Gold-laced Group*
❸ *Primula vulgaris*
❹ *Primula veris*
❺ *Viola lutea*

❻ *Ranunculus asiaticus*
❼ *Ranunculus asiaticus*
❽ *Tulipa 'Mickey Mouse'*
❾ *Tulipa tarda*
❿ *Tulipa turkestanica*

5 cm/2 in

RANUNCULUS ASIATICUS
Ranunculus, Persian buttercup

Bulb Zones: 9–10
Height: 45-55cm/18-22in

Varieties good for cutting *These semi-tender bulbs come in glowing colours, Burgundy red (see page 107), marmalade-orange, bright sunflower-yellow, and royal carmine-pink. There are forms with red veined on yellow, and yellow edged with claret, and many variations on this theme.*

The double forms are like mini peonies when they first appear, and as they open up come to look more like big anemones with their dark bulbous centres and buttercup petals. The singles look like a much bigger and more glamorous older sister of our well-known field buttercup. Use them in your spring multicoloured arrangements, mixed with tulips, anemones, ceanothus and euphorbias (see page 62). Or simply arrange them in a tightly tied posy, the rich colours mixed together with pussy willow and new maple leaves and flowers.

Conditioning *Carefully strip all but the top leaves of these plants as they quickly go slimy on contact with water. The flowers will last up to two weeks in clean water.*

Cultivation *These are plants that like a position in full sun, with a very well-drained compost. Because they are not fully hardy, it is safest to grow them in the greenhouse. Plant them out in large pots, or better still in a greenhouse bed, 8cm/3in deep and 10-15cm/4-6in apart. They are difficult to propagate, so I buy the bulbs, which are cheap and widely available.*

SALIX CAPREA
Pussy willow

Main entry: Winter Green and Silver, page 150. *Although the silver-green buds of pussy willow often appear early in winter, they rarely plump up with all their soft yellow fluff until the beginning of spring. I cut it all the time and mix it, tall or short, with almost anything for the first few weeks of spring. It also looks good on its own, cut long, the tall branches arranged in a tall vase on a windowsill where the sun will then catch the yellow haze of anthers and pollen that surrounds each flower.*

TULIPA
Tulip

Main entry: Spring Orange and Red, page 108. *In spring, tulips dominate the centre stage of cut flowers. All of the yellow ones illustrated here, ranging from the pure yellow 'West Point' to the perfect, delicate T. clusiana 'Cynthia' and the frilly 'Flaming Parrot', are stars in my book.*

VIOLA

Main entry: Spring Blue and Purple, page 113. *From early spring through to the autumn frosts, I pick little violas like the yellow V. lutea to arrange on their own in a shallow glass. Violas are almost never to be found in florist's shops and markets, and it is so easy to grow your own.*

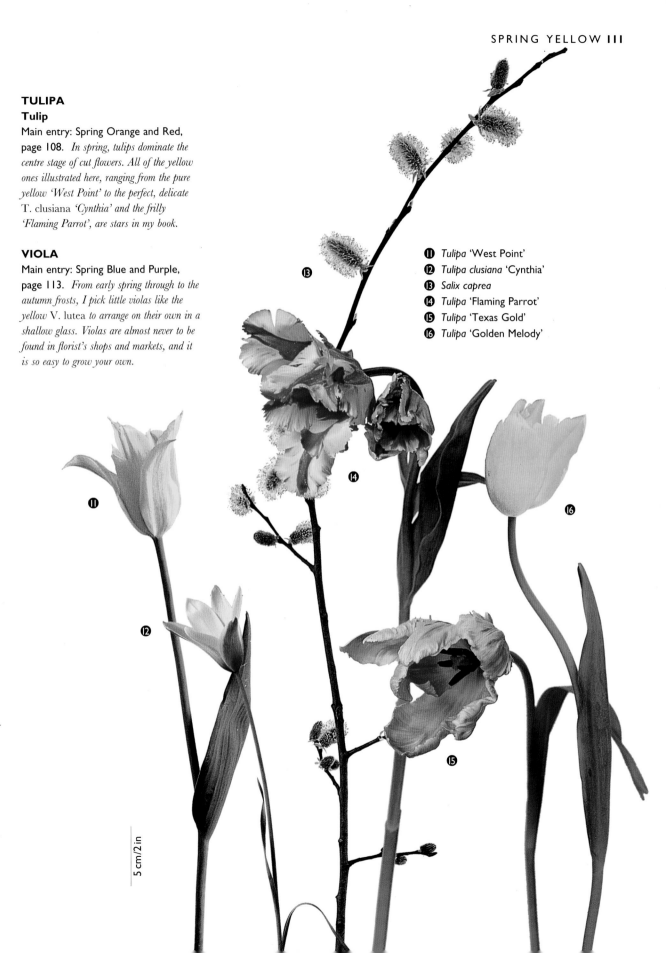

⑪ *Tulipa 'West Point'*
⑫ *Tulipa clusiana 'Cynthia'*
⑬ *Salix caprea*
⑭ *Tulipa 'Flaming Parrot'*
⑮ *Tulipa 'Texas Gold'*
⑯ *Tulipa 'Golden Melody'*

5 cm/2 in

Blue and Purple

ANEMONE
Anemone, windflower
Main entry: Spring White, page 98.
Enjoy deep blue A. blanda 'Atrocaerulea' in a glass on its own by your desk, or in a mixed posy. The velvety blue A. coronaria De Caen Group brings a plush richness to almost any colour you mix it with.

AQUILEGIA
Columbine, granny's bonnet
Main entry: Spring Orange and Red, page 106. *The purple-black, short-spurred A. vulgaris is lovely mixed with black tulips and acid-green euphorbias (see pages 60–61).*

CEANOTHUS
Californian lilac
*Evergreen and deciduous shrub and tree
Zones: C. arboreus 'Trewithen Blue',
C. 'Autumnal Blue' 9–10; C. 'Italian Skies' 8–10; C.× delileanus 'Gloire de Versailles' 7–10
Height and spread: C. × delileanus 'Gloire de Versailles' 1.5m/5ft × 1.5m/5ft;
C. 'Italian Skies' 1.5m/5ft × 3m/10ft;
C. 'Autumnal Blue' 3m/10ft × 2m/6½ft;
C. arboreus 'Trewithen Blue' 6m/20ft × 7.5m/25ft*
Varieties good for cutting *My favourites are the rich, deep blue forms, like the evergreen wall shrub C. 'Italian Skies' or C. 'Puget's Blue'. If you have room, pick one of the larger varieties, such as evergreen arboreus 'Trewithen Blue', which has paler flowers but will allow you to harvest armfuls to use as background foliage and flowers for multicoloured arrangements (see page 62). If space is restricted, choose a species that will flower over a long period. Evergreen C. 'Autumnal Blue' has pale powdery blue flowers through late summer and autumn, and sometimes in spring. 'Gloire de Versailles'*

❶ *Aquilegia vulgaris*
❷ *Ceanothus arboreus 'Trewithen Blue'*
❸ *Ceanothus 'Italian Skies'*
❹ *Syringa vulgaris 'Andenken an Ludwig Späth'*
❺ *Tulipa 'Black Parrot'*
❻ *Tulipa 'Queen of Night'*

will produce flowers from late spring until the autumn.
Conditioning *Hammer or slit the stem ends for 2.5-5cm/1-2in after picking and then stand in deep water for several hours.*
Cultivation *Plant at least one species for spring and one for autumn picking. Choose*

sites in full sun with light, well-drained soil, and try to protect them from cold and drying winds with the shelter of a sunny wall. Ceanothus can be short-lived, so take semi-ripe cuttings in summer (see pages 38 and 39). Remove only dead wood from evergreens as pruning will shorten their life. Deciduous ceanothus can have their laterals pruned in early spring, to within 8-10cm/3-4in of the previous year's growth.

HYACINTHOIDES
Bluebell
*Bulb Zones: 5–8
Height: 60cm/24in*
Varieties good for cutting *The rich blue carpet of a wild bluebell wood is a sight that lifts the spirits. The wild bluebell, H. non-scripta, is best arranged on its own, or mixed with cowslips and Solomon's*

seal in a wild-flower arrangement (see page 58). Best of all are the white forms of H. non-scripta (see pages 101–2). There are blue cultivated forms with larger flowers, but the blues tend to be washed-out.
Conditioning *Pick bluebells when they first emerge and sear the stem ends for 20 seconds. It is better to use scissors when you pick them, rather than just to pull them up, as children are inclined to do, and risk damaging the bulb. Cut above the white part of the stalk, which does not suck up water as effectively as the green part.*
Cultivation *The best place to grow bluebells is in a woody area or shrubbery, but if you do not have one, plant them in heavy soil against a damp shady wall or under a tree. Plant in autumn, 10-15cm/4-6in deep. Propagate by division in late summer, or by seed sown in the autumn.*

5 cm/2 in

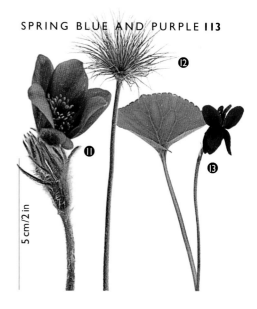

LAVANDULA STOECHAS subsp. PEDUNCULATA
Lavender

Main entry: Summer Blue and Purple, page 134. *This showy lavender is one of the first to flower in mid-spring. With deep purple 'rabbit's ear' tassels on purple and grey fragrant heads, it mixes well with almost anything. For a simple, pretty bunch, combine it with bishop's flower, white and blue anemones and yellow Persian buttercups. For a more glamorous look, cut tall sprays of it and simply poke* Tulipa *'Flaming Parrot' into its woody structure. Use it, too, in early summer party swags with alchemilla, poppies and cornflowers (see pages 64–6).*

PULSATILLA
Pasque flower

Perennial Zones: 5–9
Height: P. halleri 15-38cm/6-15in; P. vulgaris 15-23cm/6-9in; P. vernalis 5-10cm/2-4in

Varieties good for cutting *Plant this exotic-looking, plush-purple flower in generous clumps, and you may coax it to spread into a rich velvet carpet, as it still sometimes does in its wild state on its native chalk downland.*

When you pick it, place just a few stems and leaves in one or two small glasses, and find a place where they will be back-lit, to catch the fine halo of tiny hairs that covers flowers, foliage and stem. Pasque flower seed heads are also good for picking. I like to mix them with the flowers of deep-coloured Viticella clematis, which are not unlike those of P. vulgaris *itself.*

Among the various colour forms are a deep crimson and a pure white, P. vernalis. *There is also a larger-flowered purple species,* P. halleri, *with huge 8cm/3in upward-facing flowers, with a pointing, purple proboscis in the middle of the deep yellow centre. None of these, however, has quite the exquisite beauty and charm of the wild species.*

Cultivation *They thrive in full sun, in a calcareous, well-drained soil. Propagate by root cuttings during winter (see page 43), or seed sown when it is still fresh in early summer.*

SYRINGA VULGARIS
Lilac

Main entry: Spring White, page 102. *This deep purple lilac S.v. 'Andenken an Ludwig Späth' is best in bud when the intensity of its colour is greatest. Put it in a simple arrangement with* Tulipa *'Spring Green'. Or mix it with* T. *'Queen of Night',* T. *'Orange Favourite' and* Euphorbia *griffithii 'Dixter' and add the yellow-greens of* E. polychroma *and* E. palustris.

TULIPA
Tulip

Main entry: Spring Orange and Red, page 108. *The almost black* T. *'Black Parrot' and* T. *'Queen of Night', with their strong shape and colour, have great glamour. Contrast them in a tightly tied bunch with* T. *'Spring Green' and peonies and euphorbias, or with orange and acid-green euphorbias in a hanging globe (see pages 60–61).*

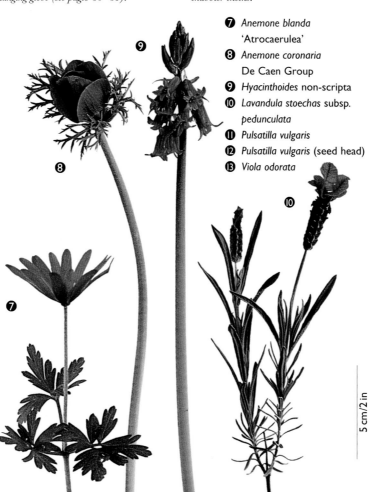

❼ Anemone blanda 'Atrocaerulea'
❽ Anemone coronaria De Caen Group
❾ Hyacinthoides non-scripta
❿ Lavandula stoechas subsp. pedunculata
⓫ Pulsatilla vulgaris
⓬ Pulsatilla vulgaris (seed head)
⓭ Viola odorata

VIOLA
Sweet violet, pansy, viola

Annual and perennial Zones: 3–9
*Height: 10-20cm/4-8in (*V. cornuta *30-60cm/12-24in)*

Varieties good for cutting *The viola genus has flowers to pick in every season of the year. In spring, the lovely deep purple, scented sweet violet,* V. odorata, *comes into flower. Its tiny flowers would be lost among others and so it should be arranged on its own (see pages 56–8). Grow other violets such as the pure white* V. obliqua alba *or the oddity* V. sororia *'Freckles', which is covered in tiny splashes of violet on white. Then there are the mini violas, like* V. tricolor *and* V. lutea *(see pages 110 and 111), in many combinations of yellow and purple. The smaller species violas tend to have less cheek and more chin than the pansies, which have rounder faces with chubbier cheeks.*

During summer the many colour forms of the rhizomatous perennial V. cornuta *will continue to flower for months. These have longer stems than most and so can be mixed with other flowers, like the deep orange, small-flowered Icelandic poppy,* Papaver nudicaule *'Matador'. The mauvy blue form combines beautifully with this. Also grow the annuals* V. *'Jolly Joker', a gaudy orange and purple, and the near-black* V. *'Molly Sanderson' or* V. *'Bowles Black' with its many tiny flowers on one stem. This lasts particularly well in water, still looking good after 10 days. If you keep picking or deadheading these will continue to flower all through summer and autumn.*

For winter, choose any of those in the catalogues designed for cold-weather flowering. Plant up pots in autumn, and put them by your back door for easy picking and deadheading, as well as for bringing indoors when there are hard frosts.

Conditioning *Strip the bottom leaves.*
Cultivation *Some species violas prefer a cool, shady site, but generally all annual violas do best in sun. Group them in good-sized clumps of five to seven plants, planted 20-30cm/8-12in apart.*

Most violas grow easily from seed. Many of them self-seed so freely that you will have violas for ever. If you sow them in early spring, they will flower later the same year. Some species have spreading rootstocks, so they can easily be propagated by division in mid-spring. Most can also be propagated from softwood cuttings. They all benefit from feeding and deadheading.

Summer

Summer is the time to have huge displays of flowers all over the house, giving a sense of luxury and abundance for everyone to enjoy. You can create statuesque and sumptuous vases of lilies, roses, bearded iris, delphiniums, sunflowers, philadelphus, eremurus, acanthus and artichokes. Who could want more? Room by room, a different glorious display will greet you. For smaller arrangements, cut fragrant sweet peas, pinks, sweet Williams, phlox, roses and honeysuckle. With all the colour and vigour of annuals in full flood at this time of year, you will never be lacking for choice.

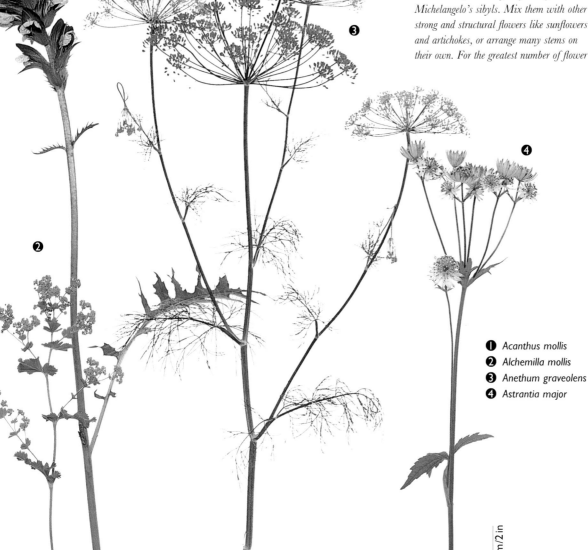

① Acanthus mollis
② Alchemilla mollis
③ Anethum graveolens
④ Astrantia major

5 cm/2 in

Green and Silver

ACANTHUS
Bear's breeches
*Semi-evergreen herbaceous perennial
Zones: A. mollis 8–10; A. spinosus,
A. hungaricus 6–10
Height: 90cm-1.5m/3-5ft; A. spinosus to
1.8m/6ft*
Varieties good for cutting
The imposing foxglove-like flower spikes of the acanthus are a mixture of green, purple, white and pink. Each is clad in 20 or 30 flowers, with their dominant purple bracts like the dark, hooded eyes of one of Michelangelo's sibyls. Mix them with other strong and structural flowers like sunflowers and artichokes, or arrange many stems on their own. For the greatest number of flower spikes choose A. spinosus, although A. hungaricus is also free-flowering. A. mollis and A. spinosus Spinosissimus Group, whose elegant, finely divided foliage is an asset in any garden, produce fewer flowers.

Conditioning Beware of the long, sharp spikes in the flowers when cutting and arranging. Plunge the stem ends into boiling water for 20 seconds and they will last for up to two weeks in water.

Cultivation Plant acanthus in groups of three or five in spring, and protect the crowns with a mulch in the first winter. They may take a year or two to settle in and start flowering, so be patient. Acanthus will grow in shade, but for lots of flower spikes choose a site with deep well-drained fertile soil in full sun where its roots can bake. They can become invasive and, once established, their long thong-like roots are difficult to eradicate. Propagate acanthus from root cuttings in winter (see page 43) or by division in autumn or early spring (see pages 37, 41).

ALCHEMILLA MOLLIS
Lady's mantle
*Deciduous perennial Zones: 4–8
Height: 30-50cm/12-20in*
Varieties good for cutting
A. mollis, with its acid-green light and frothy flowers and downy foliage, is the bread and butter of the summer florist: a robust and long-lasting cut flower. The bright plateaux of green make perfect foreground foliage with any combination. This is the diplomat among flowers; you can mix it with any and everything.

Use it in a pretty country-style bunch with nigella flowers and seed heads, blue and white cornflowers, white sweet peas and snapdragons. Better still, use its vibrant colour as a contrast to other bright and resonant tones. Mix it in a tightly tied posy with Viticella clematis 'Royal Velours', C. 'Rouge Cardinal', or C. 'Jackmanii', Cosmos 'Versailles Carmine' and bright orange and yellow tissue-paper Iceland poppies. The intensity of the green, rich crimson, deep carmine, yellow and orange will make those usually blind to the power of flowers stop in their tracks.

Alchemilla is also ideally suited for using

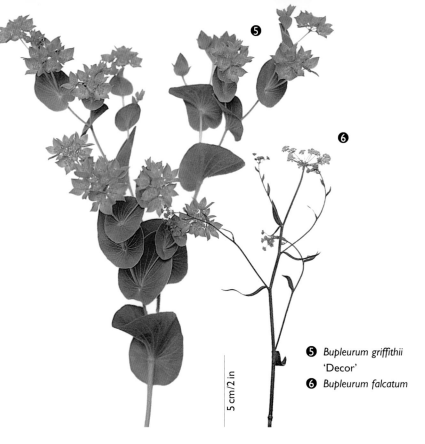

5 cm/2 in

5 *Bupleurum griffithii*
   'Decor'
6 *Bupleurum falcatum*

in oasis. The density of the flower heads will quickly cover up the ugly green blocks of foam. I use it and hornbeam seed cases as the foliage in a summer swag (see pages 64–7), where combined with blue cornflowers, lavender and poppies it lasts for three or four days if kept out of the sun.

Conditioning *To prolong their cut life, give them a good drink before arranging.*

Cultivation *Alchemilla is rewarding and easy to grow, and will thrive in all but boggy soils. It looks its best en masse, lining the sides of a path, rather than dotted throughout the garden. Plant in sun or partial shade. As the flowers lose their brightness towards the end of summer, cut the plants right to the ground. They will soon be covered in fresh, fluffy foliage and you may get a second flush of smaller blooms.*

Alchemilla will spread rapidly and readily, starting from only a few plants. It self-seeds promiscuously into any nook and cranny and these seedlings can be gathered up and replanted to flower the following year. What is more, a small plant will reach a good size by the end of one growing season, and can be divided into two or even three small plants in autumn or early spring (see pages 37 and 41).

ANETHUM GRAVEOLENS
Dill

Hardy annual
Height: 60-150cm/2-5ft

Varieties good for cutting *Grow dill in as large a quantity as space allows. It is an elegant and striking filler in the garden, and invaluable in any bunch of flowers. The tiny individual florets combine into light and fluffy yellow-green umbrellas which give a lift to any arrangement. Mix it, as your primary foliage, with startling oranges and blues, with whites and greens, or best of all as a stark contrast to the rich Venetian colours of carmine, crimson, purple and lapis-lazuli.*

Conditioning *Strip all but the top leaves, and plunge the cut stem ends into boiling water for 20 seconds. It will then last for about 10 days in water.*

Cultivation *Plant small plants or seed plugs 20-25cm/8-10in apart. Dill will thrive in any poor, well-drained soil in full sun, as long as you water the plants in well initially, and keep them moist and well weeded until they become established. Cutting and watering makes for bushy, vigorous plants, and prevents them going to seed, but will exhaust them in the end.*

Repeat sowings or plantings, every three to four weeks, are needed for a good supply.

Sow seed in situ in thick lines or blocks in the garden (see page 35). The seeds are large, so can be placed individually in the drills before being covered with soil. Thin to 20-25cm/8-10in apart in each direction, and provide some support using canes (see page 37). For early flowers, sow under cover in early spring, using pots or plug trays (do not sow into seed trays because dill does not like being transplanted). Space the seed evenly in your pot, or sow four per plug, and then cover them with perlite. Germination takes two to four weeks. Plant out when the risk of frost has passed.

Dill is another promiscuous self-seeder and can become a menace. If you fail to pick the flower heads for the house, you should cut them down before the seeds ripen and disperse. Keep dill and fennel well apart, or they will cross-pollinate.

ASTRANTIA
Masterwort

Deciduous perennial Zones: 4–8
Height: 60cm/2ft

Varieties good for cutting

This highly sculptural, dagger-petalled flower resembles those stylized plants often seen in illuminated mediaeval manuscripts. It has an elegance and presence that add character to any bunch of flowers. Each astrantia flower is in fact a collection of many, surrounded by a collar of jagged bracts. Mix the green and white A. major simply with golden-yellow-centred Lilium regale. The overpowering scent of the lilies will drown the astrantia's slight musty smell, and the pointed petals of the two together make a beautiful filigree pattern. Use the pinker A. maxima, with its broader, more petal-like bracts, with alchemilla and the heavy heads of scented pink roses R. gallica 'Versicolor' (Rosa Mundi) and R. 'Fritz Nobis'. A. major has an excellent large white-flowered form, A.m. subsp. involucrata 'Shaggy' (or 'Margery Fish'), which is showier than the rest. This is useful for bridesmaids' bunches and bridal bouquets. In my view, the best form of all for cutting is the dark claret-stemmed A.m.

'Ruby Wedding', with its interesting chiselled shape and rich plum colour.

Conditioning *Give the stems a long drink in warm water.*

Cultivation *Astrantias are rewarding and easy to grow. Plant A. major in groups of three in part shade or full sun, in a moist position. A. maxima needs a drier position and is less tolerant of a poor soil.*

These vigorous plants spread by underground runners and are therefore easily propagated by division after only one or two growing seasons (see pages 37 and 41). Buy in a small number of the varieties you want and increase your stock from these, but keep them apart, as they are self-seeding and will interbreed freely.

BUPLEURUM

Annual, perennial and shrub
Zones: B. fruticosum 7–10; B. falcatum 4–9
Height and spread: B. griffithii 50cm/20in × 30cm/12in; B. falcatum 90cm/3ft × 60cm/2ft; B. fruticosum 1.5m/5ft × 1.5m/5ft

Varieties good for cutting *The star of this genus and a superb plant for cutting is the hardy annual B. griffithii. Its euphorbia-like domes of flat, bright green flowers, with 15 or 20 to every stem, provide some of the best foreground foliage you can grow. They will last for up to two weeks in water, and give a perfect relaxed structure into which you can poke flowers of any colour to make a beautiful and informal bunch. Combine B. griffithii with bishop's flower and bells of Ireland as your foliage and then add sweet peas, sweet Williams, poppies, and trumpet or martagon lilies. It is not strong enough to balance heavy-headed plants like sunflowers, artichokes or dahlias, but is the perfect foil for almost anything else.*

The perennial bupleurum, B. falcatum, is less robust and showy but is also good cut. Its smaller yellow-green heads resemble a miniature version of dill and it combines well with the deep clarets and carmines of Cosmos bipinnatus 'Versailles Carmine', the beautiful roses 'Nuits de Young' and 'Souvenir du Docteur Jamain', and rich-coloured stocks (see page 70). Later in the year the shrubby evergreen B. fruticosum *also comes into its own. The coarser, dill-like flowers attract and are pollinated by hover flies, so avoid using them when they are fully open. I cut the buds and the seed heads for late-summer and autumn arrangements.*

Cultivation *These are sun-loving plants.* B. griffithii *should be grown in large quantities and will thrive in any good well-drained soil, in full sun.* B. falcatum *should be planted in a clump of three at the front of the border, in mid-autumn or mid-spring. It will thrive in any ordinary soil.*

B. fruticosum *is a large plant, so plant only one. It is slightly tender and will benefit from a warm site, ideally with the shelter of a wall. Cut it back periodically after flowering so it does not get too woody.*

B. griffithii *should be sown in situ in mid-spring (see pages 34 and 35). Keep it well watered, and once fully established keep picking to promote the growth of laterals to help the plant to bush out. It does not respond well to transplanting.* B. falcatum *should be propagated from seed sown in a cold frame in mid-spring, and* B. fruticosum

either from seed or from semi-ripe cuttings in late summer (see pages 38 and 39).

CYNARA
Cardoon, globe artichoke
Main entry: Summer Blue and Purple, page 132. *The edible buds of the globe artichoke,* C. cardunculus *Scolymus Group, make perfect strong foreground foliage to complement intense colours like scarlets and oranges (see page 73) or heavy-headed sunflowers, 'Casa Blanca' lilies and dahlias.*

ERYNGIUM
Sea holly
Biennial and perennial, some evergreen
Zones: Onopordum acanthium 6–10;
Eryngium planum *5–9;* E. alpinum,
E. × tripartitum, E. × zabelii *5–8*
Height: E. × tripartitum *60-75cm/*
24-30in; E. × zabelii, E. alpinum,
E. planum *75-90cm/30-36in;*
E. giganteum *1.2m/4ft; Onopordum acanthium 2.5m/8ft*
Varieties good for cutting
*Eryngiums rank with euphorbias, poppies, sunflowers and Parrot tulips as my favourite plants for cutting and for the garden. The sculpted heads in steely grey or rich royal blue are hard to beat. They are sympathetic mixers but can also be head-turning primadonnas. Grow them and grow lots of them. Among the best are the biennial or more accurately short-lived perennial Miss Willmott's ghost (*E. giganteum*), and the new* E.g. *'Silver Ghost'. These may take some years to flower, and will then die, scattering their seed. Their statuesque silver teasel-like flowers are the perfect foil to several stems of heavy-headed lilies, like* Lilium *'Casa Blanca'. Other fine sculptural beauties are the indigo-blue spiky flowers of* E. × zabelii *'Violetta' (see page 133) and the similar-structured, largest-flowered*

❶ *Cynara cardunculus* Scolymus Group
❷ *Eryngium alpinum* 'Amethyst'
❸ *Eryngium giganteum*
  (Miss Willmott's ghost)
❹ *Euphorbia lathyris*
❺ *Euphorbia schillingii*
❻ *Euphorbia seguieriana*

5 cm/2 in

eryngium, E. alpinum. *Mix these with poppy seed heads, bupleurum, orange and yellow alstroemerias, and eremurus spikes, all contrasted to the sumptuous deep-purple of lisianthus. The smaller-headed* E. planum *and* E. × tripartitum *are also excellent.* E. × tripartitum *flowers right through the summer and into the autumn, and its dominant fluffy blue centre and spiky barbed-wire-like ruff look good with almost any colour. Another fabulous plant is* Onorpordum acanthium, *the Scotch thistle. It is invaluable for huge arrangements and lasts over two weeks in water.*

Conditioning *Just give eryngiums a long drink in deep water.*

Cultivation *Eryngiums thrive and colour best in full sun. They are easy-going about soil type and will even grow with excessive lime and in poor stony soils. Most like some moisture but, being tap-rooted, they dislike becoming cold and waterlogged, so always introduce plenty of grit on planting.* E. alpinum *will tolerate some shade, but at the price of good deep blue colouring. Plant them in generous groups of three to five in spring or autumn.*

The results from seed are unreliable, so if you have a good colour form, propagation from root cuttings in winter (see page 43) is safest. If you propagate from seed, it should be sown as soon as you have gathered it in the autumn. Sow in shallow pans of light soil, and put them into a cold frame to let the frost get to them. The seed germination of eryngiums is slow: seedlings may take two years to appear. Plant them out before the tap root develops significantly.

E. giganteum, *which dies after flowering, is a free self-seeder. It can often be successfully introduced into a garden by a random sprinkling of fresh seed gathered from a friend. Alternatively, beg a young seedling or two and wait for them to colonize your garden. Learn to recognize the seedlings to avoid weeding them out before they flower.*

EUPHORBIA
Spurge, milkweed
Main entry: Spring Green and Silver, page 96. *Euphorbias are the jewel in the crown for the flower arranger. In summer,*

E. sikkimensis *is the first to flower. This is followed by* E. schillingii, *which will carry on well into autumn. Their spreading acid-green flower heads are the perfect foil for any tall and stately bunch.* E. seguieriana, *a compact and delicate plant, is invaluable for the smaller summer posy. Another must is the primeval, almost dinosaur-like, biennial caper spurge,* E. lathyris, *with its deep hooded eyes arranged regularly up the stem.*

MOLUCCELLA
Bells of Ireland, shell flower
Half-hardy annual
Height: M. laevis *60-90cm/2-3ft;*
M. laevis *'Long Spike' 90cm-1.2m/3-4ft*
Varieties good for cutting
M. laevis, *another top-rank annual cutting plant, should be grown in as large a quantity as space allows. These towering, curling and curving spikes of vivid green chalices, intricately veined with cream, are among the best that summer provides and an invaluable tall and elegant final touch to almost any arrangement. Place five to seven spikes of them to break up symmetry and add vertical emphasis to any neat dome of flowers. Look out for the handsome 'Long Spike' form of* M. laevis.

Conditioning *Remove the lower leaves and any side branches – the brittle stems break easily at these junctions so take great care. Give them a long cool drink.*

Cultivation *This plant grows easily in full sun, in rich, well-drained soil. Provide a network of twigs to support the stems. If they collapse they will regrow upright towards the light, but you will have lost some height.*

Sow seed under cover in the cool (13-15°C/55-60°F) in mid-spring. Prick out when large enough to handle, and gradually harden off for planting out after the last frosts. Or sow into a seed bed outside in late spring, for late-summer and autumn cutting.

7 *Nicotiana 'Lime Green'*
8 *Paeonia variety*
9 *Moluccella laevis*
10 *Stachys byzantina*

5 cm/2 in

5 cm/2 in

NICOTIANA
Tobacco plant
Main entry: Autumn White, page 139.
The pale chartreuse-green N. 'Lime Green' is a long, elegant, yard-of-ale-style flower. In texture and tone it is the perfect complement to any of the rich ecclesiastical colours, or to vibrant scarlets and oranges (see page 73). It lasts for up to two weeks in water.

PAEONIA
Peony
Main entry: Spring Pink, page 105.
Many of the peonies have interesting and dramatic seed heads, like the three-pointed jester's caps shown here. They combine well with any strong and sculptural summer and early-autumn flowers.

STACHYS
Lamb's ears, rabbit's ears
Perennial and sub-shrub Zones: 4–9
Height: S. byzantina *30-38cm/12-15in (flowering spikes may reach 90cm/3ft)*
Varieties good for cutting
S. byzantina *(syns.* S. lanata, S. olympica*) is an evergreen, furry, silver-leaved plant with spreading velvety rosettes. It throws up tall spikes of tiny magenta flowers swaddled in the softest, woolliest of leaves throughout the summer. These look just like the floppy ears of a domesticated rabbit. In the garden stachys makes an excellent traditional group with alchemilla and alliums for carpeting the ground beneath old roses. Cut the flowering spikes and use them as your foliage in hand-tied posies, or in little bunches for the bedside (see page 70). Or make a silver velvet frame to encircle a bridesmaid's bouquet. Look out, too, for the taller, more robust forms, which are useful for mixing in larger arrangements.*

Conditioning *Strip the bottom leaves and give the spikes a good drink in shallow water, taking care not to overwet the foliage.*

Cultivation *These plants are easy to grow in any well-drained soil, and are particularly tolerant of poor soils. Mass them along a path, or beneath your roses, choosing an open site in full sun. They can look moth-eaten as the year progresses, so cut them back after flowering in early autumn. Lots of fresh growth will soon appear.*

Propagate S. byzantina *by division (see pages 37 and 41). This is a vigorous plant which spreads rapidly by furry offshoots, and so it can be divided after only one growing season. It will also self-seed freely.*

White

AGAPANTHUS

Main entry: Summer Blue and Purple, page 130. *The white-tinged-pink pompon A. campanulatus var. albidus looks lovely in a arrangement of long stems on their own, or with white lilies and peony seed heads.*

AMMI MAJUS
Bishop's flower

Hardy annual
Height: 60-120cm/2-4ft

Varieties good for cutting *Bishop's flower is the florist's cow parsley. Like Solomon's seal or guelder rose, its tall, lacy flowers transform any bunch into a light and airy arrangement. Cut short, it mixes with nigella, cornflowers, sweet peas, snapdragons and poppies. It is also a beauty arranged on its own, 10 to 15 stems cut to their full length in a waisted glass vase for the centre of a large table. Use it, too, in stylish yet simple pompons for a summer party. Cut the stems to 30-45cm/12-18in to cover oasis globes to hang in a series from the ceiling.*

Conditioning *Strip all the bottom leaves and some of the higher ones since they will yellow way before the flowers begin to age.*

Cultivation *This is an easy plant to grow in full sun. It needs plenty of water and will flower for many weeks if it is regularly picked and not allowed to run to seed. For 90cm-1.2m/3-4ft plants, sow in autumn directly into the flowering position. The plants overwinter well and you will have flowers to pick by late spring. For smaller plants, sow in the flowering site in mid-spring. Bishop's flower self-seeds freely so transplant the seedlings into beds or rows.*

ANTIRRHINUM
Snapdragon

Main entry: Summer Orange and Red, page 125. *The cottage garden snapdragon A. majus 'White Wonder', with its large white flax-like flowers, is a great mixer for any simple, pretty bunch.*

ARCTOTIS FASTUOSA
Monarch of the veldt, Namaqualand daisy

Main entry: Summer Orange and Red, page 125. *The chocolate and orange centres of the pale creamy white sunflower-like daisies A.f. 'Zulu Prince' look like patterns on a butterfly's wings. For an eye-catching bunch, cut short some heads of the sunflower 'Velvet Queen', make them into a tight dome, and add A.f. 'Zulu Prince'. Their centres match the sunflowers perfectly.*

CAMPANULA
Bellflower

Main entry: Summer Blue and Purple, page 131. *The clear white virginal bells of campanula C. persicifolia alba are useful and long-lasting. Mix them with white foxgloves, yellow roses, deep purple lisianthus and sprays of dill for wedding posies.*

COSMOS

Half-hardy annual and tuberous perennial
Zones: C. atrosanguineus 8–9
Height: C. atrosanguineus 60cm/2ft; C. bipinnatus 1.2m/4ft

Varieties good for cutting *The annual cosmos is definitely among the plants that best earn their keep in the cutting garden. These tall bushy annuals flower and flower, providing cut flowers of sumptuous colours and fragile texture from late spring until the first hard frosts. Grow C. bipinnatus 'Purity', whose crinkled, saucer-shaped flowers mix with everything, and the deep carmine-pink C.b. 'Versailles Carmine' (see page 126). Put them on their own in a jug on a windowsill, where their thin petals will catch the light.*

❶ *Agapanthus campanulatus* var. *albidus*
❷ *Ammi majus*
❸ *Antirrhinum* majus 'White Wonder'
❹ *Arctotis fastuosa* 'Zulu Prince'
❺ *Campanula persicifolia alba*

5 cm/2 in

From late summer through autumn, the deep claret-crimson tender perennial C. atrosanguineus, *the chocolate-smelling cosmos, comes into flower (see page 142).*

Conditioning *Give these robust, long-lasting flowers a good cool drink.*

Cultivation *Cosmos like full sun and a moist but well-drained soil. The annuals thrive with regular top-dressing, watering and picking. In mild areas, tubers of half-hardy* C. atrosanguineus *may be overwintered in the ground if protected with a deep mulch. In more severe climates, lift them and store them as for tender tubers (see page 42). Start them into growth in the greenhouse and plant out in early summer.*

Propagate annuals from seed in early spring. Sow under cover, with some heat. Prick them out when they are large enough to handle, and gradually reduce the heat. Transfer to cold frames and plant out when all risk of frost has gone (see page 35). Propagate the chocolate cosmos from basal cuttings in spring or from semi-ripe cuttings in late summer (see pages 34, 36 and 39).

DELPHINIUM

Main entry: Summer Blue and Purple, page 132. *Any of the towering white delphiniums are beautiful for cutting, and the more you pick, the more the laterals will be encouraged to develop and flower. Use white delphiniums, such as 'Lilian Bassett', in a stately white arrangement, or mix with royal and deep blue delphiniums.*

DIGITALIS
Foxglove

Biennial and perennial, some evergreen
Zones: 4–8
Height: D. grandiflora *75cm/2½ft;*
D. purpurea *varieties 90cm-1.5m/3-5ft*

Varieties good for cutting *Much as I love* D. purpurea, *the biennial wild foxglove, I find its plum-pink a harsh and difficult colour to combine with other flowers, but there are many other stately foxglove species and cultivars that are perfect for cutting. Best of all is the pure white* D.p. f. albiflora, *with its great spikes of massed hanging bells, for an all-white virginal piece. Cut it short and use its soft, velvety texture to*

complement deep crimson and claret snap-dragons, stocks, and sweet Williams, with blue thistles, anchusas and viper's bugloss. Or mix it with foxgloves from D. Excelsior Group. *The smaller and finer yellow perennial* D. grandiflora, *is also good cut.*

Conditioning *As you cut foxgloves, put them into a deep bucket of warm water and leave for several hours before arranging. They will then last for over a week. The bottom flowers will brown or drop before the top buds have developed and opened. Remove any flowers hanging on by the stigma.*

Cultivation *The biennials grow best in semi-shade and acid, humus-rich, moist but well-drained soil; but they will tolerate most conditions, even seaside shingle, though here they will grow to only half the height. Plant clumps of 10 to 15, or grow them in a row. The perennial forms like sun but will take some light summer shade. Winter wet spells death. Prolong the picking season by cutting the central spike of a foxglove to promote the growth and flowering of the lateral branches.*

Sow the fine seed of biennials in late spring or early summer, under glass, without bottom heat. Do not cover with compost. Prick out at an early stage and then plant out in a seed bed for the rest of the summer. Transplant them to their final flowering position in autumn. They self-seed freely, but some will revert to the wild coloured form. Pull out any seedlings with red stems if you want to grow white flowers.

EPILOBIUM
Rosebay willowherb

Herbaceous perennial Zones: 3–7
Height: 1.5m/5ft

Varieties good for cutting *The pink rosebay willowherb,* E. angustifolium, *which covers many a motorway bank and railway cutting, is too leggy and invasive a plant for the cutting garden. But the white form* E.a. 'Album' *has a haunting and ethereal air, with its wand-like white flower*

spikes. It is an excellent bulker for white and green arrangements (see page 72).

Conditioning *Strip the lower leaves and sear the stem ends in boiling water for 20 seconds, before giving them a long cool drink.*

Cultivation *Plant in sun or shade, where it will quickly spread to brighten a corner. It prefers a moist but well-drained soil.*

Propagate by softwood cuttings of side shoots in spring (see page 39).

❻ *Cosmos bipinnatus* 'Purity'
❼ *Delphinium* 'Lilian Bassett'
❽ *Digitalis* Excelsior Group
❾ *Digitalis purpurea* f. *albiflora*
❿ *Epilobium angustifolium* 'Album'

5 cm/2 in

5 cm/2 in

LATHYRUS
Sweet pea, everlasting pea
Hardy annual and perennial climber
Zones: L. latifolius 5–9
Height: L. latifolius, L. odoratus 3m/
10ft; L. chloranthus 1.5-2.5m/5-8ft
Varieties good for cutting *Everyone*
is cheered by the scent of the sweet pea,
L. odoratus. *Grow monotone groups of your*
favourite colours over elegant hazel wigwams
in a flower border, and a colour razzmatazz
in a sunny corner of the vegetable patch for a
simple jug of clanging and clashing reds,
mauves, pinks, blues and whites. White
sweet peas such as 'White Supreme' mix
well in any country-style bunch with lark-
spur, alchemilla and cornflowers. I grow the
deep claret-black variety 'Pageantry' mixed
with the bicoloured purple and carmine
L.o.'Matucana' (see pages 70 and 134)
and the handsome but unscented lime-green
L. chloranthus 'Lemonade'.

In autumn, when your scented sweet peas
are over, the long-flowering everlasting pea,
L. latifolius, is useful with silver foliage of
artemisia and pale blue Salvia uliginosa.
Conditioning *Avoid direct sunlight and*
heat, which ages sweet peas rapidly.
Cultivation *Sweet peas like a deep,*
humus-rich, well-drained soil in full sun.
Soak seed for annuals overnight before
sowing into long pea pots. Sow in early
autumn under cold glass to give you strong

and sturdy plants for putting out in early
spring. Or sow them in late winter with
some heat, and plant them out as soon as
they begin to bulk up. They can also be
sown in situ in spring. Always pinch out the
leading shoot once you have one pair of true
leaves. Remove the climbing tendrils as they
grow. Tie the stem in to your framework on
a regular basis. This will give you nice long
strong stems for cutting. Do not let them set
seed – pick off any seed pods where you have
missed cutting the flowers.

Grow perennials from seed sown in
autumn, or by division in spring. Cut them
down to the ground in late autumn.

LILIUM
Lily
Bulb Zones: 4–8
Height: L. 'Fire King', L. longiflorum
90cm/3ft; L. monadelphum 50cm-
2m/18in-6ft; L. 'Casa Blanca', L. Pink
Perfection Group, L. regale 1.2-1.5m/4-5ft
Varieties good for cutting *For a*
heady and luxurious treat there is little to
beat the pure white 'Casa Blanca' lily. Its
huge open blooms, with crinkle-edged petals
and burnt-brick-red pollen, exude a sump-
tuous, room-filling scent – the stuff seduction
scenes are made of. These are a treat in any
bunch, but look best simply contrasted with
stark, lichen-covered branches to highlight
their beauty and drama. Any of the lilies
with an Oriental ancestry, like 'Casa Blanca',
are well worth the expense of the bulb. The
pure white Longi lily, L. longiflorum, is
used widely by florists for its delicious scent
and long life in water, but there are better,
more unusual varieties of these elegant,
trumpet-shaped lilies. L. regale, with its
alternating deep pink and white outside
petals and white with golden centre, exudes a
perfume to wake Sleeping Beauty. Even
better is the dusky, romantic, deep plum hue
of Pink Perfection Group – a silken thing of
glamour and allure. Look out, too, for the
turkscap lilies, L. martagon, and the
similar L. monadelphum (syn. L. szovit-
sianum), with their curly, reflexed, wrought-
iron-like petals and flowers arranged up the
stem like a baroque chandelier (see page
129). The coarser, unscented Asiatic lilies

are also good cut, though they last less well.
Choose the rich, deep ambers, near-clarets,
and also orange 'Fire King' (see pages 126
and 127), which is good mixed with blue
delphiniums in a hanging globe.

The seed heads of lilies can also look
beautiful cut; they are like spikes hung with
Shakespearean knickerbockers. Pick the seed
pods of L. martagon in late summer to mix
with delphiniums and dahlias.

Conditioning *When cutting lilies, leave*
enough stem and foliage to allow for photo-
synthesis and food storage to sustain the bulb
through the winter and spring. Strip the
anthers from the stamens before they cover
your clothes with their sticky, staining pollen.
Cultivation *Almost all lilies like a good,*
free-draining site in full sun, preferably with
a cool root-run. Martagon lilies also do well
in part shade. When planting, particularly

❶ *Lathyrus odoratus*
   'White Supreme'
❷ *Magnolia grandiflora*
❸ *Lilium* 'Casa Blanca'
❹ *Lilium regale*
❺ *Lupinus* Noble
   Maiden Group

on heavy soils, envelop the bulb in sharp sand, or you will lose them in a wet winter.

Buy in your lily bulbs from a good wholesaler. Experiment with the easiest to grow, like L. regale, and build up your repertoire from there. Choose bulbs that will give you flowers throughout the summer. Plant them in good generous clumps, tightly packed, so that you can cut several flowering spikes without depriving your garden. Add humus, and a fertilizer rich in potash and phosphate, like bonemeal, to the soil. Do not use strong nitrogenous fertilizers and manure.

Plant in late summer, very early autumn, or the spring, 8-15cm/3-6in deep according to the size of the bulb. Lilies can be left undisturbed for years, and only moved when they become overcrowded.

LUPINUS
Lupin
Main entry: Summer Blue and Purple, page 134. The white Noble Maiden Group lupin, with its tall spikes of solid flowers in continuous whorls, makes a fresh, strong addition to either a pure white arrangement or a multicoloured array.

MAGNOLIA
Main entry: Spring White, page 101. The huge evergreen M. grandiflora with its vast waxen frisbee-sized flowers is slow to flower but will eventually be covered in luscious lemon-scented goblets which you should put in pride of place in a simple silver cup on your table or desk.

MATTHIOLA
Stock
Main entry: Summer Pink, page 123. White stock makes an invaluable scented mixer for any country bunch.

PHILADELPHUS
Mock orange
Shrub Zones: 5–8
Height and spread: P. 'Manteau d'Hermine', 90cm-1.2m/3-4ft; P. 'Belle Etoile', P. × purpureomaculatus 1.5m/5ft × 1.5m/5ft; P. 'Beauclerk' 3-3.5m/10-11½ft × 2.5m/8ft; P. coronarius 3m/10ft × 2.5m/8ft
Varieties good for cutting Of all the philadelphus varieties, those producing white flowers with crimson hearts, like P. 'Belle Etoile' and P. × purpureomaculatus, are to me the loveliest. They merit arranging in a vase on their own, but can be cut short and mixed with pinks and deep plum roses, to highlight their rich-coloured centres.

P. coronarius and the extra-fragrant P. 'Beauclerk' are the earliest to flower of the species philadelphus. Plant them to cascade forward from the back of the border. The compact 'Manteau d'Hermine' is a superb, highly scented double form.
Conditioning Hammer the stem ends.
Cultivation Plant in sun or medium shade in any fertile, well-drained soil, even on chalk. Prune shoots to within 2.5cm/1in of the old wood immediately after flowering. This will lighten up the overall structure and

encourage new shoots that will flower in one or two years' time. Propagate by layering, or from hardwood cuttings (see page 43).

PHLOX
Annual and perennial Zones: 4–8
Height: P. maculata 90cm/3ft; P. paniculata cultivars 1.2m/4ft
Varieties good for cutting The great honey-scented heads of perennial phlox look as if they were made to be waved by cheerleaders. The slightly smaller, cylindrical-headed P. maculata forms come into flower as summer begins, while P. paniculata varieties come into their own in late summer. Grow pure white P.p. 'White Admiral', or P.p. 'Fujiyama' to fill an arrangement of white 'Iceberg' roses, with green dill and deep purple lisianthus. 'Fujiyama' and 'Graf Zeppelin' (see page 141), both late-flowerers, can be picked until the end of autumn. The purple P. paniculata 'Amethyst' is good in bright and resonant mixtures of bupleurum, yellow sunflowers, purple artichokes, scarlet lychnis, orange

arctotis and Euphorbia griffithii 'Fireglow'.
Conditioning Though phlox are long-lasting, some blooms in the flower head will fade after a week. Give the stem a good shake to dislodge any ageing flowers and clear the way for the smaller buds to open.
Cultivation Grow in full sun or light shade in a fertile, moisture-retentive soil. Stake the plants. Water in the morning to discourage mildew, and divide the clumps regularly to avoid congestion. Propagate from softwood cuttings or division in early spring. Replant the divisions immediately (see pages 37, 38 and 39).

ROSA
Rose
Main entry: Summer Pink, page 124. The climbing rose R. mulliganii has a soft, entrancing scent and lovely single flowers. Pale primrose-yellow buds open to clear white, backed by shiny bottle-green foliage. This is the perfect rose for a simple jug for a table centre; or use its lengthy stems for a summer globe (see pages 68–9).

❻ Matthiola cultivar
❼ Phlox paniculata
❽ Philadelphus 'Belle Etoile'
❾ Rosa mulliganii

5 cm/2 in

5 cm/2 in

Pink

AGROSTEMMA
Corncockle
Hardy annual
Height: 60-90cm/2-3ft
Varieties good for cutting
A. githago, *with its delicate saucer-shaped pink flower on a tall, spindly stem, was once a common sight of field edges. Combine it in a sheaf or in a wide-necked vase with oats, corn or barley, grasses, blue cornflowers, viper's bugloss, scarlet poppies and butter-cups. A. githago 'Milas' is an improved version with slightly larger 5-8cm/2-3in pink saucer blooms. Mix it with the purple-red form, A.g. 'Purple Queen'.*
Conditioning *Strip the bottom leaves and give the stems a good long drink.*
Cultivation *Corncockle thrives in full sun in well-drained, not too fertile, soil. Do not feed. Always support with a network of sticks, as the fine stems are liable to collapse. Corncockle will self-seed. Propagate by seed sown in situ in spring or early autumn. For a good supply do a second sowing two to three weeks later and thin to 15cm/6in.*

CENTAUREA
Cornflower, knapweed
Main entry: Summer Blue and Purple, page 131. *The perennial cornflower C. dealbata 'Steenbergii' has large Scotch-thistle-style flowers, and is lovely in vibrant multicoloured mixtures with oranges, blues and yellows, or in wild flower arrangements.*

COTINUS
Main entry: Autumn Orange and Red, page 142. *The frothy, fluffy flowers of C. 'Flame' form a bright pink haze as they catch the light. Use it as a foliage flower to form a structure into which you can poke intense gem-like saucer- or ball-headed flowers in contrasting colours.*

DIANTHUS
Pink, carnation, sweet William
Annual, biennial and perennial Zones: 4–8
Height: D. barbatus 45cm/18in; old-fashioned and laced pinks and modern hybrids 23-30cm/9-12in; D. chinensis, clove carnations 25-35cm/10-14in
Varieties good for cutting *It is difficult to know where to start with this huge genus of excellent cutting flowers, with their almost universal rich clove scent and durability in water. The sweet Williams, D. barbatus, are the first to bloom. Grow them in jolly coloured panels of pink, white and crimson single and bicoloured mixtures, with single or double flowers, or in groups of single colours. Of the biennial kinds, there is the small-flowered, highly scented, almost black D. barbatus Nigrescens Group (see pages 132 and 133). Grow also a rich crimson variety, best just plain with no white eye, like D.b. 'Dunnett', and a pure white, D.b. albus. Cut tall, use the deep rich-reds in fragrant combinations of claret stocks and snapdragons, contrasted to deep blue anchusas and the velvety bells of white foxgloves. Use D.b. Nigrescens Group in a bedside bunch of sweet peas and roses (see page 70). Recently developed annual forms of sweet Williams will guarantee you flowers in the same year from a late-winter sowing.*

From the huge range of perennial hybrid pinks choose the taller, larger varieties, which combine well with other flowers, or can be arranged on their own. The old-fashioned laced pinks will bloom only at midsummer, but there are some irresistible flowers in this group. Two of my favourites, with an intense clove scent, are the double-flowered pale pink D.b. 'Alice' and the rich crimson, pink-edged D. 'Laced Monarch', and for the best scent of all it is worth growing some of the old clove carnations, which flower in late summer when the pinks are over. Also look out for 'Old Crimson Clove'.
Conditioning *Dianthus lasts up to two weeks in water. Just strip the bottom leaves.*
Cultivation *All dianthus like a sunny position, good drainage and a reasonably alkaline soil. Sow the biennial sweet Williams inside in late spring to plant out in a seed bed in summer. Alternatively, sow them directly into the seed bed in early summer and transplant to their flowering position in autumn. Annual sweet Williams need sowing early for strong, healthy plants.*

The perennial pinks all root easily from cuttings. Put heeled cuttings into open ground with added sand, or in pots of well-drained sandy compost in early autumn (see page 42).

DIGITALIS
Foxglove
Main entry: Summer White, page 119. *The D. Excelsior Group contains some lovely pale pink plain and spotty foxgloves. Arrange seven to fifteen stems in an explosion of flowers for the middle of a large table.*

GLADIOLUS
Main entry: Autumn Orange and Red, page 143. *The rich carmine flowers of the species gladiolus G. communis subsp.*

❶ *Agrostemma githago 'Milas'*
❷ *Dianthus barbatus 'Alice'*
❸ *Dianthus 'Laced Monarch'*
❹ *Centaurea dealbata 'Steenbergii'*
❺ *Cotinus 'Flame'*

5 cm/2 in

byzantinus *are the colour of the bravest silk sari, to be worn on special occasions. For a stunning contrast, mix with acid-green euphorbias and spikes of bells of Ireland, purple-blue anchusas and lisianthus.*

LONICERA
Honeysuckle

Evergreen and deciduous shrub and climber
Zones: L. splendida *9–10;*
L. periclymenum *5–9;* L. × brownii,
L. sempervirens *4–9*
Height: 4-6m/13-20ft
Varieties good for cutting
Honeysuckle twisting and twining about an arrangement, disturbing all symmetry and tidiness, is reason enough to encourage you to grow lots. *The sweet, spicy scent filling the evening or early-morning air makes them irresistible. If you have room, grow a selection of two or three scented varieties to flower at different times. Choose one of the yellows, one of the pinky-reds, and perhaps one of the rich intense oranges. Avoid the most rampant (*L. japonica *or* L. henryi*), for the flowers will soon be out of reach of your nose and your secateurs. Of the yellows, grow* L. periclymenum *'Graham Thomas' (see page 129). Of the reds and pinks, grow* L. × americana *and the strongest-scented of all,* L. periclymenum *'Serotina', which flowers from midsummer to mid-autumn. Combine this deep carmine-pink and yellow honeysuckle with* Cosmos bipinnatus *'Versailles Carmine' and green dill for a light and fragrant bunch. During winter, the highly fragrant shrub honeysuckles such as* Lonicera × purpusii *come into their own (see page 157).*

Cultivation *Plant honeysuckles in sun or part shade. Like clematis, they need a cool root-run but are not fussy about soil. Enrich it with organic matter, keep it moist in summer and give an annual mulch of leaf mould. On planting, it is worth shortening the main stems in order to promote early branching and ultimately create the maximum possible spread. Once this is achieved, regular pruning is not necessary, though it is worth periodically pruning out the flowered wood of the climbing forms. For summer-flowerers, do this after flowering; with plants that flower in autumn, wait until early spring.*

Propagate by semi-ripe cuttings in summer, or by hardwood cuttings in late autumn (see pages 38, 39 and 42).

MATTHIOLA
Stock

Annual, biennial and perennial
Height: M. incana *Brompton Group and white perennial matthiola 45cm/18in;*
M.i. *Giant Imperial Group and Giant Excelsior Group 60-75cm/24-30in*
Varieties good for cutting
The heady warm clove-like scent of stocks reminds me of optimistic balmy summer evenings. Plant them in clumps around a

⑥ Digitalis Excelsior Group
⑦ Gladiolus communis subsp. byzantinus
⑧ Matthiola cultivar
⑨ Lonicera periclymenum 'Serotina'

garden seat or by your kitchen window, so *you can enjoy their wafting perfume, getting stronger and stronger into the night. The dark smoky-purple-pink and rich wine-red varieties of annuals and biennials are the most striking for cutting. Mark the good colour forms and collect seed from them for sowing the next year. Combine them with bright acid-greens and oranges for a rich, glowing bunch of flowers (see page 70).*

Grow, too, the pure white varieties in any of the giant forms, like the annual Giant Imperial or Giant Excelsior Groups. You can always cut down a tall stem, but cannot elongate a short one. The bushy white perennial matthiola, with its white flowers held on short stems set against a mound of grey leaves, is useful for small scented bedside posies. Stocks are best used with other cut flowers as their value is in their scent rather than their appearance.

Conditioning *Strip all leaves below the water line. These will taint the water quickly and exude a pungent smell.*

Cultivation *Plant stocks in sun or semi-shade, in fertile, well-drained, ideally lime-rich soil. Sow seeds of annuals under glass in late winter, or in situ outdoors in mid-spring. Sow biennials, like the Brompton stocks, in frames in high summer to flower the following spring. Sow seeds of perennials under glass in spring (see pages 32–4).*

ROSA
Rose

Deciduous and semi-evergreen shrub and climber Zones: 6–10 except: R. mulliganii 5–10; R. 'Souvenir du Docteur Jamain', 6-9; 'Cardinal de Richelieu', R. 'Charles de Mills', R. gallica 'Versicolor', R. moyesii 'Geranium', R. 'Nevada', R. 'Nuits de Young', R. 'Tuscany Superb', R. xanthina 'Canary Bird' 5–9; R. glauca 4–9 Height and spread: R. 'Iceberg' 90cm/3ft × 60cm/2ft; R. 'Cardinal de Richelieu', R. 'Charles de Mills', R. 'Felicia', R. gallica 'Versicolor', R. 'Graham Thomas', R. 'Heritage', R. 'Nuits de Young', R. 'Tuscany Superb' 1.2m/4ft × 1.2m/4ft; R. 'Fritz Nobis' 1.5m/5ft × 1.2m/4ft; R. glauca, R. 'Nevada', R. xanthina 'Canary Bird', R. moyesii 'Geranium' 2.5m/8ft × 1.8m/6ft; R. 'New Dawn', R. 'Souvenir du Docteur Jamain',3m/10ft × 2.5m/8ft; R. mulliganii 4.5m/15ft × 3m/10ft

❶ *Rosa 'Charles de Mills'*
❷ *Rosa 'Fritz Nobis'*
❸ *Rosa gallica 'Versicolor'*
❹ *Rosa 'Nuits de Young'*

Varieties good for cutting *Choose roses that are irresistible to you on grounds of colour or scent, but check that they will last in water. I would choose any of the deep rich chocolate-crimsons or deep purples, such as 'Cardinal de Richelieu', or even better those with golden-yellow centres and enveloping perfume, such as 'Nuits de Young' or 'Tuscany Superb', which has the colour and texture of the most luxurious silk-velvet, gold-leaf brocaded curtain. Also, grow a rich deep pink like the vibrant, intense 'Charles de Mills'. 'Fritz Nobis' is another sumptuous rose, with more open flowers and less dense petals. I have a passion for the old-fashioned striped bicoloured roses. Grow R. gallica 'Versicolor' (Rosa Mundi), the oldest, with its carmine and pink dapples and stripes. It is excellent for cutting.*

Arrange any of these on their own in a shallow rose bowl, with a pin-holder for support, or combine them with other regal,

velvet beauties. Choose, too, some easy-to-grow, good hard-working scented roses which will flower over long periods. Widely known, though much maligned, pure white 'Iceberg' is a superb, productive rose. It will flower from summer to winter, with perhaps a flower or two for picking on Christmas Day. There are three pale pink roses, 'New Dawn', 'Felicia' and the modern English rose 'Heritage', which fit into this category, too. They all pick well, flower from early summer until the first frosts, require minimal care and have good scent. For a similar hard-working yellow rose, try the modern English rose 'Graham Thomas' (see page 146). 'Souvenir du Docteur Jamain' is another good 'doer', and one of the most sumptuous in colour and scent. It will flower for many months, well into the autumn.

If you have room, grow a vigorous early-flowering rose for spring picking. The cream rose 'Nevada' and primrose-yellow R. xanthina 'Canary Bird' will both be in flower by mid- to late spring and are rampant enough to take some heavy picking. Fill a jug with several twisting and turning boughs and place it at the centre of a large table. They will only last a few days but are lovely while they do.

If you have a wall or pergola, think of growing one of the summer-flowering single Rambler roses. R. mulliganii, with its yellow buds and simple white flowers, is

ideal and not too rampant (see page 121). In autumn R. moyesii 'Geranium' (see pages 144 and 145) and R. glauca are both excellent to cut for their elegant hips.

Conditioning *Always cut the stem ends of roses at a sharp angle, revealing more of the pithy stem centre that absorbs water. This increases the surface area for drinking. Plunge the cut ends in boiling water for 20 seconds, before giving them a long drink in tepid water (see page 48).*

Cultivation *All the roses named above are easy to grow and will tolerate even the poorest soil. Most prefer full sun and all like a moist but well-drained position. If you buy bare-rooted plants, ensure that you dig a hole large enough to accommodate all the roots without cramping. Place the bush in the hole, with the union (the point where the shoots join the rootstock) about 2.5cm/1in below the soil level. Replace the soil in two or three stages, shaking it down and treading firmly with the heel each time. Top-dress with bonemeal. Do not plant where roses have been grown before, or you may have problems with Specific Replant Disease.*

Feed in late winter or early spring with a balanced fertilizer, and apply a mulch of manure. Roses will benefit from a monthly feed during spring and summer. Deadhead repeat-flowerers. Propagate by semi-ripe cuttings in summer (see pages 38 and 39) or hardwood cuttings in winter (see page 43).

5 cm/2 in

Orange and Red

ALSTROEMERIA
Peruvian lily
Tuberous perennial Zones: 7–10
Height: A. ligtu hybrids 50-75cm/20-30in; large-flowered A. aurea hybrids 60-90cm/2-3ft

Varieties good for cutting *The cellophane-wrapped supermarket combination of alstroemerias, chrysanthemums and a few sprigs of fern does not do the alstroemeria justice. They are popular because they last so long in water, they have a long flowering season and come in a good medley of colours. So do not throw the baby out with the bath water. Start by selecting named varieties from among the listed tall large-flowered A. aurea hybrids which are raised for the cut-flower trade. Choose a deep resonant orange like A. 'Princess Margaret' and also a white with tiger stripes like A. 'Bianca' for calmer, quieter bunches. The hardier A. ligtu hybrids have smaller flowers and shorter stems but come in a range of rich deep pinks, corals, oranges, buffs and yellows.*

Conditioning *Give them a good drink.*

Cultivation *Alstroemerias may be difficult to establish. Plant groups of three to five in sites of rich, well-drained soil in full sun. They spread by underground fleshy roots and if happy may become invasive, so plant them in a spot where you will not mind if they run riot. In cold winters, protect the roots with a good mulch of dry compost.*

Propagate alstroemerias by division or if possible by seed, as they do not enjoy disturbance (some A. aurea hybrids do not set seed, so must be propagated by division).

ANTIRRHINUM
Snapdragon
Perennial and semi-evergreen sub-shrub, usually grown as an annual Zones: 5–9
Height: dwarf cultivars (e.g. A. majus 'Black Prince') 45cm/18in; tall cultivars e.g. A. Forerunner Series, 90cm/36in

Varieties good for cutting *The cottage garden snapdragon always reminds me of old-fashioned front gardens and has no less charm for that. Antirrhinums can look handsome and regal, if the right colours are chosen. Grow the aptly named A. majus 'Black Prince', with its tall spikes of deep chocolate-crimson and dark foliage. A.m. 'Crimson Monarch' is a slightly pinker, less black version of the same, with green foliage. They are both an impressive sight if arranged 15 to 20 stems on their own, but also combine well with other rich and velvety flowers. The white cultivar 'White Wonder' is another fine one (see page 118). There are taller varieties, but while many of these would be excellent to grow for cutting, they are rarely available as single colours. Look out for Rocket or Forerunner Series, which will reach 90cm/36in. Avoid the dwarf dumpy forms, as the stems are too short to be of much use for cutting, and certainly avoid the doubles, which confuse the simple and lovely top and bottom lip 'snap' structure.*

Conditioning *Strip the bottom leaves and give the stems a long drink.*

Cultivation *Nurseries and garden centres sell trays of snapdragons, but they are usually of mixed colours. It is better to sow your own. Treat them as half-hardy annuals and sow under glass or in a propagator in late winter (see pages 32–4). Don't pinch out the leaders of your seedlings if you want a nice tall stem for cutting. Plant out into pre-fed ground when the risk of frost is over: snapdragons need sun and rich, well-drained soil. Plant closer than the seed packet directs so that a little competition for light helps the plants to maximize their height. Water and pick antirrhinums regularly, and they will go on flowering well into autumn.*

Older snapdragons are more susceptible to rust fungus. In a sheltered spot, snapdragons will also self-seed.

ARCTOTIS FASTUOSA
Monarch of the veldt, Namaqualand daisy
Half-hardy annual and perennial Zone: 10
Height: 60cm/24in

Varieties good for cutting *This bright orange South African daisy (syn. Venidium fastuosum) is like a marigold dolled-up for a party, with extra-black markings on each petal and a deep chocolate-brown-flecked orange centre. Arrange arctotis on their own with 15 to 20 stems in a china jug for your kitchen table, or with bupleurum and the indigo-blue spires of Salvia patens. They last twice as long in water as the marigold. Also grow the large-flowered, creamy-white, chocolate-centred A.f. 'Zulu Prince', with its unusual sunflower-like flowers (see page 118).*

Conditioning *Strip the bottom leaves.*

Cultivation *Grow them in full sun in very well-drained, ideally sandy soil. Plant them creeping out over a path or lawn. The stems tend to grow soft and floppy rather than straight and upstanding, so they are best suited to the front of the border. Water and pick regularly and they will reward you with flowers well into the autumn.*

Sow in early spring, under cover, with some heat. Germination is usually excellent. Prick out when large enough to handle, and plant out after all risk of frost has passed.

CALENDULA
English marigold, pot marigold
Hardy annual
Height: 60cm/24in

Varieties good for cutting *The common-or-garden marigold is many people's least favourite plant. It has an odd smell, which you either like or hate, and it comes in some pretty brash and brassy colours. I used to be a subscriber to the anti-orange-and-yellow-in-your-garden club. Since I started arranging flowers regularly, I have joined the opposite camp. The more easy-to-grow, jolly, bright cottage garden plants the better, and now English marigolds rank high on my list.*

Pick one of the better mixtures, like the double Art Shades Group, and you will have the typical orange, plus yellows (see page 128), cream, buff and apricot with dark

❶ *Alstroemeria ligtu hybrid*
❷ *Antirrhinum majus 'Black Prince'*
❸ *Arctotis fastuosa*
❹ *Calendula Art Shades Group*

5 cm/2 in

① Clematis 'Royal Velours'
② Cosmos bipinnatus 'Versailles Carmine'
③ Knautia macedonica
④ Helianthus annuus 'Velvet Queen'
⑤ Iris 'Ruby Mine'

chocolate centres. Of the single colours, 'Indian Prince' is one of the best, with a deep orange centre and burnt-marmalade back. The yellow single C. 'Muselli' is another good one to mix with deep crimsons and clarets. Avoid the dwarf varieties, which are too stubby for picking.

Arrange them all jumbled up together in a blue ceramic jug for the kitchen, or make up a tightly tied posy mixing the oranges with blue cornflowers. Their brightness, brilliance and strong flower structure also make them a useful contrast in large and grand arrangements (see pages 70–71).

Conditioning *Just strip the bottom leaves. They will last for a week.*

Cultivation *Grow in sun and any well-drained soil. Keep picking, or deadhead, to ensure flowers until the first frosts. Sow directly in their flowering position in the spring, and thin to 25-30cm/10-12in apart. For very strong plants sow in situ in the autumn. Calendula will also self-seed.*

CLEMATIS
Main entry: Spring White, page 99. *Of the summer clematis I particularly like the deep crimson-claret Viticellas 'Royal Velours', 'Rouge Cardinal' and 'Jackmanii'. Rather than take whole branches as I do with the montanas, I simply cut the flowering stem of these less vigorous plants back to the wood.*

COSMOS
Main entry: Summer White, page 118. *I probably use the open daisy-like cosmos more than any other flower. C. bipinnatus 'Versailles Carmine' has a velvety colour and texture that mix perfectly with 'Royal Velours' clematis, yellow and orange Iceland poppies and green tobacco flowers for a head-turning wedding bouquet. Make matching headdresses for the bride and bridesmaids.*

HELIANTHUS
Sunflower
Main entry: Summer Yellow, page 128. *The rich red H. annuus 'Velvet Queen' looks exotic one stem on its own in a tall decanter, and equally striking mixed with other bright and warm colours (see pages 74–5).*

5 cm/2 in

IRIS
Main entry: Winter Blue and Purple, page 158. *I grow the deep bronze-claret Iris 'Ruby Mine', a lovely long-flowering late Tall Bearded iris, to combine with oranges and yellows.*

KNAUTIA MACEDONICA
Main entry: Scabiosa, Summer Blue and Purple, page 135. *The scabious-like perennial knautia blooms from the end of spring to mid-autumn, producing lovely, richly hued flowers to combine or contrast with almost any colour you choose. It comes in a range of whites, pinks and mauves, but my favourite is the deep claret form. Its cultivation is as for scabious.*

LILIUM
Lily
Main entry: Summer White, page 120. *The zingy rich orange lily 'Fire King' looks wonderful with a clashing bunch of opposing colours and acid-greens.*

5 cm/2 in

LYCHNIS
Jerusalem cross, Maltese cross

Annual, biennial and perennial Zones: 4–8
*Height and spread: L. × arkwrightii
'Vesuvius' 45cm/18in; L. chalcedonica
90cm-1.2m/3-4ft × 30-45cm/12-18in*

Varieties good for cutting *You do
not get much brighter than the true scarlet
L. chalcedonica and the shocking brick-
red-orange L. × arkwrightii 'Vesuvius'.
Both are colours for a fashion show. The
neat star-shaped flowers, with their indented
petals like a snake's forked tongue, add to
their strength and beauty. The hybrid L.
× a. 'Vesuvius' has a longer flowering season
than the species, and the intense flower colour
contrasts with deep purple-maroon foliage.
Mix them both with calming rich blue
anchusas and green artichoke buds and
tobacco plants (see page 73). Or use them as
a component of a zingy multicoloured mix,
with lime-green bupleurum and dill, golden-
yellow sunflowers and deep blue umbrellas of
agapanthus. There is nothing subtle about
the reds, so have fun dreaming up the
brashest colour collisions!*

Cultivation *Lychnis grows easily in good
moist soil in full sun in a sheltered position.
L. × arkwrightii is short-lived and best
treated as an annual. Sow singly in warmth
and plant out after the frosts. Propagate
L. chalcedonica by division or seed in
autumn or spring; it will flower in the second
year from seed.*

PAPAVER
Poppy

*Hardy annual, biennial and perennial
Zone: 4–9*
*Height: P. nudicaule 35-50cm/14-20in;
P. commutatum 45cm/18in;
P. somniferum 'Danebrog', P. rhoeas
cultivars 45-60cm/18-24in; P. orientale
'Ladybird' 60-90cm/2-3ft*

Varieties good for cutting *Many
people think poppies far too frail and fragile
to survive cutting. Think again. Poppies are
some of the best flowers you can grow in the
cutting garden. The biennial Iceland poppy,
P. nudicaule, is the most robust and long-
lasting in water. Once the stems have been
seared, the petals will emerge from tight buds*
*and you will have a series of new flowers for
up to two weeks. What could be better than
a plain glass vase of 10 to 15 stems of these
crinkly tissue-paper flowers in their various
whites, creams, yellows, pinks, oranges and
brick-reds.*

*The best deep rich scarlet-orange forms,
P.n. 'Matador' or 'Red Sail', are perfect
mixed with Euphorbia cornigera, the
similar-coloured Lychnis × arkwrightii
'Vesuvius', and purple Salvia × superba.
Use them also in a flag-like multicoloured
summer swag (see pages 64–7). Also perfect
for several days' admiration are all the wild
corn poppy varieties. Arrange the scarlet-red
P. rhoeas on its own, with its elegant
hanging hairy buds and stem, or mix it in a
medley from one of the mixtures (P.r. Shirley
Group or P.r. Mother of Pearl Group) of
whites, pinks, mauves, doubles and singles in
an arrangement of great delicacy and grace.
Just keep the vase out of the wind and away
from open windows, or a gust of wind may
destroy the lot, scattering every petal on the
table. Grow some of the annual freaks too,
like the extraordinary P. somniferum
'Danebrog' (syn. P.s. 'Danish Flag'), with
its huge flowers with serrated petals in
scarlet and white. Also grow the red with
black-spotted P. commutatum 'Ladybird',
which looks exactly as it should.*

*The perennial Oriental poppies,
P. orientale, will hold on to their petals for
several days if seared as soon as you pick
them. All are fabulous cut, from the white
P.o. 'Perry's White' to the greyish-crimson
'Patty's Plum'. Grey-green P. somniferum
or P. orientale seed heads are also good cut.*

Conditioning *Plunge the cut ends into
boiling water for 20 seconds and then into
tepid water for a long drink (see page 48).
P. nudicaule buds may need helping out of
their tight glove-like calyces, which if torn in
one place will gradually unravel.*

Cultivation *These are easy plants to
grow and thrive if planted in sun or semi-
shade, in a moist but well-drained soil.
Plant the annuals and biennials in generous
clumps in the border, at 25-30cm/10-12in
spacings. Plant the perennials in groups of
three, 45cm/18in apart.*

The hardy annuals can be sown either in
*autumn or in spring. They will not survive
transplantation, so must be sown in situ and
then thinned to 20-25cm/8-10in in their
intended flowering position. The biennial
P. nudicaule varieties can be sown under
glass in late spring and then potted up, to be
planted out in their flowering position in
autumn (see page 38). Or sow them in a
seed bed and thin to 25-30cm/10-12in.
P. orientale cultivars are best propagated by
root cuttings in winter (see page 43).*

6 *Lilium 'Fire King'*
7 *Lychnis chalcedonica*
8 *Papaver nudicaule 'Matador'*
9 *Papaver orientale*
10 *Papaver rhoeas*
11 *Papaver somniferum 'Danebrog'*

5 cm/2 in

Yellow

ALCEA
Hollyhock

Annual, biennial and short-lived perennial
Zones: 3–9
Height: 1.5-2m / 5-6½ft

Varieties good for cutting *Few
arrangements could be more impressive than
a collection of towering hollyhock spikes,
with their large, open, crinkled crêpe-paper
flowers arranged all the way up the stem.
Use their full height, and either several
colours jumbled up together or many stems of
a single colour in a stately vase. Avoid the
Powder Puff double varieties and any dwarf
forms, but grow the pale yellow perennials
A. rugosa and A. pallida and the deep
purple-black A. rosea 'Nigra'. If you have a
place for mixed colours, grow the A. rosea
white, pink, yellow and red forms. These
will all flower from late spring, producing
new flower spikes until the end of autumn.*

Conditioning *Sear the stem ends in
boiling water for 20 seconds, before giving
them a deep cool drink.*

Cultivation *Plant hollyhocks 45cm /
18in apart, in groups of three to seven,
depending on space. Easy to grow, they will
thrive in full sun in fairly poor but well-
drained soil. Of the single types, A. rugosa
is the most resistant to rust. If rust occurs,
cut off all the foliage and drench the plant
with fungicide. If this inorganic treatment
offends you, grow them as half-hardy annuals
or biennials.*

*Grow hollyhocks from seed. The annual
varieties, if sown early in the year and
planted out after the frosts, will flower the
same year. For larger, finer plants, grow as
biennials, sowing under glass in summer and
planting out that autumn to flower the
following year. They will self-seed freely.*

CALENDULA
English marigold, pot marigold
Main entry: Summer Orange and Red,
page 125. *Mix the bright buttercup-yellow
marigold from the Art Shades Group with
other marigolds in orange, cream and buff, or
use it to highlight the middle of a bunch of
roses and sweet peas (see page 70).*

EREMURUS
Foxtail lily, king's spear

Bulbous perennial Zones: E. robustus,
E. *Ruiter Hybrid 6–9;* E. stenophyllus
subsp. stenophyllus *5–9;*
E. himalaicus *3–9*
Height: E. stenophyllus *90cm-1.2m / 3-
4ft;* E. *Ruiter Hybrid 1.5m / 5ft;* E.
himalaicus, E. robustus *1.8-2.5m / 6-8ft*

Varieties good for cutting *These
tapering, towering spikes of small starry
flowers look more like the tail feathers of a
giant exotic jungle parrot than a fox's brush
– you can imagine them trailing down from
a high branch of a mahogony tree, entirely
surrounded by orchids and ferns, and humid
mossy smells.*

*They make luxurious and opulent cut
flowers in white, cream, pink, orange and
bright yellow. Mix them in any great
summer arrangement (see pages 70–71), or
have them on their own, the colours jumbled
like a collection of coloured sparklers. For a
mixture of colours and real statuesque height,
grow the early-flowering Ruiter Hybrids.
The earliest eremurus to flower, E.
himalaicus, also tall, has immense, pure
white, cylindrical spikes. E. robustus, in
pale pink, flowers next and E. stenophyllus
last. If your space is limited, this is the one
to grow: it is shorter and more compact than
the others, with golden-yellow flowers.*

Conditioning *As with other flower
spikes, the bottom flowers die before the top
blooms open. Cut when the bottom half is in
flower, and remove flowers as they wilt. The
spike should last seven to ten days if kept out
of strong heat.*

Cultivation *Buy in tuberous roots from
good bulb wholesalers, making sure that you
obtain freshly lifted crowns with succulent-
looking roots. Plant 30-35cm / 12-14in
apart into holes filled with horticultural grit
in a sheltered sunny position and you may
have flowers the first year. Set the crown just
below the surface. Mark each tuber with a
cane, so that you do not pierce the roots when
you are planting around them. In a windy
site support the stem with a hazel pea-stick.*

*Eremurus are best propagated by division
in early spring or autumn (see page 37). Dig
a wide circle around their radiating roots.*

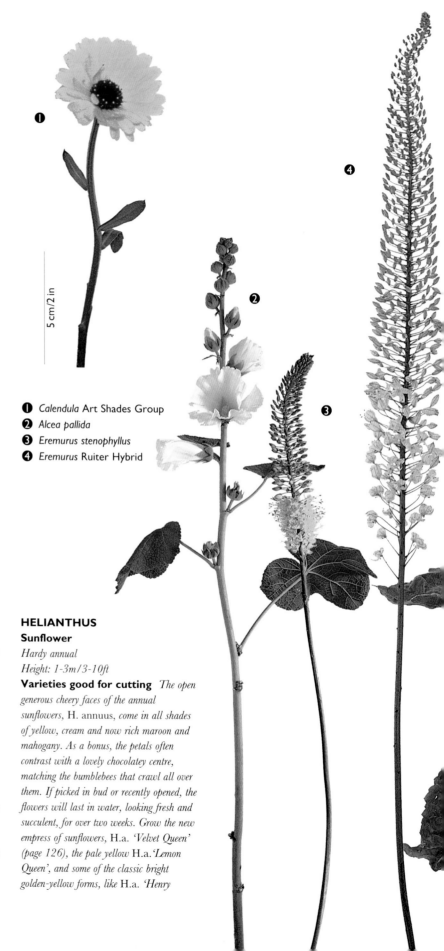

❶ Calendula Art Shades Group
❷ Alcea pallida
❸ Eremurus stenophyllus
❹ Eremurus Ruiter Hybrid

5 cm/2 in

HELIANTHUS
Sunflower

Hardy annual
Height: 1-3m / 3-10ft

Varieties good for cutting *The open
generous cheery faces of the annual
sunflowers, H. annuus, come in all shades
of yellow, cream and now rich maroon and
mahogany. As a bonus, the petals often
contrast with a lovely chocolatey centre,
matching the bumblebees that crawl all over
them. If picked in bud or recently opened, the
flowers will last in water, looking fresh and
succulent, for over two weeks. Grow the new
empress of sunflowers, H.a. 'Velvet Queen'
(page 126), the pale yellow H.a.'Lemon
Queen', and some of the classic bright
golden-yellow forms, like H.a. 'Henry*

5 *Helianthus annuus* 'Henry Wilde'
6 *Lilium monadelphum*
7 *Helianthus annuus* 'Italian White'
8 *Lonicera periclymenum* 'Graham Thomas'
9 *Papaver nudicaule* Oregon Rainbow Group

5 cm/2 in

*Wilde' and 'Valentine', and grow too some
of the multicoloured cream, yellow, orange,
crimson and mahogany mixtures. The pale
cream H.a. 'Italian White' flowers through
summer and autumn until the first frost.*

Conditioning *Put straight into water
and keep them away from heat.*

Cultivation *Plant six to eight plants per
square metre/yard, in full sun, in a moist
but well-drained soil. They will tolerate
light shade, but remember that the flowers
will always face the sun. Provide support,
for the wind may catch the giant heavy heads.*

*Sow them directly into their flowering
position in the spring. Place the large, flat
seeds in groups in the border, or in lines in
the cutting patch. Keep them well watered.
Or sow early under cover in individual pots
in a propagator or greenhouse, planting them
out when risk of frost is over (see page 34).*

LILIUM MONADELPHUM
Turkscap lily

Main entry: Summer White, page 120.
*The elegant golden-yellow turkscap lily
L. monadelphum is beautiful arranged tall
with blues and purples. Combine it with*

*bupleurum and cotinus, larkspur, lupins and
lisianthus. Cut it short and use it to highlight the golden centres of crimson and claret
roses 'Tuscany Superb' or 'Nuits de Young'.*

LONICERA
Honeysuckle

Main entry: Summer Pink, page 123.
*The long-flowering deciduous L. pericly-
menum 'Graham Thomas' is one of the
best of the yellow honeysuckles. If pruned
back in spring, it will flower continuously
until late autumn. Combine with its name-
sake Rosa 'Graham Thomas' for a simple,
pretty, fragrant posy.*

PAPAVER
Poppy

Main entry: Summer Orange and Red,
page 127. *Iceland poppies come in all
shades of yellow, cream, orange and pink.
The calm pale yellow P. nudicaule Oregon
Rainbow Group with its crisp, papery
flowers is a beauty for arranging in a tall
glass on its own, to put on your desk. Or
arrange it with smoky purples: a few sprigs
of purple sage and some sweet peas.*

5 cm/2 in

Blue and Purple

AGAPANTHUS
African lily
Perennial, some evergreen
Zones: 8–10; A. Headbourne Hybrids 6–9
Height: most are 60-150cm/2-5ft
Varieties good for cutting *These many-flowered blue pompons on their long straight stalks look like maces in an ecclesiastical procession. Arrange them in tall*

❶ *Agapanthus 'Loch Hope'*
❷ *Allium cernuum*
❸ *Allium cristophii*
❹ *Allium giganteum*
❺ *Anchusa azurea 'Royal Blue'*

narrow vases on their own, or combined, in an explosion of flower colour, with eremurus and alliums (see pages 70–71). Grow the hardiest, the Headbourne Hybrids, which come in a range of colours from deep blue to white. For the tall and stately, choose the mid-blue 'Loch Hope' with flower spikes of 1.5m/5ft. 'Buckingham Palace' is a richer blue and even taller, but with a less generous number of flowers. Of the smaller varieties to mix with roses, phlox and bupleurum, choose

the dark blue A. 'Lilliput' which stands only 30cm/12in high. The paler-coloured deciduous A. campanulatus *varieties are almost completely hardy, too. Look out for the hardiest of all, A.c. subsp.* patens *and handsome* A.c. var. albidus *(see page 118). The angular agapanthus seed heads are lovely in autumn arrangements (see page 136).*

Conditioning *Pick when there are still many unopened flowers, and remove dead florets as they age.*

Cultivation *To get the best midnight-blue varieties, choose your agapanthus plants when in flower. Plant generous clumps of three to five, depending on their size. These are sun-loving plants which thrive in a fertile soil that is moist but well drained, particularly during the winter months. They will do best with the shelter of a sunny wall. Protect the crowns in winter with a good layer of mulch (see page 37). Clumps increase slowly, but after some years can be divided in the spring.*

ALLIUM
Ornamental onion
Bulbous perennial Zones: Triteleia laxa 7–10; Allium giganteum, A. 'Globemaster', A narcissiflorum 6–10; Triteleia hyacintha 5–10; Allium aflatunense, A. cristophii, Nectaroscordum siculum 4–10; Allium flavum 3–9; A. cernuum, A. sphaerocephalon 3–8
Height: A. narcissiflorum to 30cm/12in; Triteleia laxa 30-50cm/12-20in; Allium cernuum, A. cristophii, A. flavum 30-70cm/12-28in; A. sphaerocephalon to 90cm/3ft; A. 'Globemaster' 90cm-1.2m/3-4ft; Triteleia hyacinthina, Nectaroscordum siculum 1.2m/4ft; Allium aflatunense 1.5m/5ft; A. giganteum 2m/6½ft

Varieties good for cutting *There are so many excellent alliums for cutting that it is impossible to mention them all. Together they look like a starry globe of exploding fireworks. A. cristophii, with its green-centred spiny stars, A. giganteum and A. 'Globemaster' are the largest and most impressive. Grow these for combining in a giant arrangement (see pages 70–71). Use*

the melon-sized globes of A. giganteum *with heavy-headed, deliciously scented white lilies like* L. 'Casa Blanca' *to counteract the indisputably oniony smell of the allium as it ages. What is more, both flowers will continue to look good for 10 to 14 days, without any rearranging. Just change the water every other day. For similar, slightly smaller flowers, which will be produced up to six weeks earlier, plant A. aflatunense.*

Among the shorter-stemmed and smaller-headed varieties, grow A. sphaerocephalon. Its magenta-purple shuttlecock-shaped heads are beautiful with whites and greens, or in a mixture of hotter colours. Look out, too, for the lemon-yellow A. flavum, with flowers like a cascading rocket. A pretty rosy-purple version of this is A. cernuum.

Grow also the less hardy, related Triteleia (syn. Brodiaea) with six-petalled starry blooms like a twice-magnified allium flower. T. hyacinthina, a pretty white flushed pink, looks like wild garlic but is without the smell. T. laxa is a good mid-blue (see pages 134 and 135). Another impressive plant related to the alliums is Nectaroscordum siculum subsp. bulgaricum. The pendant bell-shaped early-summer flower in white flushed with purple and green is followed by angular agapanthus-style seed heads.

Conditioning *Change the water of the larger varieties regularly to minimize their oniony smell.*

Cultivation *Alliums are easy to grow in an open sunny situation with good drainage. Plant generous quantities in the autumn, 13cm/5in deep. Left undisturbed, most alliums will quickly form clumps. These can be divided: the spring-flowering varieties in late summer, the summer-flowering forms in spring (see pages 37 and 41). Alliums can be grown from seed – most will self-seed all over the garden, and some can become quite a menace, so be careful where you put them.*

ANCHUSA
Annual, biennial and perennial, some evergreen Zones: 4–8
Height and spread: A. azurea cultivars 1.2m/4ft × 60cm/2ft; A. capensis varieties 20-45cm/8-18in × 20cm/8in

5 cm/2 in

Varieties good for cutting A. azurea *flower spikes remind me of a circus clown balancing 30 or 40 plates on a series of canes. Each of the anchusa's stack of fine bone-china plates has a clear white centre and a wide rich blue surround. They make robust, long-lasting, graceful cut flowers. Of the short-lived perennials, grow the deepest and richest, A. azurea (syn. A. italica) 'Loddon Royalist' with indigo-blue, almost purple, flowers, and the gentian-blue A.a. 'Royal Blue'. Combine either with rich scarlets and oranges for a strong contrasting arrangement (see page 73). Avoid the pinks and whites, which look washed out.*

A. capensis, the bushy South African biennial, usually grown as a half-hardy annual, is good for smaller bunches. A.c. 'Blue Angel' is too small, except for little posies, but the purplish forget-me-not-like 'Blue Bird' reaches nearly 60cm/24in and is well worth growing as a filler at the front of a border in the cutting garden.

Conditioning *Dislodge any ageing flowers by turning the stem upside-down and giving it a good shake.*

Cultivation *This is a Mediterranean wild flower and so needs sun and very well-drained soil, without too much winter wet. Plant perennials 45cm/18in apart in clumps of three to five. Stake the tall flower spikes. If you keep picking anchusas to stop them going to seed, they will flower from the beginning of summer to mid-autumn.*

You can propagate perennials easily from root cuttings in winter. A. azurea varieties can also be successfully grown as biennials, sown in late spring and transplanted to rows in a seed bed for the summer. Plant into their flowering position in the autumn and they will be in bloom by late spring the following year. Propagate half-hardy annuals, such as A. capensis, from a spring sowing under cover with heat, planting out when the risk of frost is over (see pages 32–4 and 35). They all self-seed freely and are easily transplanted.

CAMPANULA
Bellflower
Annual, biennial and perennial, some evergreen Zones: 3–8; C. pyramidalis 8

Height: C. 'G.F. Wilson' *8-10cm/3-4in;* C. portenschlagiana *15cm/6in;* C. glomerata, C. persicifolia *75-90cm/2½-3ft;* C. lactiflora, C. pyramidalis *1.5-2m/5-6½ft*

Varieties good for cutting
Campanulas, with their simple silhouettes of hanging bells, seem to me the most serene of flowers. Grow the simple bellflower, C. persicifolia, in blue and white (see page 118), and mix it with alchemilla, snapdragons, roses and other cottage garden plants. It is a robust cut flower and also good for using in oasis to fill out a summer swag. Avoid the double forms of C. persicifolia, *'Fleur de Neige' and 'Pride of Exmouth'; the flower's charm lies in its simplicity. Grow also the long-flowering tall and stately spikes of the biennial* C. pyramidalis *in blue and white and the other magnificent giant late-summer-flowering* C. lactiflora *'Superba'. Arrange these on their own in a huge ceramic jug for the middle of a large table, or mix them simply with boughs of roses. Right at the other end of the scale, grow the harebell-like* C. 'G.F. Wilson' *or the more vigorous* C. portenschlagiana *for your small posies.*

The stronger, richer-coloured and quickly spreading C. glomerata *'Superba' has a more cultivated feel, but is also excellent for cutting. Mix this with intense oranges and scarlets, all contrasted with lime-greens.*

Conditioning *Plunge the cut ends of* C. lactiflora *cultivars in boiling water for 20 seconds.*

Cultivation *Campanulas are easy and unfussy plants to grow, and will thrive in sun or partial shade. They like a moist but well-drained soil. The more vigorous varieties, like* C. glomerata, *should be dug up and replanted regularly or the centres of the ever-expanding clumps will begin to die off. The tall* C. pyramidalis *and* C. lactiflora *will need staking (see page 37).*

Propagate the perennials by softwood or basal cuttings in summer (see pages 36, 38 and 39), or by division in autumn or spring (see pages 37 and 41). Use this method for good colour forms and named varieties. They are also easy to grow from seed. Sow the biennial C. pyramidalis *under cover in late spring, planting it out in a seed bed for the summer.*

CENTAUREA
Cornflower, knapweed
Annual and perennial Zones: 4–8
Height: C. moschata *cultivars (correctly* Amberboa moschata*) 45-60cm/18-24in;* C. cyanus *vars 30-90cm/1-3ft;* C. dealbata, C. macrocephala *90cm/3ft*

Varieties good for cutting *The bright thistle-like heads of the clear blue cornflower* C. cyanus *combine well with any colour. Grow the improved and larger-flowered* C.c. *'Blue Diadem' for a more showy variety. Try the almost black cornflower* C.c. *'Black Ball', which makes a good mixture with the very dark sweet pea 'Pageantry', contrasted with the orange-scarlet* Lychnis × arkwrightii *'Vesuvius'.*

5 cm/2 in

6 *Campanula persicifolia*
7 *Centaurea cyanus* 'Black Ball'
8 *Centaurea cyanus* 'Blue Diadem'

5 cm/2 in

Avoid the stumpy dwarf varieties, which are less useful for cutting. Many of the perennial centaureas also make good cut flowers. The pink C. dealbata *varieties like 'Steenbergii' (see page 122) are also excellent for cutting.*

Conditioning *Pick cornflowers when the flowers are half open, and strip the bottom leaves. They will last four to five days.*

Cultivation *Cornflowers will grow in even quite poor soil, in full sun. If you want really bumper-sized flowers you can de-bud the young plants, but this seems unnecessary to me; lots of slightly smaller flowers are just as nice as fewer giant ones. If you do not pick very regularly, remove the bleached flowers before they set seed. They may suffer from powdery mildew in hot summers.*

Sow the hardy annual forms in situ in spring, and thin to 10-15cm/4-6in. Even better, sow in early autumn so they can build up large rosettes and good energy stores before they have to produce a flower spike. Grow the perennial forms from seed, division or root cuttings (see pages 32–4, 37 and 43).

CLEMATIS
Main entry: Spring White, page 99.

I put a few velvety heads of the herbaceous blue-purple C. × durandii *on its own, for the middle of a table.*

In late summer and autumn I mix its feathery, spiralling seed heads with honeysuckle berries and late roses like the pink English Rose 'Heritage'.

CYNARA
Cardoon, globe artichoke
Perennial Zones: 7–9
Height and spread: C. cardunculus *2-2.5m/6½-8ft × 1m/3ft;* C.c. *Scolymus Group 1-1.2m/3-4ft × 60cm/2ft*

Varieties good for cutting *This genus, which includes both cardoons and globe artichokes, is excellent for huge arrangements in tall vases or party urns. Pick leaves of the cardoon,* C. cardunculus, *to combine with bright blue delphiniums and eremurus, cutting them so they stand about 90cm/3ft tall. Young globe artichoke leaves,* C.c. *Scolymus Group, are also lovely in spring, mixed with* Helleborus orientalis *seedlings (see pages 56–8). Cut artichoke and cardoon flowers both in bud and in full flower. While still green, they provide perfect strong architectural stems for mixing with startling scarlets and oranges (see page 73). When they have opened and are showing their rich purple plumes, combine them with huge-headed sunflowers and acanthus, or simply arrange them on their own.*

Conditioning *Strip the bottom leaves on the flowering spikes and change the water regularly, as it may turn brown.*

Cultivation *Plant a good clump of three to five artichokes and, if you have room, at least one cardoon. Plant in spring, in a warm, well-drained, sunny site. Cut your artichokes down in the late autumn and protect the crowns with a thick mulch of straw or leaves. Stake the cardoon flower spikes when they reach their giant height. Propagate by division or from seed in spring.*

DELPHINIUM and CONSOLIDA
Annual and perennial Zones: Delphinium *Belladonna Group 3–8; large-flowered hybrids 2–8;* D. grandiflorum *4–9*
Height: D. grandiflorum *45cm/18in; dwarf large-flowered hybrids,* Consolida regalis, D. *Belladonna Group 90 cm-1.5m/3-5ft; large-flowered hybrids 1.5-1.8m/5-6ft*

Varieties good for cutting
Delphiniums make a graceful addition to any bunch of flowers and to the flower border. They come in blues, white and pink, and more recently, yellows, reds and creams have

been developed. *Of the large-flowered hybrids, grow the rich violet-blue Black Knight Group,* D. 'Nobility' *or the paler D. 'Cristella' (see pages 70–71), which will all produce spike after spike of flowers from midsummer into autumn. Put them at the back of the border beside a stately cardoon and pick them together for a 1.5m/5ft display of flowers and foliage. Also choose a white (see page 119) and perhaps a cream. Good dwarf forms include the indigo-blue 'Blue Tit', which reaches 1.2m/4ft.*

Many of the species and old hybrid delphiniums are also excellent cut. D. *Belladonna Group is a delicate branched variety with lovely single open-winged flowers in a deep rich blue with a white eye. Try also* D. grandiflorum *(often listed as* D. chinense*), which is a short-lived perennial usually grown as an annual.* D.g. *'Blue Butterfly' has large rich royal blue flowers and is well worth growing.*

Others invaluable for cutting are the annual delphiniums, Consolida regalis *or larkspur. Grow the deep rich purple-blues like* C. *(Exquisite Series) 'Blue Spire' and the pure white 'White King', from the Giant Imperial type. Avoid the pinks, which are in my experience either a sickly powder-pink or a deep greyish-pink, both very difficult colours to mix.*

Conditioning *Pick delphiniums when most of the flowers on the spike are open. They are very sensitive to ethylene gas, which is emitted as fruit ripens, so do not put them near a bowl of fruit.*

Cultivation *Delphiniums grow vigorously on most types of soil with good drainage and full sun. Some will thrive in part shade, if given ample water and feed and kept weed-free. Mulch in spring and give regular feeds throughout the flowering season.*

Plant perennials 60cm/24in apart, in groups of three to five. Plant annuals closer,

in blocks in the border or lines in your cutting patch. Adequate spacing to allow a good air-flow through the foliage is important, as both perennial and annual delphiniums have a problem with mildew, particularly in late summer. Regular cutting of delphiniums will promote the development of lateral shoots and prolong the flowering season. The taller varieties will need staking (see page 37).

Annuals can either be sown under cover in early spring, to be planted out when the frosts are over, or be sown in situ in early autumn or spring (see pages 32–4 and 35). Named cultivars of perennial delphiniums and D. *Belladonna Group should be propagated from basal cuttings of young shoots in spring. Take them, 5-8cm/2-3in long, when the shoots first emerge in early spring, before they develop a hollow centre. Put them in individual 8cm/3in pots and allow them to develop roots, without heat.*

❶ *Clematis* × *durandii*

❷ *Dianthus barbatus* Nigrescens Group

❸ *Consolida* (Exquisite Series) 'Blue Spire'

❹ *Eustoma grandiflorum* F₁ Hybrid

5 cm/2 in

DIANTHUS BARBATUS
Sweet William
Main entry: Summer Pink, page 122.
D.b. *Nigrescens Group has blackish-purple flowers that complement pink roses or sweet peas in a rich-scented bouquet (see page 70).*

ECHIUM
Viper's bugloss
Annual and biennial; also perennial and shrub
Height: E. plantagineum *'Blue Bedder' 30cm/12in;* E. vulgare *60cm/24in*
Varieties good for cutting *The biennial species of echium,* E. vulgare, *is a wild flower that grows around shingly coasts. Its blue, pink and purple flowers surrounded by a hairy, spiky calyx look lovely mixed with anchusas and contrasted with acid-green dill, claret stocks and sweet Williams. Use the spike to break up the symmetry of a bunch.* E. plantagineum *'Blue Bedder' is the best and most widely available of the hardy annual varieties.*
Conditioning *Strip the bottom leaves.*
Cultivation *Grow them in clumps of five in a sunny, well-drained, even stony, site.* E. vulgare *is best grown as a biennial, sown under cover in late spring, planted out for the summer, and transplanted to its flowering position (see page 38). It can also be treated as a hardy annual but it will produce smaller plants.* E.p. *'Blue Bedder' should be grown in the same way. Both will self-seed freely and can be transplanted.*

ERYNGIUM
Sea holly
Main entry: Summer Green and Silver, page 116. *Mix the indigo-blue spiky flower of* E. × zabelii *'Violetta' with poppy seed heads, bupleurum, orange and yellow alstroemerias and eremurus spikes, contrasted with the sumptuous deep purple lisianthus.*

EUSTOMA
Lisianthus, prairie gentian, Texas bluebell
Hardy perennial grown as half-hardy annual
Height: 45-60cm/18-24in
Varieties good for cutting *The deep purple lisianthus* E. grandiflorum *(syn.*

Lisianthus russellianus), is one of the most richly textured and coloured of all annuals. Lisianthus make long-lasting and robust cut flowers. Grow lots for mixing and enriching any bunch – combine them with oranges, blues and greens for a luxurious hot, exotic display. Or mix them with whites and greens for a bride's wedding bouquet. Grow the E.g. Yodel Series, which are improved F$_1$ hybrids. The pure white and cream forms are well worth growing to take centre stage in any calming, cool-coloured bunch. Their open tubular flowers are like large poppies. Avoid the ruched double forms.

5 *Cynara cardunculus*
6 *Delphinium 'Nobility'*
7 *Echium vulgare*
8 *Eryngium × zabelii 'Violetta'*
9 *Iris 'Jane Phillips'*

Conditioning *Recut the stem ends, removing at least 2.5cm/1in. Do not allow the flowers to get wet for they will become transparent and brown quickly.*
Cultivation *This is a difficult annual to grow, though well worth the bother. Sow seed when fresh in winter, under cover with some heat and plant out in a well-drained site in full sun. Pinch out the growing points for maximum flowers on branching plants.*

IRIS
Main entry: Winter Blue and Purple, page 158. *The mid-season soft violet-blue Tall Bearded iris 'Jane Phillips' is a stunning sculptural flower with a sweet, rather exotic smell. It lasts for over a week in water as buds continue to open out.*

5 cm/2 in

5 cm/2 in

LATHYRUS ODORATUS
Sweet pea

Main entry: Summer White, page 120.
The deep claret-black L.o. 'Pageantry' is beautiful mixed with the bicoloured purple and carmine L.o. 'Matucana'. They can be grown in the main part of the garden in an elegant combination with deep purple climbing French beans, and arranged on their own or combined in a fragrant mixture of clarets and reds with roses, stocks and sweet Williams (see page 70).

LAVANDULA
Lavender

*Evergreen shrub Zones: L. stoechas 8–9; L. angustifolia varieties 6
Height and spread: both 60-90cm/2-3ft*
Varieties good for cutting *Although deliciously scented, lavender can appear scraggy as a cut flower. You need to mass several stems together before you get much of a show. Both L.a. 'Munstead', a mauve-purple, and L.a. 'Hidcote', a deeper violet, are worth growing and cutting. On the whole, though, it is the tender lavenders with large showy bracts that win the day in the cutting garden. L. stoechas subsp. pedun-culata is a superb flower for cutting (see page 113). If you are worried about its*

hardiness in your area, grow it in large terracotta pots and bring the plants in for the winter.
Conditioning *To preserve the scent, pick flowers for drying at mid-morning and dry them in a cool, dry room, not in the sun.*
Cultivation *For a good flower crop, plant lavender in full sun on well-drained, preferably limy, soil. Sadly for me, they do not like boggy clay. Prune well after flowering in late summer, but do not cut into old wood. Lavender is easily propagated by semi-ripe cuttings in summer (see pages 38 and 39).*

LUPINUS
Lupin

*Annual, perennial and shrub Zones: 3–9
Height: all 90cm-1.5m/3-5ft except:
L. luteus, L. varius 45-60cm/18-24in;
L. mutabilis var. cruckshanksii 'Sunrise' 90cm/3ft;*

❶ *Lathyrus odoratus* 'Pageantry'
❷ *Lathyrus odoratus* 'Matucana'
❸ *Lavandula angustifolia* 'Munstead'
❹ *Salvia* x *superba*
❺ *Triteleia laxa*

5 cm/2 in

Varieties good for cutting *I love lupin flower spikes, which look like the tail feathers of an exotic parrot or tropical pheasant. There are many good colour forms, which are best grown clumped together. Grow the indigo-blue L. polyphyllus and the white and blue cultivar L. 'The Governor'. Another excellent deep purple-blue and white is L. 'Blue Jacket', which has the added bonus of being highly scented and long-flowering. The white lupin L. Noble Maiden Group is also an exotic beauty and a good mixer (see pages 120 and 121). Lupins also look spectacular grown in a great jumble of different colours, if you have the right self-contained spot. Plant L. 'The Page' in shades of carmine next to L. 'Chandelier' in many shades of yellow. Put in some reds, pinks and purples for good measure. You could also try one of the better mixtures, like the L. Band of Nobles Series.*

Cut and arrange them as they come, in a huge jug of clashing and contrasting colours.

There are some annual lupins which are also worth growing. The hardy, and scented, L. mutabilis var. cruckshanksii 'Sunrise', with its white, egg-yolk yellow and blue flowers, is an excellent one. The half-hardy, exceptionally bright yellow L. luteus and deep blue-black L. varius also make lovely cut flowers. As ever, avoid the dwarf varieties, which are not much use for cutting.
Conditioning *To prevent the flower spikes bending up towards the sun, do not put them in a trug or basket, but plunge them in a bucket of water straight away. They tend to drop their pea-like flowers after four or five days, even sooner in heat.*
Cultivation *Lupins thrive in sun or part shade in ordinary lime-free soil (L. poly-phyllus particularly hates lime), but they need good drainage and do best in a sandy soil. Picking the flower spikes will encourage the development of laterals and a longer flowering season. It also prevents them from setting seed, which weakens the plant. Mildew can be a problem on the foliage. To avoid this, treat lupins as biennials and remove them when they finish flowering.*

The perennial lupins can be propagated by spring cuttings (see pages 38 and 39). Most can also be grown from seed sown in mid-spring. They will flower in the second year. Rub the large seeds briefly with sand-paper and then soak them until they have plumped up. This may take a day or two. Sow them individually about 5mm/¼in deep, in 8cm/3in pots. Pot on when they have three or four true leaves and then out to a seed bed to grow on. Hardy annual L. mutabilis var. cruckshanksii 'Sunrise' is easily grown from seed. It must be sown where it is to flower. The half-hardy annuals are best sown in autumn, so they have time to thicken up before flowering.

MATTHIOLA
Stock

Main entry: Summer Pink, page 123.
This smoky-purple stock is dramatic mixed with bupleurum and moluccella; any of the dark-coloured forms are good for adding richness and scent to summer arrangements.

NIGELLA
Love-in-a-mist
Hardy annual
Height: N. damascena *cultivars,* N. hispanica *35-45cm/14-18in;* N. damascena *'Oxford Blue',* N. hispanica *'Curiosity' 75cm/30in*

Varieties good for cutting *Both the blooms, like a Tudor ruff, and the purse-like seed pods of love-in-a-mist make excellent cut flowers. Grow nigella as a filler for the front of your cutting borders and to mix in country-style bunches for the house. Make hand-tied posies of the seed pods and pretty feathery foliage. Grow the showiest variety,* N. hispanica, *with its large deep blue flowers and pronounced black and maroon stamens. Or try the tallest, richest blue form of* N. damascena, *'Oxford Blue', which has dark-striped seed heads. There are also fine pink and white forms of* N. damascena *and good coloured mixtures, like Persian Jewel Group.* N. orientalis *is also well worth growing.*

Conditioning *Strip the bottom leaves.*
Cultivation *Nigella grows best in sun in fertile, well-drained soil. Keep picking, but leave a few flowers to form seed pods for mixing with later flowers. Sow in situ, broadcasting seed in the flowering position. Nigella hates being transplanted. For large early-flowering plants sow in early autumn in preference to mid-spring. Nigella seeds germinate quickly and will need thinning to about 10cm/4in. Nigella self-seeds freely in all your nooks and crannies, and if not weeded out will become self-perpetuating.*

SALVIA
Main entry: Autumn Blue and Purple, page 147. *The rich purple* S. × superba, *one of the earliest to flower, is good mixed in borders and in your arrangements with deep orange 'Matador' Iceland poppies, Lychnis × arkwrightii 'Vesuvius' and the green and orange unripe seed cases of Chinese lanterns.*

SCABIOSA
Scabious, pincushion flower
Hardy annual and perennial Zone: 4
Height: S. caucasica *cultivars 60cm/24in;* Double Mixed S. atropurpurea *90cm/3ft*

Varieties good for cutting *The mauves, dark oranges, whites and pinks of the annual mixture Double Mixed* S. atropurpurea *are pretty for informal bunches but it is the deep crimson form that I like best. The large-domed dark flowers on their long stems make a fine duo with Zinnia 'Envy' and mix well with crimson stocks, sweet Williams and snapdragons, contrasted with viper's bugloss and anchusas. The perennials include many handsome large-flowered varieties in pale blue, mauve and white. Grow the long-flowering* S. caucasica *'Fama', a strong bright 1970s-style mauve, to mix with flowering teasels, nigella seed pods and dill. Pinkish-mauve* S.c. *'Clive Greaves' mixes well with acid-green and orange. I use the white* S.c. *'Perfecta Alba' or cream 'Miss Willmott' in conventional bridal and bridesmaids' bouquets.*

Conditioning *Give them a good drink before arranging.*
Cultivation *Scabious thrives in sun, in fertile, well-drained, alkaline soil. Plant a good clump of three to five plants of each perennial variety, as one plant will not have an enormous number of flowers at one time. They will, however, flower for many months, particularly if you keep picking and prevent them setting seed. Support the pincushion flower with a network of cotton and twigs for each clump. If you keep picking they will continue to flower until the first frosts.*

Grow the annuals from seed sown in situ or under cover in spring. They can also be sown under cover in early autumn for an earlier start to flowering. Overwinter them in a cold frame and plant them out in mid-spring. Pinch out growing points from seedlings to encourage branching.

Grow the perennials from young basal cuttings in summer, from seed in autumn or from division in early spring as growth begins.

TRITELEIA LAXA
Main entry: see Allium, page 130. *This mauve-blue allium relative is one of the longest-lasting cut flowers. Use it in a bright mix with orange and yellow alstroemerias, different-coloured poppies and bupleurum.*

❻ *Lupinus*
❼ *Matthiola* cultivar
❽ *Nigella damascena* 'Oxford Blue'
❾ *Scabiosa atropurpurea*
❿ *Scabiosa caucasica* 'Clive Greaves'

5 cm/2 in

Autumn

Once autumn arrives, it is time to create wild, ragged vases of turning leaves, seed heads, berries and hips. Make relaxed and generous towering beauties and, as the outdoor light fades, bring inside the hot colours of rich velvety clashing dahlias, gladioli and zinnias that are now flowering.

Silver, Green and Brown

AGAPANTHUS

Main entry: Summer Blue and Purple, page 130. *Tall and statuesque agapanthus*

seed heads, with their droplets of jade held on delicate stems, look like Fabergé jewels. Mix them with richly coloured dahlias, Chinese lanterns and late sunflowers.

AMARANTHUS CAUDATUS
Love-lies-bleeding

Half-hardy annual
Height: 90cm-1.2m/3-4 ft

Varieties good for cutting *The bright green version of love-lies-bleeding makes an invaluable addition to any large autumn bunch. This late-maturing annual mixes well with whites and blues, and contrasts dramatically with the oranges, crimsons, browns and scarlets of berries and turning leaves. Arrange it or the more usual red-tasselled form (see page 22) tall and stately, the tassels hanging in a staggered curtain, like icicles in a frozen waterfall. Some of the more upright amaranthus, like*

'Green Thumb' and 'Pygmy Torch', are rather too pert and too unrelaxed for my liking. Keep to the tall, laid-back, hanging varieties and you won't go wrong.

Conditioning *Remove the lower leaves and sear the stem ends in boiling water for 20 seconds, before giving them a long drink.*

Cultivation *Plant out at 45-60cm/ 18in-24in intervals (amaranthus become large plants). Choose a site in full sun with fertile, well-drained soil. They will not reach full height and maturity until late summer or early autumn but will continue to flower until the early part of the winter – one of the last flowers to be picked. Feed them well and you may produce 1.5m/5ft giants.*

Amaranthus are easy to grow from an early-spring sowing under cover. The tiny seeds produce little spindly seedlings which should be pricked out at the one or two true leaf stage (see page 34). They also self-seed.

ARTEMISIA
Absinth, lad's love, wormwood

Perennial and deciduous or semi-evergreen shrub or sub-shrub Zones: A. arborescens 'Faith Raven', A. 'Powis Castle' 7–10; A. pontica 5–10; A. absinthium 'Lambrook Silver' 4–10

Height and spread: A. pontica 60cm/ 24in × 20cm/8in; A. absinthium 'Lambrook Silver' 80cm/32in × 50cm/ 20in; A. 'Powis Castle' 60–90cm/2–3ft × 90cm–1.2m/3–4ft; A. arborescens varieties 90cm-1.2m/ 3-4ft × 90cm/3ft

Varieties good for cutting *The bright silver-filigree foliage of many aromatic artemisias provides excellent contrast to the hot and intense colours that are so common in the garden at this time of year. It enlivens and lightens what can become a cloying richness when the oranges, reds and ochres are left on their own. While it is pretty combined with nigella, bishop's flower and roses in summer, in autumn it becomes invaluable.*

A. arborescens 'Faith Raven' (named after my mother, who found this variety on top of a mountain in Rhodes) will quickly form a brilliant silver mound; if you pick carefully around its underskirts, you will leave no sign of your harvest. Like the similar 'Powis Castle', it retains its compact dome-like structure because it flowers little in colder climates. More delicate in appearance are A. absinthium 'Lambrook Silver', with widely spaced feathery foliage, and the very upright elegant A. pontica, perfect for poking into a small intense-coloured hand-tied bunch. They all mix well with salvias, dahlias and asters (see page 78).

Conditioning *Artemisias flop easily. Sear the cut end of the stems (see page 48), then give them a cool drink overnight.*

Cultivation *These Mediterranean plants thrive in open, sunny, well-drained sites. Neaten established shrubs and sub-shrubs with a hard prune in spring, to encourage a neat hummocky shape. They will quickly*

5 cm/2 in

❶ *Agapanthus (seed head)*
❷ *Amaranthus caudatus 'Viridis'*
❸ *Artemisia absinthium*
　'Lambrook Silver'
❹ *Artemisia arborescens 'Faith Raven'*

❺

❻

❼

5 cm/2 in

H. lupulus, *is still commercially grown in pockets of Sussex and Kent for flavouring bitter beer. H.l. 'Aureus' flowers and fruits less freely, but its bright yellow-green foliage is more ornamental.*

Conditioning *Hang hops immediately, so that they dry quickly without becoming mildewed or musty. Spray the entire structure with odourless hairspray to hold seed heads in place and slow up the inevitable moulting.*

Cultivation *Grow hops in sun or semi-shade in any well-drained soil; they thrive in a warm sheltered position. Hops need some support to clamber over. H.l. 'Aureus' is best grown in full sun in a soil that doesn't dry out. Propagate by division in early spring.*

NICANDRA PHYSALODES
Shoo-fly plant
Hardy annual
Height: 1m/3ft

Varieties good for cutting *The bright green or green-and-black fruit calyces of the shoo-fly plant make elegant additions to a bunch of almost black dahlias or bright pink, orange and yellow zinnias as a strong foliage to balance these vigorous colours. Look out for the large-flowered variety, which has bell-shaped sky-blue and white flowers in summer and sculptural fruit calyces. The flowers make pretty fillers for an immature garden, but bear in mind they last only a day picked (see pages 78–9).*

Conditioning *Remove some or all of the leaves, as the seed cases last much longer.*

Cultivation *An easy annual to grow, the shoo-fly plant likes full sun and a rich, well-drained soil. Sow under cover in early spring and plant out after the frosts have finished. It can also be sown direct into the ground as the soil warms up in mid-spring.*

PENNISETUM
Feather-top
Herbaceous perennial
Zones: P. alopecuroides 'Woodside' 7–10; P. orientale 5–6; P. villosum 5–10
Height: P. alopecuroides 'Woodside' 60cm/24in; P. orientale 75cm/30in; P. villosum 90cm/36in

Varieties good for cutting *The fluffy squirrel-tail grasses with their green centres*

and pinkish-white hairy outlines are among the queens of autumn foliage. Grow both the bright brownish-pink P. orientale and the lighter P. villosum, and cut either to stand up above a dome of bright rich salvias and asters (see page 78) or deep crimson dahlias and Zinnia 'Envy'. Place on a windowsill, so the light enhances their radiant halo. The free-flowering P. alopecuroides 'Woodside', with its indigo bottlebrush appearance, is another good almost hardy variety.

Cultivation *Grow pennisetums in any well-drained but not too fertile soil, but choose a warm open site in full sun. If you feed pennisetums too generously you will*

❺ *Clematis* 'Bill Mackenzie'
❻ *Cyperus albostriatus*
❼ *Humulus lupulus*
❽ *Euphorbia marginata*
❾ *Nicandra physalodes* (seed pods)

❾

❽

5 cm/2 in

refurbish themselves from their woody basal shoots. Pinch out the tips of young plants to encourage a bushy habit, and subsequently nip out any wayward long shoots.

Propagate the suckering A. pontica by division in spring or autumn. The shrubs and sub-shrubs are easily struck from soft-wood or semi-ripe cuttings in summer.

CLEMATIS
Main entry: Spring White, page 99. *The wispy seed heads of C. 'Bill Mackenzie', like those of C. × durandii or C. tangutica, remind me of immaculately groomed Old English sheepdogs ready to trot out at Crufts' dog show. Team them with Cosmos 'Versailles Carmine' and tithonia.*

CYPERUS
Papyrus, galingale
Evergreen perennial Zones: 4–8
Height: C. albostriatus 60cm/24in

Varieties good for cutting *Most of the papyrus family, like C. involucratus and C. papyrus, are tender greenhouse plants. This is a great loss because they are excellent cutting plants, adding real spice and interest to any bunch. C. albostriatus, however, will grow happily in a cold climate and is invaluable in autumn, providing bright lime-green foliage at a time when the euphorbias are mostly over, and annual foliage plants such as bupleurum are at an*

end. Try it or the similar C. eragrostis with asters, dahlias and Iris foetidissima (see page 78), or with zingy pink nerines.

Cultivation *Cyperus will grow in almost any soil in sun or shade. It needs little care or maintenance. Propagate by division in spring or autumn. It self-seeds freely.*

EUPHORBIA
Spurge, milkweed
Main entry: Spring Green and Silver, page 96. *The pretty greyish-green annual E. marginata with its white-striped margins comes into its own in late summer and autumn. Mix it with 'Iceberg' roses, trailing hops and crinum lilies for a cool and fresh-looking table centre for a party.*

HUMULUS LUPULUS
Hop
Deciduous twining climber Zones: 3–9
Height and spread: 3-6m/10-20ft

Varieties good for cutting *The twisting and twirling stems of the hop are one of the real boons of autumn, with their crop of bright green, heavily scented fruit that follows on from the flowers of the female plant. Cut them long or short for arranging around the house. Use them trailing for a hand-tied bunch, or make a medallion (see pages 78–9); a series of these hung for a party will intoxicate the guests as they arrive. The ordinary dark-green-leaved form,*

❶ *Pennisetum villosum*

❷ *Rubus cockburnianus* 'Golden Vale'

❸ *Rubus fruticosus*

❹ *Typha latifolia*

❺ *Zinnia* 'Envy'

promote soft growth and sudden winter death. They will, however, need a good mulch to protect them in a cold winter.

Propagate by division in late spring or autumn. Keep recent offsets in the cold frame during winter. P. orientale, in particular, is not reliably hardy, and this way you will have a fall-back stock to rely on.

RUBUS
Blackberry, raspberry, wineberry

Deciduous shrub Zone: 6
Height: R. cockburnianus 3.7m/12ft
R. fruticosus, R. idaeus 90cm-1.8m/3-6ft; R. phoenicolasius 1.8-2.5m/6-8ft
Varieties good for cutting *A bough of red or black berries is often the making of a late-summer or early-autumn arrangement. The luscious and shiny berries stand in contrast with brilliant reds, yellows and*

oranges, *mixing perfectly with red or yellow chillis, zinnias and deep red snapdragons. Grow a thornless variety of blackberry like R. fruticosus 'Loch Ness'. The brilliant red fuzzy-stemmed Japanese wineberry, R. phoenicolasius, with its packed branches of long-lasting berries, is also excellent cut.*

In summer, mix the acid-green leaves of fruiting raspberry canes, R. idaeus, and the contrasting fruit with boughs of pink roses or white 'Casa Blanca' lilies. For a huge sculptural arrangement in late autumn or winter, consider growing the towering white stems of R. cockburnianus.

Conditioning *Invest in a pair of thorn-proof gloves for picking rubus. Keep the fruiting varieties as cool as you can, as mildew can become a problem.*

Cultivation *Most rubus are best planted in autumn, in a deep, rich, well-drained but moist soil in sun. Cut the fruited stems of raspberries and blackberries to the ground, tying in the new growth. Cut out about one-third of the stems of R. phoenicolasius and R. cockburnianus each spring, to encourage new growth. Mulch all rubus with manure in late autumn and again in spring. Give raspberries a high-potash feed (wood ash spread around the roots is good) and keep them well watered as they fruit.*

Propagate by semi-ripe cuttings in summer (see pages 38 and 39) or by division in autumn. R. phoenicolasius is also easily grown from seed. Blackberries are best propagated by layering tips in summer or by transplanting suckers in autumn.

TYPHA
Bulrush

Deciduous perennial Zones: 3–9
Height: 1.8-2.5m/6-8ft
Varieties good for cutting *The cylindrical brown frankfurter that we think of as a bulrush flower is the seed case produced from the female part of the flower. Grow T. latifolia or the slightly smaller T. angustifolia and mix them, very dramatically, in a vase with many stems of white crinum lilies, or use them as the vertical addition to a huge autumn jug of dahlias, salvias, leaves turning colour and hips (see pages 82–3).*

Conditioning *Do not keep bulrushes too long in the house; after two or three weeks the seed heads will disintegrate and seeds will pour out like bubbles from a newly opened champagne bottle.*
Cultivation *Grow bulrushes, in sun or shade, in the shallows of a pond edge, or in a damp swampy area. They are invasive plants, so take care where you plant them. Propagate in spring by seed or division.*

ZINNIA

Half-hardy annual
Height: 30–90cm/12–36in
Varieties good for cutting *This huge family ranges from Las Vegas to Venetian silks, from Manhattan blare to Old World richness. I love all of them, but the very best is the double lime-green 'Envy'. Mix it with contrasting deep crimsons and reds, or arrange one or two stems simply on their own, to appreciate its exquisite and dramatic but calming colour. For reds and oranges choose from the Giant Cactus Group and Scabious-flowered Group (see page 145).*
Conditioning *Just strip the bottom leaves. These long-lived cut flowers should look good for at least two weeks.*
Cultivation *Plant zinnias out in full sun in fertile, well-drained soil. Pick them regularly from the moment they start flowering and they will continue to flower until winter. They do best in baking hot summers, but take care not to overwater them once they are in the ground; they can suffer from mildew. Propagate from seed sown under cover in late spring. Prick the seedlings out and pot them up, taking care not to overwater.*

White

ANEMONE × HYBRIDA
Japanese anemone
Main entry: Spring White, page 98.
*The clear white saucer-shaped flowers of
A. × h. 'Honorine Jobert' with their crisp
yellow and green centres make a perfect foil
to intense hot colours. Use tall in huge
autumn jugs or cut short in delicate arrangements of autumn crocus and colchicums.*

CRINUM × POWELLII
Crinum lily
Bulb Zones: 7–10
Height: 1.2m/4ft
Varieties good for cutting *When
your lilies are over, crinums will do more
than merely replace them. The pure white
trumpets of C. × p. 'Album' are beautiful to
behold. The five to seven buds held on each
tall stem will open in succession, while their
fabulous scent pulses out in great bursts.
Seven or nine stems arranged on their own,
with their scent suffusing the air, will give a
feeling of rare luxury. Or mix them with the
variegated annual Euphorbia marginata
and heavy-headed white roses, as the glamorous stars of a table for an evening party.*

*   Crinum lilies also come in pink. Look
out for the deeper pink C. × p. 'Krelagei'
and 'Ellen Bosanquet', and try mixing them
with white crinums, or combining them with
Euphorbia schillingii and Rosa 'New
Dawn' for a pretty and fragrant vase.*
Cultivation *Plant crinums in a sunny
well-drained site with the bulb necks above
ground. They like a rich, deep soil, with
adequate moisture. Mulch thickly with
manure every second year. Buy five to ten of
the mini football-sized bulbs from a good
wholesalers. You can propagate by offsets in
spring, but they take several years to flower.*

NICOTIANA
Tobacco plant
*Half-hardy annual, and perennial grown as
an annual*
Height: N. alata 60cm/24in;
N. langsdorffii, N. sylvestris *1.5m/5ft*
Varieties good for cutting *Many of
the tobacco plants, with their elegant tubular*

*flowers and powerful evening fragrance,
make excellent cut flowers. The giant
N. sylvestris is dramatic in the autumn
garden and arranged on its own (see page
82). Combine it with the towering tassels of
Amaranthus caudatus 'Viridis' and the
purple and white Dahlia 'Edinburgh'.*

*   For summer and autumn picking grow
the annual N. 'Lime Green' (see page 117),
or the pretty lime-green N. langsdorffii,
with its ball-dress-shaped small flowers, for
small delicate bunches.*
Conditioning *Nicotianas last well in
water. Give them a good drink before
arranging, and remove fading flowers.*
Cultivation *Grow in full sun or part
shade in a fertile, well-drained soil. Picking
the flowers will encourage lateral growth and
prolong flowering. Tobacco plants are easily
grown from seed sown under cover in early
spring (see pages 32–4). Plant out after the
last frosts. N. sylvestris readily self-seeds.*

① Anemone × hybrida 'Honorine Jobert'
② Crinum × powellii 'Album'
③ Nicotiana sylvestris
④ Rosa 'Iceberg'

ROSA
Main entry: Summer Pink, page 124.
*Whether grown as a standard or a shrub,
Rosa 'Iceberg' is definitely a must for even
the smallest cutting garden. It will continue
to flower, producing faintly scented but
generous bosomy white roses, from early
summer right up until the really cold weather
of late autumn.*

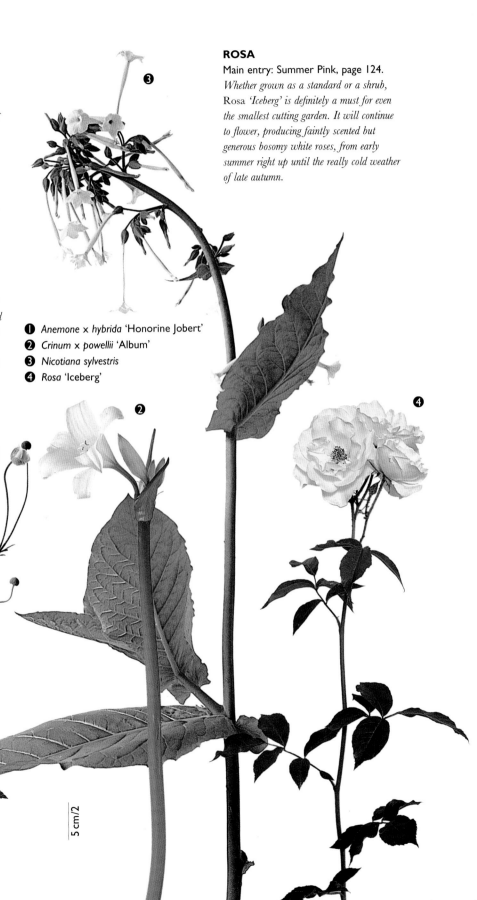

5 cm/2

Pink

ASTER

Daisy, Michaelmas daisy

Herbaceous perennial Zones: 5–10
Height: A. amellus 30cm/12in;
A. × frikartii 'Mönch', 90cm/36in;
A. novi-belgii 90-120cm/3-4ft

Varieties good for cutting *These frothy single and double daisies come in a full range of blue, purple, mauve and white. I especially like the long-flowering pale mauve A. × frikartii 'Mönch' with its yellow centre, the richer purple with yellow A. amellus 'Veilchenkönigin', the mid-purple A. novi-belgii 'Sailor Boy' and the deep cerise-pink A. n.-b. 'Carnival'. Arrange them mixed in a brilliant colour jamboree with salvias and dahlias (see pages 76–8).*

Conditioning *Strip the bottom leaves, give them a drink overnight, and the flowers will last up to two weeks in water.*

Cultivation *Grow asters in sun or partial shade, in a rich but well-drained soil, with adequate moisture throughout the summer. Taller varieties may need staking. The modern* novi-belgii *cultivars in particular may need spraying against mildew.*

These plants are easy to grow from soft-wood cuttings or division in spring.

COLCHICUM

Bulb Zone: 6
Height: C. autumnale 10-15cm/4-6in;
C. speciosum 'Album', C. 'The Giant'
15-20cm/6-8in

Varieties good for cutting *The large goblet-shaped flowers of colchicums are like robust and strapping crocuses. Arrange many stems on their own, or mixed only with the fresh green grass in which they grow. Choose the chunky large-flowered white-based violet or pink 'The Giant', handsome in a shallow coloured glass on its own or mixed with the pure white C. speciosum 'Album', or its deep wine-purple brother, C.s. 'Atrorubens'. Grow also the classic C. autumnale.*

Cultivation *Order corms from a bulb wholesaler in late winter for summer delivery and planting. Colchicums do best in a dry, well-drained soil in full sun or light shade.*

They are perfect for planting under fruit trees in an orchard. Cut a hole in the turf, plant them 5-8cm/2-3in below the surface, and replace the turf. As the buds emerge, place slug pellets around each clump, or you will have no more than a few ragged scraps left. Slugs or colchicums, that's your choice.

Propagate established colchicums by division immediately after flowering.

CYCLAMEN

Main entry: Winter Pink, page 153.
The delicate pink C. hederifolium is lovely arranged on its own, many stems in a saucer placed on a windowsill or in the pool of light from a table lamp. Mix it, too, with its own leaves and its white colour form.

DAHLIA

Main entry: Autumn Orange and Red, page 143. *The handsome long-stemmed D. 'Edinburgh' with its great pompon heads of rich purple-pink with white tips, makes a fabulous cutting plant. Arrange it with boughs of acorns or mix it with autumn leaves, hips and berries (see pages 82–3).*

NERINE

Bulb Zones: 8–10
Height: 45-60cm/18-24in

Varieties good for cutting *I used to have an aversion to nerines. The hardiest, the harsh nail-varnish pink N. bowdenii, often shouts too loudly from its sunny flower bed. You can have fun with them, though. Place*

5 cm/2 in

● Colchicum autumnale
❷ Colchicum 'The Giant'
❸ Cyclamen hederifolium
❹ Aster novi-belgii 'Carnival'
❺ Dahlia 'Edinburgh'
❻ Penstemon 'Blackbird'
❼ Rosa 'New Dawn'
❽ Schizostylis coccinea 'Major'
❾ Nerine bowdenii 'Mark Fenwick'
❿ Phlox paniculata 'Graf Zeppelin'

5 cm/2 in

vase for a fabulous modern still-life, or mix with bright green cyperus, shrubby bupleurum and sky-blue Salvia uliginosa. Avoid a conventional mix with whites and blues. There are some beautiful but tender cultivars. Try the white N. flexuosa 'Alba' or the deeper pink large-flowered clone N.b. 'Mark Fenwick'. Mix the even more brazen salmon-orangey-pink colour forms with crimson-black dahlias and Chinese lanterns.

Conditioning Give them a good drink and they will last for over a week in water.

Cultivation Plant the hardy varieties in late summer or after flowering, with the noses of the bulbs showing above the soil. Choose a sheltered site, in full sun, preferably with the shelter and warmth of a sunny wall. They do best on a light sandy soil. Grow the more tender forms in a greenhouse, and plant out after the frosts.

The leaves appear after the flower spike and disappear by the summer. To get the best flowers, water until the leaves die down, then let them dry off. Protect with a good mulch through winter. Nerines dislike being disturbed, but as they become congested lift and replant every four to five years in autumn or when the leaves die down. They can also be grown from fresh seed.

PENSTEMON

Evergreen herbaceous perennial and sub-shrub Zones: 8–10
Height and spread: 45-90cm/18-36in × 30-60cm/12-24in

Varieties good for cutting The lovely flower spikes of the large-flowered border penstemon hybrids, with their many tubular flowers arranged up the stem like an array of trumpets, are a real mainstay of the autumn cutting garden. Their velvety colours range from white to pink, and bright scarlet to nearly black. My favourites are 'Raven' or 'Blackbird' mixed with orange and yellow red hot pokers and Chinese lanterns (see pages 80–81), the bluish-purple 'Sour Grapes' and 'Stapleford Gem', the clear blue-mauve 'Blue Bedder' and the lovely rich 'Burgundy'. For subtler tones, choose the large-flowered 'White Bedder' or the P. campanulatus hybrids that come in paler pinks and mauves.

Conditioning Some penstemons droop after cutting. Strip the bottom leaves and sear the stem before soaking overnight.

Cultivation Plant penstemons in full sun in a fertile, well-drained soil, facing south or west and well sheltered from wind. If you pick or deadhead regularly, you will have three or four months of flowering well into the autumn. They are best treated as half-hardy perennials, with stock replenished from cuttings in late summer to early autumn. Overwinter away from frost in a cool greenhouse or a cold frame. The parent plant can be potted up and kept in frost-free conditions. Cut it right back in late winter and by the time it can be planted out after the last frosts it will be covered in shiny new leaves and shoots.

PHLOX

Main entry: Summer White, page 121.
The faintly scented, white-flushed deep pink P. paniculata 'Graf Zeppelin' is an excellent late-flowerer for combining with white Japanese anemones and 'Iceberg' roses.

ROSA

Main entry: Summer Pink, page 124.
The climber 'New Dawn' is a very free- and long-flowering pale pink rose with a pretty, open flower and gentle scent.

SCHIZOSTYLIS COCCINEA

Bulb Zones: 8–9
Height: 60cm/24in

Varieties good for cutting Pick a generous bunch of these miniature, gladiolus-like deep pink and red flowers. The delicate flower spikes with neat cup-shaped blooms held on thin stems look best en masse.

When they are fully open in sun, the darker colours shine as if cut from the finest iridescent silk. These slightly tender bulbs will provide a strong splash of colour even after the first frosts have clobbered almost everything else. Grow the rich scarlet-pink S. coccinea 'Major' or the smaller-flowered white S.c. alba, and the salmon-pink 'Sunrise'.

Cultivation These bulbs do well in full sun in almost any soil, but need a lot of moisture during the summer to enable them to throw up good flower spikes in autumn.

The thick matting roots become rapidly congested. To keep up good flower production, they should be divided every few years and moved to a fresh place.

5 cm/2 in

Orange and Red

ABUTILON

Herbaceous perennial and deciduous shrub,
Zones: 9–10
Height and spread: A. 'Ashford Red', 'Can-
ary Bird' 90cm-1.8m/3-6ft × 45-90cm/
18in-3ft; A. × suntense cultivars,
A. vitifolium 1.8-3m/6-10ft × 90cm/3ft

Varieties good for cutting *With*
generous, open, saucer- and bell-shaped
flowers in rich reds, yellows, oranges, purples
and whites, abutilons make statuesque
additions to any bunch and are also perfect
as single stems for a desk or bedside table.
'Ashford Red', with its papery, deep orange-
red flowers and contrasting pale green calyx,

will flower from summer right through to the
first frosts. 'Canary Bird' is an excellent
clear vibrant yellow form of similar habit.
For summer flowering, the lovely pale mauve
A. vitifolium 'Veronica Tennant' has huge
disc-shaped flowers with brilliant golden
anthers. Look out, too, for the pure white
A.v. var. album. Best of all these earlier
flowerers for a sheltered spot is the lovely rich
dark blue-purple A. × suntense 'Violetta'.

Conditioning *Strip most of the leaves,*
which tend to flop. Sear the stems in boiling
water for 20 seconds.

Cultivation *Grow the more tender vari-*
eties, such as 'Ashford Red' and 'Canary
Bird', in large pots so that they can be
moved inside during winter. They like moist
but not wet soil. Feed them well for a good
long flowering season. Cut them to the
ground in winter and they will be covered in
new growth and leaves by mid-spring.

A. vitifolium and A. × suntense are
best grown against a warm wall, or as free-
standing specimens in a sheltered sunny site.
They do well in any average dryish soil.
Pick smallish sprigs, cutting back lightly to
avoid spoiling the shrub's elegant form.
Cover them in a frost-protective netting
during the winter, to be safe.

Propagate from semi-ripe cuttings taken
in mid- to late summer. A. vitifolium also
grows quickly from seed and self-seeds abun-
dantly around the parent plant.

ASCLEPIAS
Butterfly weed, silkweed

Tuberous perennial Zones: 4–9
Height and spread: A. tuberosa, A.t. Gay
Butterflies Group 45-60cm/18-24in ×
30-60cm/12-24in

Varieties good for cutting *I long*
believed that these rather waxy, exotic-
looking plants were hot-house grown. There
are indeed some tender varieties, but others

❶ *Asclepias tuberosa*
❷ *Abutilon 'Ashford Red'*
❸ *Cosmos atrosanguineus*
❹ *Dahlia 'Arabian Night'*
❺ *Dahlia 'Bishop of Llandaff'*
❻ *Dahlia 'Queen Fabiola'*

are fully frost-hardy and do well in
temperate climates. A. tuberosa is an excel-
lent plant that flowers for many weeks in
late summer and early autumn. The light
and airy flowers of A. tuberosa combine
well with tithonia and contrast with acid-
green dill, bupleurum and purple lisianthus.
Use it to make a lovely autumn mixture with
red crabapples; add pale yellow sunflowers
and the combination will be stunning.

Conditioning *Remove the bottom leaves*
and sear the stems in boiling water immedi-
ately after picking. Like euphorbias, the cut
stems exude a sticky sap which will block
water uptake.

Cultivation *Plant the wandering fleshy*
roots 10cm/4in deep. A. tuberosa thrives
in shelter and full sun in a deep, sandy, dry
soil where the roots can make a good run.

Propagate by division in spring.
A. tuberosa germinates freely and easily
from fresh seed, but seeds from a packet
produce unreliable results.

COSMOS

Main entry: Summer White, page 119.
C. atrosanguineus, a spectacularly rich
chocolate-red ruby of a flower, exudes the
sort of exotic scent you might imagine
wafting from the seraglio in Istanbul. The
flowers are best on their own or grouped with
other single flowers (see pages 78–9).

COTINUS
Burning bush, smokebush

Deciduous shrub and tree Zones: 5–8
Height and spread: C. coggygria 2.5-
4m/8-13ft × 2.5-4m/8-13ft; C. obovatus
6m/20ft × 4.5m/15ft

Varieties good for cutting

C. coggygria is a large plant for the
average-sized cutting garden, but its summer
foliage and flowers (see page 122), and even
better its autumnal vibrant orange, pink, red
and purple leaves, are spectacular for cutting.
Grow the claret-coloured C.c. 'Royal
Purple' or 'Notcutt's Variety' for the richest,
deepest autumn foliage. If you have room for
an even bigger shrub, grow C. obovatus (see
pages 82–3), which has larger leaves in a
mix of crimson, deep carmine-pink, golden-
yellow, tangerine-orange and flame-red.

Conditioning *Hammer the stem ends.*

Cultivation *These are easily grown*
shrubs which will thrive in any reasonably
drained soil. Too fertile a soil can inhibit the
development of autumn colours and make the
shrubs coarse and sappy. They do best and
colour most dramatically in full sun; the
purple-leaved varieties tend to revert to green
in shade. Prune to remove dead wood in
spring. If you cut them back hard you will
not get the feathery haze of summer flowers,
which are produced on wood three years old
or more. You will, however, get larger leaves.

DAHLIA

Tuberous perennial   Zone: 9
Height: 90cm-2m/3-7ft

Varieties good for cutting *I grow dahlias in nearly all their shapes and forms. You can grow tall voluptuous herbaceous ones like 'Edinburgh' (see page 140), or jazzy rich burnt-orange 'Glow' to mix with deep crimson 'Queen Fabiola' or almost black 'Natal' or 'Arabian Night' (see pages 76-8). More subtle varieties are 'Bishop of Llandaff' with its scarlet petals and central ruff, and rich crimson 'Mount Noddy'. Both have exotic dark crimson foliage and combine effectively with lime-green Zinnia 'Envy'.*

Conditioning *Only pick dahlias in full flower. The buds tend to wither and die without opening. Recut the hollow stem ends under water to avoid airlocks.*

Cultivation *Select tubers in flower at a good nursery, or from a reliably illustrated list; colour descriptions are always misleading. Start them into growth in spring and they will have formed good plants by early summer, when you can plant them out in a sunny position in well-drained soil. Add a handful of bonemeal to the planting hole and plant the tubers 10cm/4in below the surface. When they are growing strongly, pinch out the tip of the main stem to encourage bushy growth. Stake the taller varieties. Keep the plants well watered in the summer and, if you are not picking them, deadhead them as the flowers fade. After flowering, lift the tubers and store them in a frost-free place. Propagate dahlias from basal cuttings (see page 36) .*

EUPHORBIA

Spurge, milkweed

Main entry: Spring Green and Silver, page 96. *The vibrant orange E. griffithii, the colour of tomato soup in spring and summer, turns a mixture of reds and yellows in the autumn, and adds vim and zest to any autumn arrangement (see pages 82–3).*

GLADIOLUS

Corm   Zones: G. communis subsp. byzantinus 6–9; Guildhall hybrids 9–10 Height and spread: 90cm-1.5 m/3-5ft 10-15cm/4-6in

Varieties good for cutting *Gladioli have had their reputation ruined by the hideous pinks, pale butterscotch-oranges and washed-out yellows that you inevitably find in funeral wreaths and floral tributes. Poor flower! There are sumptuous crimson, violet, lime-green, burnt-orange and nearly black gladiolus hybrids, not to mention the head-turning deep carmine-pink G. communis subsp. byzantinus (see pages 122-3). Look for 'Green Woodpecker', with its crimson throat and good sulphurous-green flowers, to mix with the chocolatey-crimson, almost black 'Queen of Night', the lovely rich reddish-purple 'Plum Tart' and the purple, white-throated 'Video'. One of my favourites is the claret-red 'Black Lash' – perfect when used as a strong spike with huge sunflowers, thistles and dahlias to break up the symmetry of a hanging globe (see pages 74–5).*

Conditioning *Remove the bottom leaves. Some people cut off the top 5cm/2in of the flower spike to make sure the flowers lower down all come out; I think this a shame, as the twists and turns of the spike end are an integral part of the plant's appeal.*

Cultivation *Choose summer-flowering gladioli when in flower, or order corms from a well-illustrated list of a good bulb wholesaler, to make sure you get the best colours. Plant them out after the last spring frosts, and stagger the planting at 10-day intervals from mid-spring to midsummer, to prolong the season. Choose a site in full sun with light soil rich in organic material. Plant them 10cm/4in deep and 10-15cm/4-6in apart in clumps or lines in the cutting garden. Water regularly and plentifully during the growing season, and stake the taller varieties. Lift your corms after the first*

❼ *Cotinus coggygria* 'Royal Purple'
❽ *Euphorbia griffithii* 'Dixter'
❾ *Gladiolus* 'Black Lash'
❿ *Helenium* 'Moerheim Beauty'
　 (see page 144)

5 cm/2 in

① *Iris foetidissima*
(seed heads)
② *Leonotis ocymifolia*
③ *Physalis alkekengi*
var. *franchetii*
④ *Rosa moyesii*
'Geranium' (hips)

5 cm/2 in

frost, cut off their stems, dry and clean them, and rigorously discard any with signs of disease. Dust them with fungicide and store them in a frost-free, cool, airy place for next year. Plant spring-flowerers, like G.c. subsp. byzantinus, *in the autumn.*

Propagate by removing young cormlets from the parent plant after lifting in the autumn. Be patient; they will flower in one or two years.

HELENIUM
Sneezeweed

Herbaceous perennial Zones: 4–8
Height: 90cm-1.5m/3-5ft

Varieties good for cutting *The petals of these big-boned daisy-like flowers fold back from the fuzzy central hub, almost like the wings of an insect. The heleniums have an air that somehow combines the obvious with the delicate; they do everything that an aster does but more so. My favourite is the rich orange-brown 'Moerheim Beauty' (see page 143) with its bum of a bumblebee centre and its ring of jagged crinkled petals. Combine it in a tightly tied bunch, with orange and green Chinese lanterns and*

nutmeg rudbeckias, all contrasted with rich purple Gladiolus *'Video' and acid-green bupleurum. Or mix it or the spicy yellow 'Butterpat' (see page 146) simply with deep blue salvias.*

Conditioning *Strip the bottom leaves and they will last over a week in water.*

Cultivation *Plant in full sun. These tolerant, easily grown plants will survive in any soil short of a bog. Support the heavy flowering stems with a network of hazel sticks. The clumps quickly get congested and thrive on regular division (see pages 37 and 41) in spring or autumn. If you buy one plant, you will soon have a good colony.*

IRIS

Main entry: Winter Blue and Purple, page 158. *The fruits of* I. foetidissima, *whether picked unripe with their angular green pods or bursting open with glistening pomegranate-like seeds, make a spicy addition to any autumn bunch (see pages 76–8).*

LEONOTIS OCYMIFOLIA
Lion's ear

Semi-evergreen shrub Zones: 9–10
Height and spread: 1.5m/5ft × 75cm/30in

Varieties good for cutting *The tall, rich orange spikes of leonotis carry whorls of flowers, divided by expanses of empty stem, which look like occasional brightly lit floors in a high-rise building. Contrast their vibrant colour with purple* Dahlia *'Edinburgh' in an arrangement with bulrushes and autumn leaves (see pages 82–3), or mix them with tall* Gladiolus *'Queen of Night' and* Helianthus annuus *'Velvet Queen'.*

Conditioning *Sear the bottom 2.5cm/ 1in of the stems, and give them a long drink.*

Cultivation *This tender plant will not survive winter in any but the mildest climate. Dig it up, cut it right back, and pot it in a well-drained compost to overwinter in the greenhouse. It will start into life again in late spring, and you can plant it out after the last frosts. It will not flower until late summer or early autumn. Choose a sunny position with well-drained, fertile soil.*

Propagate from seed sown in spring or from softwood cuttings taken in late summer and overwintered under glass.

PHYSALIS ALKEKENGI
Chinese lantern

Herbaceous perennial Zones: 5–8
Height: 60cm/24in

Varieties good for cutting P.a. *var.* franchetii, *with its fragile green or orange fruits like hanging lights made from coloured*

paper, is a glamorous autumn foliage plant. The lanterns are light at the top and dark at the bottom as if lit from inside. The stems twist and turn and the whole effect is like a Christmas decoration. Look out, too, for the showier P.a. *var.* f. *'Gigantea', with larger leaves and larger, more impressive, pointed lanterns. Mix them with deep crimson* Penstemon *'Blackbird', red hot pokers and*

5 cm/2 in

chestnut, mahogany and orange rudbeckias (see pages 80–81). Or simply mix them with rich royal blue gentians. During the summer the unripe green pods make fine foliage to contrast with the rich cardinal colours of cosmos, roses or snapdragons.

Conditioning *Remove the leaves, because they flop within a week or so. The lanterns continue to look as good as new for months.*

Cultivation *Physalis is invaluable for filling in awkward corners, since it will thrive in sun or shade and is not fussy about soil. But when you choose the site do keep in mind that the running roots of physalis can become invasive, so they should be kept well away from your more delicate plants. The tall stems tend to flop but can be held up by a network of sticks and thin twine or thread (see page 37).*

Propagate by division in autumn or spring, planting the tendrily roots 8cm/3in deep, or sow seed in early spring. It will fruit in the autumn of the same year.

❺ *Rudbeckia 'Nutmeg'*
❻ *Tithonia rotundifolia*
❼ and **❽** *Viburnum opulus*
❾ *Zinnia Scabious-flowered Group*
❿ *Zinnia Giant Cactus Group*

ROSA
Rose
Main entry: Summer Pink, page 124.
For long-lasting hips, grow R. moyesii and R. glauca. R.m. 'Geranium' forms tall, long-limbed bushes, which have lovely single silk-scarlet flowers in summer, followed by bright scarlet hips which last for several weeks without ageing, even out of water. I collect these hips to mix with fallen leaves and anything else I can find in the garden, to fill bowls and vases around the house. Try them with stems of cotinus and red oak, cattails, and snowberry berries (see pages 82–83), or with clematis seed heads, acorns and hazel nuts. Add any flowers there are around.

The pretty but discreet flowers of R. glauca are followed by shiny red balloon-shaped hips that look beautiful against the fine grey foliage. The branches are elegant enough to be arranged on their own.

Many of the Rugosa roses also have wonderful hips – shiny red balls the size of crabapples. Growing on shorter stems, they are especially useful for smaller posies.

RUDBECKIA
Coneflower, gloriosa daisy
Main entry: Autumn Yellow, page 146.
The large-flowered gloriosa daisy R. 'Nutmeg' comes in a variety of rich oranges and browns. Any of them look appealing in a large jug on the kitchen table. I like to pick out the most chocolatey-coloured flowers and mix them in a tight bunch with sunflower 'Velvet Queen'.

TITHONIA ROTUNDIFOLIA
Half-hardy annual
Height and spread: 1.2m/4ft × 60cm/2ft
Varieties good for cutting *Think of the sort of sofa that Liberace would have lounged in: velvet, cushioned, full, plush, receptive. That is the tithonia: as comfortable as flowers get. Grow the vibrant orange T.r. 'Torch' or the slightly less blatantly rich 'Goldfinger'. Mix them with velvety blue salvias, deep crimson dahlias, and gladioli.*
Conditioning *Tithonia flower heads have hollow bulbous bases which easily bend and break, so handle them carefully after picking.*

Cultivation. *Plant tithonia out in full sun in a well-drained soil 30cm/12in apart, or to fill gaps left by early-summer flowerers.*

To propagate, sow under cover in late spring. Keep seedlings out of cold draughts or they will yellow and die.

VIBURNUM
Main entry: Winter Pink, page 154.
The glistening redcurrant-like berries of V. opulus come in red, orange and yellow (V.o. 'Xanthocarpum'). They are perfect fillers for any autumn bunch (see pages 80–81). In early autumn V. lantanoides has a mophead of red and green cranberries.

ZINNIA
Main entry: Autumn Silver, Green and Brown, page 138. *The shaggy Giant Cactus Group looks like the sort of hat grandes dames wore to 1950s weddings. The Scabious-flowered Group, with its sharp-edged ring of petals around a central hub, appears positively Boadicean: a flash of knives, a slice through the air.*

❶ *Capsicum annuum*
❷ *Helenium* 'Butterpat'
❸ *Kniphofia* 'Yellow Hammer'
❹ *Rosa* 'Graham Thomas'
❺ *Rudbeckia hirta* 'Green Eyes'

5 cm / 2 in

Yellow

CAPSICUM ANNUUM
Chilli pepper
Half-hardy annual
Height: 45cm/18in
Varieties good for cutting *Chilli peppers come in oranges, reds and yellows, and when unripe they are a deep bottle green. Mix the ripe fruits with blackberries, sloes and Chinese lanterns, or use them to jolly up any autumn bunch.*
Conditioning *Strip all the leaves and the fruit will last for well over a month in water before beginning to age. You can also hang them upside-down in a warm, well-ventilated place and use them dried.*
Cultivation *Sow under cover in early spring, prick out and grow on in the greenhouse and plant out against a sunny wall, or in some other sheltered spot.*

HELENIUM
Sneezeweed
Main entry: Autumn Orange and Red, page 144. *One of the brightest heleniums, yellow 'Butterpat' can be cut 90cm/3ft tall to mix with sunflowers and boughs of green and red crabapples.*

KNIPHOFIA
Red hot poker, torch lily
Perennial, some evergreen Zones: 5–9
Height: 90cm-1.2m/3-4ft
Varieties good for cutting *The bottlebrush flowers of the kniphofia cultivars come in a variety of bright and brilliant colours. Try the more delicate, slender dwarf hybrids where the majority of flowers on each spike are at their peak at the same time. Look out for the dazzling yellow-flowered green-budded 'Yellow Hammer' to contrast with penstemon 'Blackbird' or mix with nutmeg and yellow rudbeckias and orange* Viburnum opulus *berries (see pages 80-81). Grow too the pinkish-orange-budded and pale yellow-flowered 'Mount Etna'. This is beautiful mixed with the turquoise* Salvia uliginosa *and* S. patens *'Cambridge Blue'.*
Conditioning *If the bottom few whorls of flowers are going over, pull them off.*

Cultivation *Plant in full sun in sandy soil that does not dry right out in the summer. Winter wet is the kniphofia's main enemy, so drainage must be excellent. In colder districts, give them a heavy mulch in late autumn. Propagate by division in spring, though clumps are slow to increase (see page 37). Kniphofias set seed freely, but a motley crew of offspring usually results.*

ROSA
Rose
Main entry: Summer Pink, page 124.
The new English rose R. 'Graham Thomas' has huge cabbage flowers the colour of pale yellow butterscotch and is an unbelievably productive performer, pumping out flowers from midsummer to late autumn.

RUDBECKIA
Coneflower, gloriosa daisy
Half-hardy annual and herbaceous perennial Zones: 4–9 Height: 60–90cm/24–36in
Varieties good for cutting *In your florist's, you will find rudbeckias stripped down to their bald central heads. The petals are stripped because they only last three to four days and would look past it before they reached the customer. All the more reason to grow your own. Rudbeckias come in a sumptuous mix of mahogany, nutmeg, yellow and burnt-marmalade colours. Grow the annual gloriosa daisies with 18cm/7in diameter flowers: R. hirta 'Green Eyes' is bright yellow with a contrasting green centre, and R. 'Nutmeg' (see page 145), produces a wide range of browns. A slightly weird variety is the 1.5m/5ft perennial R. occidentalis 'Green Wizard', which has black liquorice-allsort centres surrounded by eau-de-nil green sepals. This cool curiosity is best arranged on its own or with similar strong-coloured flowers.*
Conditioning *Pick these flowers regularly, use and chuck. Strip the leaves and give them a long drink.*
Cultivation *Plant in sun, shade, wet, dry – anywhere, short of a bog. Keep cutting and they'll keep coming. Propagate perennials by division in spring (see page 37) and annuals by a mid-spring sowing under cover (see pages 32–4).*

❶ *Ampelopsis glandulosa* var. *brevipedunculata*
❷ *Salvia viridis*
❸ *Salvia patens*

Blue and Purple

AMPELOPSIS

Deciduous climber Zones: 5–8
Height: 5m/16ft
Varieties good for cutting A. glandulosa *var.* brevipedunculata, *with its three- or five-lobed hop-like leaves, is covered with porcelain-blue berries in autumn. Arrange them on their own, leaves stripped to reveal the fruits better, with the stems writhing here, there and everywhere, or use them as foliage with* Salvia uliginosa, *orange zinnias and late marigolds. Look out for the pretty and less vigorous cultivar* A.g. var. b. 'Elegans', *with small leaves delicately splashed with pink. You sometimes see it for sale in a florist's as a house plant.*
Cultivation Ampelopsis, *a fast-growing self-clinging plant, needs plenty of room, so pick your site with care. Grow on a hot sunny wall in poor soil for the most fruit. Propagate by semi-ripe cuttings in mid-summer (see pages 38 and 39), by layering (see page 42) or from seed.*

ECHINOPS
Globe thistle

Herbaceous perennial Zones: 3–9
Height: 1.2-1.8m/4-6ft
Varieties good for cutting *The grey-blue fluffy sphere of* Echinops ritro 'Veitch's Blue' *looks like the pompons we made as children to go on top of woolly hats. Pick it in spiny silver bud or in full flower when its dense lustred heads, as weighty and substantial as wrought-iron balls, lend authority to any arrangement, underpinning the frothier flowers. They look beautiful mixed with orange marigolds in a jug for the kitchen, or cut long in with sunflowers.*
Conditioning *Just strip the slightly prickly lower leaves.*
Cultivation *Plant in full sun, though* E. ritro *varieties will flower in partial shade. These plants do best in poor soil, so omit them when you are feeding the garden. They otherwise become lank and leggy. Propagate by division in autumn or by root cuttings in winter (see pages 41 and 43).*

GENTIANA
Gentian, willow gentian

Herbaceous or alpine perennial Zones: 6–9
Height: G. triflora 45cm/18in;
G. asclepiadea 90cm/36in
Varieties good for cutting *The taller gentians are a must for autumn arrangements. The flowers of* G. triflora, *arranged in pairs up the stem, are the true blue of Moroccan tiles. A few stems will bring any bunch to life. Contrast it powerfully with orange dahlias and butterfly weed or, even better, in a multicoloured arrangement with pink and orange zinnias, orange and yellow rudbeckias, and deep rich-coloured asters and dahlias. Look for* G.t. var. japonica, *whose flower spikes can reach 80cm/32in. Also excellent is the slightly paler blue* G. asclepiadea, *or willow gentian, and a less showy white form,* G.a. alba.
Conditioning *Strip the bottom leaves and give an overnight drink before arranging. They like a bright warm place to open fully.*

Cultivation G. asclepiadea *and* G. triflora *do best in acid soil but will tolerate lime.* G. triflora *likes a moist peaty well-drained soil in full sun or partial shade. Find* G. asclepiadea, *a woodland plant, a deep moist soil in shade with lots of humus.*
Propagate in autumn from ripe seed. To help germination, stand the containers where frost can reach them. Do not cover the seed. G. asclepiadea *self-seeds freely.*

SALVIA
Sage

Annual, tender perennial and shrub
Zones: S. patens 9–10; S. uliginosa 8–9;
S. × superba 5–9
Height: S. patens, S. × superba 75cm/30in; S. uliginosa to 1.5m/5ft
Varieties good for cutting *The huge sage family, with its simple double-lipped flowers in resonant colours and soft tempting textures, is vital in autumn.* S. patens *has pretty pale blue 'Cambridge Blue' and pale mauve 'Chilcombe' that begin flowering in summer, while 'Royal Blue', is good with autumnal scarlets and reds (see page 73). The giant-flowered 'Guanajuato' is in the original royal blue. Another must is* S. uliginosa, *with sky-blue spikes. Grow, too, the early-flowering* S. × superba, *with its treacly-purple flowers, and* S. guaranitica *in the darkest purple-blue. I also cut bright red* S. elegans *and* S. fulgens *to mix with oranges and ochres. Of the many good annual salvias, look out for* S. viridis *with green-veined bracts of purple, blue or pink and* S. farinacea *'Victoria', with its deep violet flowers; both are 45cm/18in tall.*
Conditioning *Strip the bottom leaves of* S. patens. *For the others, sear the bottom 2.5cm/1in of stem and give a cool drink.*
Cultivation *Plant sages in a sunny, well-protected site to get the maximum number of flowers. Most like plenty of moisture during summer, and the tender varieties especially need well-drained soil. Stake the tallest forms. Protect the underground roots of* S. uliginosa *in winter with straw.*

❹ *Echinops ritro 'Veitch's Blue'*
❺ *Gentiana triflora*
❻ *Salvia uliginosa*

Propagate more tender varieties from cuttings taken in late summer and over-wintered in a frost-free cold frame or cool greenhouse. Dig up the parent plant, allow it to die down during the winter, and it will re-shoot in spring. Plant out after the risk of frost has passed. For robust plants, treat S. patens *as a half-hardy annual and sow every year.* S. uliginosa *and* S. × superba *are best propagated by division. Direct sow seed of the annuals in mid-spring (see pages 34 and 35).*

Winter

Few people seem to grow or gather flowers for arrangements during the winter months, yet many of the winter-flowering plants are among the most fragrant of all – they need to be powerfully scented to attract the few insects still around for pollination. Think of the exotic perfume of the winter-flowering loniceras or the sweet-scented daphnes.

Many winter flowers have a delicacy and elegance, qualities that are best appreciated when they are displayed in small bunches or as solitary stems. The fine, spidery flowers of the witch hazels are best on their own and I always prefer to have the different varieties of *Iris unguicularis* arranged singly, each in a narrow, tall, coloured glass.

I have included some spring bulbs for early forcing, and amaryllis, which is a winter indoor bulb. They are easy to grow indoors and provide a welcome addition to the flower arranger's repertoire in the garden's least productive season. I was married on New Year's Eve in Scotland, and my husband filled every room for the wedding party with nothing but the fragrant Tazetta narcissi 'Paper White' and 'Soleil d'Or'. They covered all the tables, the window ledges and the mantelpieces. These narcissi also look beautiful arranged for a table centrepiece with ivory candles.

Green and Silver

ARUM
Cuckoo pint, lords and ladies
Tuberous perennial Zones: 7–9
Height: 20-30cm/8-12in
Varieties good for cutting *For interesting and elegant foliage throughout the winter, choose* A. italicum *'Marmoratum', the cultivated variety of the wild southern European* A. italicum. *When almost everything else is dying back in autumn, this, along with cyclamen, behaves in reverse and its leaves begin to appear.*

A.i. 'Marmoratum' has arrow-shaped,

cream-veined, glossy, bright green leaves with bending and curling edges. Mix them with cyclamen leaves, scented narcissi and winter honeysuckle for a pretty and fragrant arrangement (see pages 84–6).

A. creticum, which comes in pale yellow and white forms, is also good for special picking, as a rarity. In spring it produces a few dramatic, sweetly scented phallic flowers with the spathe wrapped, like a napkin on a table in a smart restaurant, around a protruding spadix.

Rarely available but even more dramatic are A. palaestinum, A. rupicola *(syn. A. conophalloides) and* A. nigrum, *with deep, chocolatey purple-black spathes in summer. (The similar, and extraordinary, deep velvety purple-black dragon arum,* Dracunculus vulgaris, *sadly smells of rotting meat – it would otherwise be sensational in arrangements.)*

Cultivation *Plant in autumn or spring in a sunny or lightly shaded spot. A. italicum 'Marmoratum' is easy to grow in a moist, well-drained soil. Protect it with a covering of leaves if a hard frost is expected. A. creticum is less easy and is probably best grown in a pot. Protect it from severe winter frosts and keep it dry in summer.*

Increase your stock from seed or by division in autumn (see pages 34, 35 and 41). When digging for division, remember that the tubers go deep into the soil. Once established, A.i. 'Marmoratum' should seed itself and increase freely.

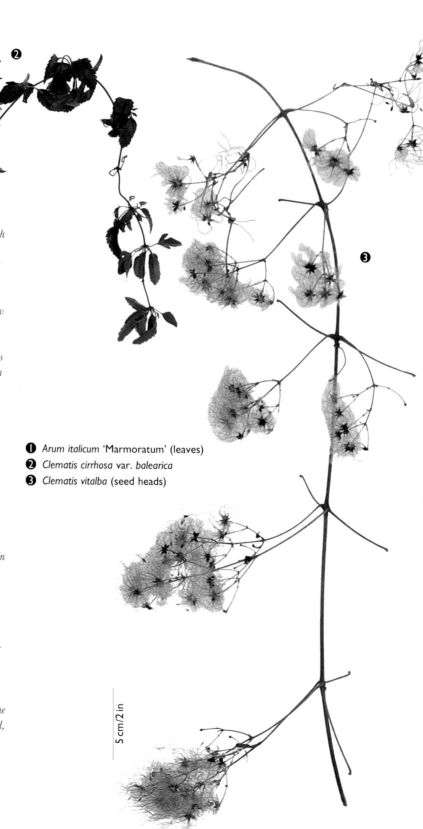

❶ *Arum italicum* 'Marmoratum' (leaves)
❷ *Clematis cirrhosa* var. *balearica*
❸ *Clematis vitalba* (seed heads)

5 cm/2 in

5 cm/2 in

4 Daphne laureola
5 Helleborus argutifolius
6 Helleborus foetidus
7 Helleborus orientalis of gardens

CLEMATIS

Main entry: Spring White, page 99.

In winter arrangements one of my absolute mainstays are great fluffy boughs of old man's beard, the seed heads of the wild C. vitalba (see pages 88–9). Less rampant and better for the garden, with pretty yellow bell-flowers in autumn, are C. tangutica and C. 'Bill Mackenzie', which always add an interesting twist and turn to any arrangement. Their seed heads seem to stay intact better than those of old man's beard.

I also cut the green and freckled flowers of C. cirrhosa var. balearica or C.c. 'Freckles'. I love almost all green-flowered plants, and this is a great winter favourite – not least because it is so surprising that it pumps its flowers out with such enthusiasm at this time of year.

No special conditioning is needed for these flowers, but it is worth spraying the delicate seed heads with odourless hair spray if you want them to last well. This makes them hold better, and you won't end up, as I so often have, with bare branches and all the fluffy stuff sitting on the floor beneath you.

DAPHNE

Main entry: Winter Pink, page 153.

D. laureola is a handsome plant for winter picking and is most scented in the evening. Strip the lower, larger leaves from the stem to reveal the cool green flowers, and combine a few short sprigs with hellebores and snowdrops in a small arrangement, or longer ones with willow and clematis stems in a looser display (see pages 84–6).

HELLEBORUS

Hellebore, Corsican hellebore, Lenten rose, stinking hellebore

Herbaceous perennial
Zones: H. argutifolius, H. foetidus 6–9; H. orientalis 4–8
Height and spread: 45-60cm/18-24in × 30-60cm/12-24in

Varieties good for cutting *All of them! Hellebores, with their fascinating forms and subtle green, pink and cloudy purple hues, are stars of the winter garden and winter arrangements (see pages 84–6).*

The Lenten rose, H. orientalis, bears cup-like flowers in various tones of green, pink (see page 154), claret, white and almost black (see page 158). Some have beautiful freckling all over their faces. Choose plants when they are in flower to make sure you get your favourite colours, and select those cultivars that hold their flower heads horizontally, not modestly bowed with their faces hidden. These are better for arranging.

The Corsican hellebore, H. argutifolius, is the most vigorous. This serrated-leaved evergreen has open clear green flowers from mid-winter to mid-spring, and the angular geometric-shaped seed pods make a sculptural addition to any large late-winter or spring arrangement.

The stinking hellebore, H. foetidus, has lovely hanging green bell-shaped flowers that look as if the petal edge has been dipped in a deep purple dye. The unpleasant odour recorded in its name is only released when leaves are crushed between the fingers. It is, however, worth looking out for the sweetly scented strain H.f. 'Gertrude Jekyll'.

Conditioning *Immediately after cutting, put the bottom 2.5cm/1in of the stem in boiling water for about 20 seconds, then plunge it into deep tepid water. Given this treatment, they should stay fresh for three or four days or more. If the flower heads droop, cut the stems again, repeat the searing process, and they should pick up. They do not last well in oasis.*

Cultivation *All these hellebores are easy to grow. They like cool conditions with light shade and a heavy, rich, limey soil that does not dry out in summer. This makes them an ideal choice for a well-drained shady border.*

Plant them in autumn or early spring in well-manured soil and then leave them alone: none likes to be moved and H. orientalis in particular dislikes disturbance. The different varieties will interbreed, so keep them well apart unless you wish gradually to develop a new colony of mixed hybrids. Mulch with well-decayed manure or compost in mid-spring and apply a liquid manure through the summer. Feed again with bonemeal in autumn. Water freely in very dry weather.

H. argutifolius likes protection from strong winds and the worst frosts. Cut back all hellebore leaves and spent flowering stems in spring. This will minimize any problem with leaf spot, make room for new growth and allow more light in for any young seedlings around the parents' skirts.

Propagate hellebores by division in early spring, or dig up seedlings from your own garden or from a friend's. To encourage seedling growth, clear the area around the parent plants as they flower. Transplant the offspring when still small in early summer. They can also be grown from seed, sown 3mm/⅛in deep in shallow trays of sandy soil in a cold frame in summer. Transplant the seedlings outdoors when one year old. They will flower the following year. Most hellebores will then self-seed freely.

SALIX
Willow

Deciduous tree and shrub Zones: 5–9
Height and spread: S. daphnoides 7.5m/
25ft × 7.5m/25ft; S. caprea 10m/33ft ×
7.5m/25ft; S. alba varieties 15m/50ft ×
7.5m/25ft; S. × sepulcralis var. chryso-
coma 12m/40ft × 12m/40ft

Varieties good for cutting *I prize*
willows mainly for their catkins, but they
have other excellent features that are equally
valuable for the flower arranger. Their
pliable young branches (up to two years old)
can be used to form the base for wreaths,
globes and medallions (see pages 88–9).
Their colour and habit can also be exploited:
the brightly coloured stems of species such as
S. alba var. vitellina (golden yellow) and
S.a. var. v. 'Britzensis' (scarlet-orange),
both of which are upright in form, mix well
with the golden weeping willow,
S. × sepulcralis var. chrysocoma, which
is more flowing in habit. They make an eye-
catching combination in a simple tall glass
vase. The pussy willow (S. caprea) bears
catkins from late winter. The female catkins
are silky grey and the male are grey with
yellow anthers. The giant pussy willow,
S. acutifolia, has silvery catkins up to
8cm/3in long.

The smaller violet willow, S. daph-
noides, is my favourite willow in winter for
its catkins, and S.d. 'Aglaia' is its best
form. This is a loose-growing willow with
elegantly twisting branches and a fluid shape
which makes for relaxed arrangements. It
mixes beautifully with amaryllis and hazels
(see page 87).

If you cut a branch of the pussy willow in
early winter you will have to remove the
female catkins' black glove-like coverings. As
the winter goes on they split open naturally.
Then the bright, plump pussy willows look
from a distance like silver-white blossom,
those of S.d. 'Aglaia' contrasting dramati-
cally with its plum-purple branches.

Cultivation *Willows are, in the main,*
as tough as old boots and will grow
anywhere with some moisture (exceptions are
S. daphnoides and S. caprea, which do
not need damp conditions). Left alone, most
willows will become large trees, but you can

coppice them and thus restrict their growth.
Do this by allowing them to become
established for a couple of years and then cut
the stems where you want new growth to
break at the beginning of spring, just before
the sap starts to rise. This will give brighter
coloured branches, but if done every year will
reduce the number of catkins, which are best

on wood that is at least two years old.
Compromise and remove half the stems each
year rather than cutting them all to the
ground, and you will always have vivid
stems and some flowers.

All varieties of willow root easily from
semi-ripe cuttings (see pages 38 and 39).
Insert the cuttings with at least half their

length below ground in a damp place, or
even in a bottle of water, in summer. If you
cannot push them into the ground easily, it is
not damp enough to be planting. If you plant
hardwood cuttings of young branches, 60-
90cm/2-3ft long, in late autumn or early
spring, pushing half their length into the
ground, they soon grow into young trees.

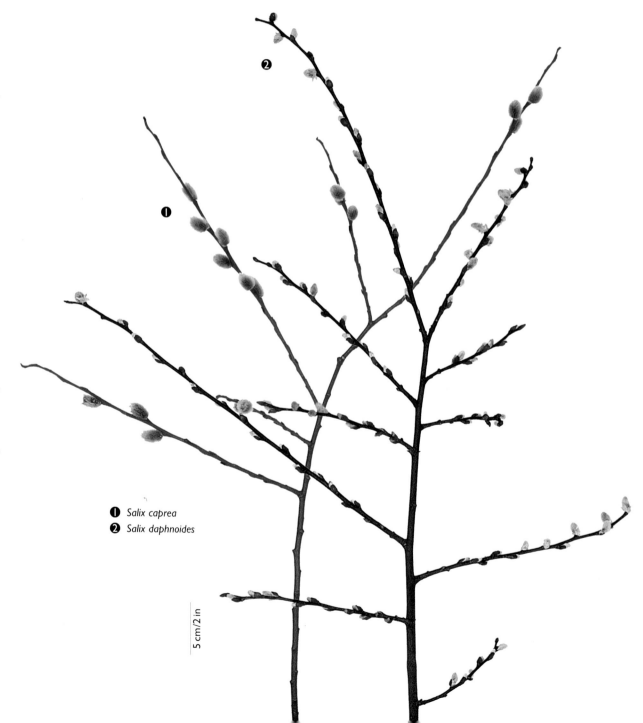

❶ *Salix caprea*
❷ *Salix daphnoides*

5 cm/2 in

5 cm/2 in

White

CAMELLIA

Evergreen shrub and tree Zones: C.
japonica *and* C. × williamsii *7–10*
Height and spread: C. × williamsii
1.2m/4ft × 2.5m/8ft; C. japonica
3m/10ft × 8m/26ft

Varieties good for cutting *Some
camellias drop their petals too quickly to be
of use for cutting, but my favourites, the pure
white single varieties such as* C. japonica
'Alba Simplex' or C.j. *'Devonia' and, at the
other end of the spectrum, the flamboyant
raspberry-ripple semi-double ones such as*
C.j. *'Tricolor', last well with buds still
opening on a sprig a week after cutting.*

*I am less keen on the solid red and pink
camellias – they remind me too much of
plastic flowers in Mediterranean graveyards
– but if you like these colours, go for* C.
williamsii *varieties. These, the easiest to
grow, are the most reliable and hardy and
drop their flowers as they brown and die;
with some* C. japonica *varieties you have to
remove the browning flowers by hand.*

Conditioning *Just slit the stem ends
before immersing in water.*

Cultivation *Camellias grow well in a
lime-free (pH4–6.5), moist soil with good
drainage and plenty of organic matter.*

*Although they can cope with occasional
windy blasts, they will suffer if they are
constantly in a draught. They are ideally
suited to sheltered, shady spots such as walls
that get little sun. Do not put them where
they get early-morning sun or the frozen
flowers will thaw too quickly and go brown.*

*Plant during autumn or spring. Dig a
large hole twice the diameter plus the depth
of the pot and part fill the hole with peat (in
the case of acid-loving plants there is no
alternative to using peat). Put in your root
ball and backfill with soil mixed with leaf
mould or peat. This will give your plant a
good start, and you will not lose your flowers.*

*In mid-spring, scatter blood, fish and
bonemeal on the soil around the roots and
then mulch with leaf mould. For a good
flower crop it is vital to keep plants well
watered between midsummer and early
autumn when the flower buds are produced.
Otherwise they will drop without opening.*

*You can propagate camellias by semi-ripe
or hardwood cuttings from midsummer to
early winter (see pages 38, 39 and 43).*

CHAENOMELES
Japonica, flowering quince

*Deciduous shrub Zones: 5–9
Height and spread: both up to 3m/10ft, but
plants are usually trained*

① *Camellia japonica 'Alba Simplex'*
② *Chaenomeles speciosa 'Nivalis'*
③ *Galanthus nivalis 'Flore Pleno'*
④ *Galanthus 'S. Arnott'*

Varieties good for cutting *The*
C. speciosa *cultivars are among the earliest
to flower, from late winter to mid-spring.
My favourites are the pure white large-
flowered varieties such as* C.s. *'Nivalis'. The
blossom appears all over the bare branches.
Trained on a high wall, the startling, plump
flowers jut out directly from the main
branches, as if they have been stuck there to
cheer up the winter garden. The flowers are
followed by sweet-smelling yellow fruits.*

Cultivation *Plant japonicas in a well-
drained soil in a sheltered, warm position.
Prevent sparrows and starlings stripping the
flowers of their fat blossom buds, to which
they are very partial, by covering the entire
plant with a fine mesh of black cotton. Cut
back side shoots, or those growing away from
the wall in wall-trained plants, to two to
three buds immediately after flowering. This
promotes strong new growth to provide next
year's flowering branches.*

*Propagate by softwood cuttings in summer
(see pages 38 and 39) if you need to.*

CROCUS
Main entry: see Winter Yellow, page
156. *One of the loveliest winter crocuses is
the see-through white* C. versicolor
*'Picturatus' with its feathery purple veins and
contrasting orange centre.*

GALANTHUS
Snowdrop

*Bulb Zones: 2–9
Height: 10-15cm/4-6in*

Varieties good for cutting *All
snowdrops look fresh and pretty when cut.
They are often best displayed in a clump, for
individual stems may easily be swamped.
They look lovely teamed simply with ivy.*

*G. nivalis is the delicate species form. Its
cultivar G. 'S. Arnott' has broad outer petals
and is fragrant and long-flowering. G. 'John
Gray' and G. 'Atkinsii' have the largest
flowers, while the showy double G.n. 'Flore
Pleno' lasts very well in water. If you are
keen on snowdrops and want a longer
flowering season, include the autumn-
flowering G. reginae-olgae in your garden.*

Cultivation *The hardy winter and early-
spring bulbs need cold to make them flower,
and thus are ideally suited to places where
the winter is severe. Find them a shady and
damp, but not boggy, position, in a humus-
rich heavy soil, and be careful not to let
bulbs dry out excessively in the ground.
However you will need a sunnier spot for
G. reginae-olgae, which requires more
summer ripening.*

*Snowdrops do not do well if planted as
dry bulbs, so if you are starting from scratch,
persuade a friend to let you divide a clump.
They increase rapidly once they are established, so you will soon be able to divide
your own clumps. Always divide when the
plants are 'in the green', that is just after
flowering and before the leaves have started
yellowing, usually in late winter or early
spring. Dig deep under large clumps to lift
them; split them by hand into smaller clumps
and replant these at the same depth.*

⑤ *Crocus versicolor 'Picturatus'*
⑥ *Muscari azureum 'Album'*
  (see page 152)

5 cm/2 in

MUSCARI
Grape hyacinth

Bulb Zones: M. armeniacum, M. azureum *4–9;* M. macrocarpum *7–10*
Height: 15-20 cm / 6-8in

Varieties good for cutting M. azureum *'Album', the white form of grape hyacinth, looks lovely in a colour jamboree with other early bulbs. Of the deep blue forms, choose* M. armeniacum *with intense, compact flower heads (see page 159). If planted in a sunny spot they often start appearing when snow is still on the ground. If you have a warm, sunny spot protected by a wall, consider growing the odd, fragrant, slightly tender* M. macrocarpum, *with its greeny yellow and black flowers.*

Cultivation *These bulbs are cheap to buy from catalogue suppliers. Plant them in autumn, 5-8cm/2-3in deep and 8-10cm/3-4in apart, in clumps of 15 to 20 in many sunny sites in the garden. They will rapidly form good solid patches and you will be able to divide them by the second autumn. They thrive in full sun, in a well-drained soil.*

NARCISSUS

Main entry: Spring Yellow, page 109. *'Paper White' narcissi are one of the joys of winter. Pot them up at two-week intervals from early autumn, keeping unplanted bulbs dry and cool, and you will have fabulous scented fresh flowers right through winter. Keep the compost moist and the pots cold but frost-free while leaves and buds form.*

PULMONARIA
Lungwort

Main entry: Winter Blue and Purple, page 159. *Mix* P. officinalis *'Sissinghurst White', a striking pure white variety with bright, faintly dappled leaves, with snow-drops and other early bulbs (see page 93).*

SARCOCOCCA
Christmas box, sweet box

Evergreen shrub Zones: 6–8
Height and spread: S. humilis *60cm/2ft;* S. hookeriana *var.* digyna *60-90cm/2-3ft × 90cm/3ft*

Varieties good for cutting *When I first saw a sarcococca I thought it looked green and insignificant – only when I picked a piece and smelled the tiny flowers did I discover the sensational scent.* S. humilis *has deep green, glossy, strap-shaped leaves and little white spiky flowers followed by black berries in spring. Combine sarcococca with pink hellebores.*

Cultivation *Plant in autumn or spring in a fertile, not too dry soil, in sun or shade. Sarcococcas will thrive under trees.*

Propagate by semi-ripe cuttings taken in summer or early autumn (see pages 38, 39) and planted in sandy soil in a cold frame.

VIBURNUM

Main entry: Winter Pink, page 154. *Use the evergreen laurustinus,* V. tinus, *with its big flat white to pink flower heads, as a background to large or small arrangements.*

❶ *Hyacinthus orientalis 'Sneeuwwitje'*
❷ *Pulmonaria officinalis 'Sissinghurst White'*

HELLEBORUS
Hellebore, Lenten rose

Main entry: Winter Green and Silver, page 149. *White varieties of the Lenten rose,* H. orientalis, *are commonly available. This one has the creamy white flowers and yellow anthers of the Christmas rose (*H. niger*), but is much more free-flowering.*

HIPPEASTRUM
Amaryllis

Main entry: Winter Orange and Red, page 155.
H. *'White Dazzler', with its large, open, veined face, really is a winter lily. Arrange simply on its own in a tall vase, or at most mix with a few lichened branches or catkins.*

HYACINTHUS
Hyacinth

Main entry: Spring White, page 101. *The lovely white Fairy or Roman hyacinth* H. orientalis *'Sneeuwwitje' has a purer, more natural look than the more usual showier and chunkier forms.*

❸ *Helleborus orientalis*
❹ *Hippeastrum 'White Dazzler'*
❺ *Narcissus 'Paper White'*
❻ *Sarcococca humilis*
❼ *Viburnum tinus 'Eve Price'*

Pink

CARDAMINE
Cuckoo flower, lady's smock
Main entry: Spring Pink, page 104. *The very early-flowering cardamine C. quinque-folia is a welcome surprise at this time of year. Arrange on its own or mix its clear pinkish-mauve flowers with early anemones or with deep blue pulmonarias.*

CHAENOMELES
Japonica, flowering quince
Main entry: Winter White, page 151. *The pale pink forms of the flowering quince, C. speciosa, are among the prettiest of all. Like the harsher red forms, such as C. speciosa 'Simonii', they look impressive in sparse, minimalist, Japanese-style arrange-ments, with just a few sprigs displayed on their own.*

❶ *Cardamine quinquefolia*
❷ *Chaenomeles speciosa*
❸ *Daphne odora 'Aureomarginata'*
❹ *Cyclamen coum*
❺ *Cyclamen hederifolium (leaf)*

CYCLAMEN
Corm Zones: C. coum 6–9; C. repandum 7; C. hederifolium 5 Height: 10cm/4in
Varieties good for cutting *The rich deep pink forms of the winter-flowering C. coum are my favourites for cutting at this time of year, until the similar, carmine-coloured C. repandum, with its honey-scented flowers, takes over in spring. Both look pretty and intense contrasted with bright orange or purple crocuses and purple and blue pulmonarias in tiny bunches. With their scalloped edges and white, lacy veining, the leaves of C. hederifolium appear after the pink or white autumn flowers (see page 140) and are excellent for winter cutting.*

Cultivation *Cyclamen do well in rich, well-drained, friable soil containing plenty of leaf mould. Dry, shaded nooks and crannies under trees or among rocks are ideal except for C. coum, which prefers moist sun or part shade. Provide protection against hard frosts in winter for C. repandum. Top-dress with manure and compost annually once the leaves die down, after first raking last year's mulch away. Do this in early summer for C. hederifolium and in the autumn for C. coum and C. repandum. Take care not to bury the corms too deeply.*

Cyclamen are great self-seeders, so it is easiest to buy a few corms and leave them to spread naturally. Plant the corms in late summer or early autumn, 5-8cm/2-3in apart and 2.5cm/1in deep, with the flattest side down and the tops visible at soil level.

DAPHNE
Evergreen shrub Zones: D. laureola, D. odora 8–9; D. mezereum 3–7 Height and spread: D. mezereum 60cm/2ft × 60cm/2ft; D. laureola 90cm/3ft × 90cm/3ft; D. odora 1.5m/5ft × 1.5m/5ft
Varieties good for cutting *D. odora and its cultivars have a fragrance that is a perfect mix of sharp citrus with spicy incense and ginger. Three sprigs by your bedside are enough to scent the whole room for up to two weeks. This compact shrub has deep pink buds and paler flowers grouped above a whorl of mid-green leaves. D.o. 'Aureo-marginata', which is hardier than the species, has a cream margin to the leaf, which makes it more interesting when not in flower. D. mezereum has striking pink flowers and is also scented, but with less of a punch. D. × burkwoodii 'Somerset' is another lovely one (see page 104).*

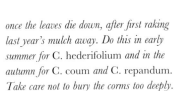
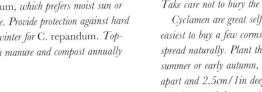

5 cm/2 in

❶
❷
❸

5 cm/2 in

Cultivation *Daphnes do not like being disturbed, so plant them when they are young, preferably in groups of three because one plant will not tolerate excessive cutting. They thrive on fertile, well-drained but not over-dry soil; both* D. mezereum *and* D. laureola *do well on chalk. Most like full sun, although* D. laureola *prefers a cool, shaded spot. Provide them with some shelter and protect* D. odora *from severe frosts.*

Keep daphnes well fed with regular top-dressings. They are quite easy to propagate from semi-ripe cuttings in summer, or from seed when it is fresh; D. mezereum, *in particular, seeds set freely. It makes good sense to nurture the offspring as replacements, since daphnes tend to be short-lived.*

HELLEBORUS
Hellebore, Lenten rose
Main entry: Winter Green and Silver, page 149.
The Lenten rose, H. orientalis, *has lovely pink forms. Some, like 'Zodiac', have been cultivated for their freckles, while others are chance seedlings.*

HYACINTHUS
Hyacinth
Main entry: Spring White, page 101.
The zany pink H. orientalis *'Jan Bos' is a bit shocking in the garden but I love to see a few stems on their own in a lime-green cup.*

PRIMULA
Polyanthus, primrose
Main entry: Spring Yellow, page 110.
The pretty pink primroses are invaluable with other early bulbs and pulmonarias in a bright, cheering winter posy (see page 93).

SARCOCOCCA
Christmas box, sweet box
Main entry: Winter White, page 152.
S. hookeriana var. digyna, with its red stem and rose-pink calyx and petals, is one of my favourite varieties of this headily perfumed species.

VIBURNUM
Deciduous and evergreen shrub Zones:
V. tinus *8–10;* V. × bodnantense, V. sargentii *7–8;* V. farreri *6–8;* V. carlesii,

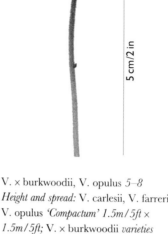

V. × burkwoodii, V. opulus *5–8*
Height and spread: V. carlesii, V. farreri, V. opulus *'Compactum' 1.5m/5ft × 1.5m/5ft;* V. × burkwoodii *varieties 2.5m/8ft × 2.5m/8ft;* V. × bodnantense *varieties 3m/10ft × 2m/6½ft;* V. tinus, V. sargentii *3m/10ft × 3m/10ft*
Varieties good for cutting *As a family, the viburnums have to be in my top ten for year-round picking – the winter-flowerers are certainly mainstays of the winter cutting garden. The evergreen laurustinus,* V. tinus *(see page 152), with its white or pink flower heads, is good in arrangements of any size. For smaller bunches, though, I tend to strip some of the leaves, otherwise the overall effect may be too dense. Metallic-blue berries, left over from the previous year of flowering, are a bonus of this handsome shrub, and the pale pink 'Gwenllian' has the best berries of all.*

Highly recommended for larger gardens are varieties of the winter-flowering V. × bodnantense, *such as 'Dawn' with deep pink buds and paler pink flowers, and*

'Deben', with white flowers tinted pink. Both last well cut and their clumps of white or pale pink flowers on bare branches are ideal at the bedside – wake to enjoy their gentle scent. V. farerri *(syn.* V. fragrans) *does not last so well and its flowers tend to drop. Varieties of the late-winter and spring-flowering* V. × burkwoodii *(see page 103) and of* V. carlesii *are also pretty and scented. Good in late spring and early summer is* V. opulus *'Roseum', and in autumn the wild form of* V. opulus *with its red, orange or yellow berries (see page 145).*

Cultivation *All viburnums thrive in any fertile moist soil and most grow happily on lime or acid soils. Plant them in late autumn in sun or semi-shade and mulch in late winter. In general viburnums do not need pruning, but when you cut branches for the house do so with the resulting shape of the bush in mind. With big shrubs like these, I recommend buying one specimen, as it takes years before you can pick from newly propagated plants. If you are patient, you can take semi-ripe cuttings in summer, and insert them in a sandy mix (see pages 38 and 39).* V. tinus *can also be layered (see page 42).*

❶ *Helleborus orientalis*
❷ *Hyacinthus orientalis* 'Jan Bos'
❸ *Sarcococca hookeriana* var. *digyna*
❹ *Primula* variety
❺ *Viburnum* x *bodnantense* 'Dawn'
❻ *Viburnum* x *burkwoodii*

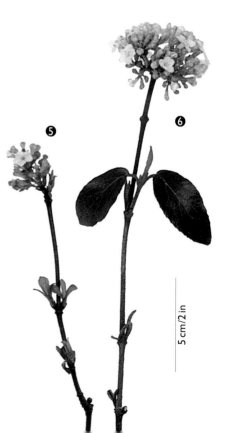

Orange and Red

HAMAMELIS
Witch hazel
Main entry: Winter Yellow, page 157.
H. × intermedia *'Diane'* bears flowers of a
rich burnt copper with a deeper red calyx.
H. × i. *'Jelena'*, the most vigorous of the
witch hazels, grows to 4.5-6m/15-20ft
high and has more delicate orange-red
flowers with the petal tips fading out to a
buttercup-yellow. Both have vivid autumn
leaves in hot orange, red and scarlet.

HIPPEASTRUM
Amaryllis
Indoor bulb
Minimum temperature: 13°C/55°F
Height: 30-50cm/12-20in
Varieties good for cutting *All these
chunky indoor bulbs are excellent for cutting.
My favourites are the deep rich red shades
'Red Lion' and 'Clove', and the delicate pale
green 'Lemons and Lime'. For late-spring
flowering, look out for the similar species
with vivid orange-scarlet flowers,
Rhodophiala pratensis. The larger
blooms, up to 15-20cm/6-8in across, look*

glamorous with a few simple branches of
hazel or willow (see page 87); or make them
the central focus of a tight, vibrantly coloured
arrangement with Narcissus 'Soleil d'Or'.
The smaller blooms look best on their own.
Conditioning *Always cut and arrange
them while still in bud and then leave them
alone. The large flower heads bruise easily
and lose the density of their colour where they
have been damaged. They last for up to three
weeks, but their stems often collapse much
earlier because of their length and the weight
of the flower. Prevent this by inserting a cane
into the hollow stem and blocking it in with
a cotton wool plug. The bases of the flower
stems have a tendency to split and roll
upwards in water after a few days. Again,*

this can be prevented by securing the stem
end with a rubber band.
Cultivation *Plant them in autumn. The
best soil mix for these bulbs is 1 part well-
rotted manure, 1 part sand and 2 parts leaf*
mould. *Put some crocks (they need good
drainage) in a pot 5cm/2in wider than the
diameter of the bulb and plant them half in
and half out of the soil. Do not water much
initially. Keep bulbs in a warm place near a
radiator or other source of heat until they
have made a growth of 10cm/4in; they can
then be moved somewhere cooler, in either
full sun or partial shade.*

*Feed with liquid fertilizer until one week
before flowering. After flowering, feed every
10 days. Cut the foliage in summer and
leave dormant with no water until the buds
begin to show again. When they do, give the
pot a top-dressing to a depth of 5cm/2in.
Repot only every three to four years.*

*Treat Rhodophiala pratensis, the late-
spring flowerer, in reverse. Give it some
moisture in summer and keep it dormant in
the winter season. It also requires a rich,
sandy soil. While it is safest grown in a pot,
it can be grown against a sunny wall in
milder regions.*

*If you are prepared to wait for three years
for flowers, you can propagate from seed
sown in spring or from offsets planted in
autumn. I lack the patience for this and
simply buy bulbs every year.*

PULMONARIA
Main entry: Winter Blue and Purple,
page 159. P. rubra *'Redstart'* is the most
upright of the red forms. The flowers have a
slightly muddy redness to them but brighten
when mixed with P. officinalis *'Sissinghurst
White'* (see page 152) or white crocus.

❶ *Hamamelis × intermedia 'Jelena'*
❷ *Hippeastrum 'Red Lion'*
❸ *Hippeastrum 'Clove'*
❹ *Pulmonaria rubra 'Redstart'*

5 cm/2 in

5 cm/2 in

5 cm/2 in

Yellow

ACACIA
Mimosa, wattle

Evergreen shrub and small tree Zones: 9–10
Height and spread: A. dealbata *and*
A. longifolia *8m/26ft × 8m/26ft (twice this height in Mediterranean climates)*

Varieties good for cutting *Not many of us will have a spot sheltered enough for an acacia tree, but I include it for the fortunate few who have. Mimosa makes a staggering sight in full, fluffy, primrose-yellow flower in the depths of winter, so grow it if you can. Quantities of it arranged on its own in a huge jug brighten gloomy winter days, not only looking but also smelling lovely.* A. dealbata *has feathery grey-green leaves and pompon flowers.* A. longifolia *has strap-shaped leaves and long strands of flowers.*

Conditioning *Strip the bottom leaves.*

Cultivation *In temperate climates, plant in full sun in a sheltered site away from winds. Most acacias prefer a moist, acid soil although* A. longifolia *can tolerate some lime and drought. They may well be cut down by long and severe frosts, but often come again from the base. Unless you start with a reasonably mature plant, you will have several years to wait before you can cut much. Acacias are fast growers though, so you can increase your stock by semi-ripe cuttings in summer (see pages 38 and 39).*

CORNUS
Dogwood, cornel

Mainly deciduous shrub and tree Zones: 2–8 except C. mas *5–8*
Height and spread: C. mas *to 5.5m/18ft × 5.5m/18ft;* C. alba *'Sibirica' and* C.a. *'Elegantissima' to 2.2m/7ft × 2.2m/ 7ft;* C. stolonifera *'Flaviramea' to 2m/6½ft × 4m/13ft*

Varieties good for cutting *One of my favourite dogwoods for cutting is* C. mas, *the Cornelian cherry, with its starry bright yellow flowers in late winter. A few sprigs cut and arranged on their own look lovely; or mix them with hamamelis. If you have space, it is also worth planting a small clump of* C. stolonifera *'Flaviramea', with greeny yellow stems. Cut the bare winter*

branches for a huge arrangement in a simple glass vase or use them to make the basis of wreaths and globes at any time of year. The stems, like those of willow, are pliable and soft when newly cut. On into late spring and summer, there is no better foliage than variegated* C. alba *'Elegantissima' as the base of a large white and green arrangement.*

Conditioning *Branches cut for foliage should have the last 2.5cm/1in of their stems plunged in boiling water for one minute, before having a good soaking in deep tepid water. They have a tendency to droop.*

Cultivation *Most dogwoods are tough plants and thrive almost anywhere, but* C. mas *prefers a sunny, sheltered position against a wall. Plant in early winter.*

If left to their own devices all dogwoods become large shrubs or small trees. Like willows, their size can be kept in check by coppicing in late winter and by regular cutting. If you are growing them for their winter stems cut them back in early spring every year or every two years, since it is the new growth that provides the bright colour.

You can take softwood cuttings in summer or hardwood cuttings in autumn or winter (see pages 38, 39, and 43).

CORYLUS AVELLANA
Hazel, cobnut

Deciduous shrub and tree Zones: 3–8
Height and spread: C. avellana *4m/13ft × 6m/20ft;* C.a. *'Contorta' 5.5m/18ft × 5.5m/18ft*

Varieties good for cutting *Good throughout the winter as a source of lovely boughs of catkins which gradually elongate while still on the tree, the hazel reaches its resplendent climax towards the end of the season when the pollen emerges. Dazzling displays of yellow male catkins radiate from woods and hedges all around where I live in south-east England. Even before the catkins are smothered with pollen, they look glamorous teamed with* Salix daphnoides *and amaryllis (see page 87). The corkscrew hazel,* C.a. *'Contorta', with twisty stems and 5cm/2in-long yellow catkins, looks dramatic in the garden or in a vase.*

Cultivation *Group hazels 3m/10ft apart each way. They will thrive in sun or*

part shade. Prune in early spring, cutting back to the base shoots that are more than two years old. The tree will then provide easily reached catkin-laden branches for the next winter. Grow hazels from seeds (nuts) planted 5cm/2in deep in the open ground and transplant the seedlings two years later. Alternatively, take suckers from the parent plant in mid-autumn.*

CROCUS

Corm Zones: C. tommasinianus, C. versicolor *'Picturatus' 5–9;* C. chrysanthus *varieties 4–9;* C. vernus *varieties 3–9*
Height: C. chrysanthus *varieties 5-8cm/ 2-3in;* C. tommasinianus, C. versicolor *'Picturatus' 5-8cm/2-3in;* C. vernus, *larger-flowering varieties 9-10cm/3½-4in*

Varieties good for cutting *Crocuses always seem bright and optimistic and these qualities are to be enjoyed indoors as much as out. As soon as there is any sun they open so wide that their petals double right back, echoing one's own feelings about the sun at the end of a long winter. All of the smaller-flowered* C. chrysanthus *varieties, the first to come into flower, are good for winter picking. Try* C.c. *'Ladykiller', with the outside of its petals a deep purple-violet, and inside a pale lilac. I like the bright, brassy oranges like* C.c. *var.* fuscotinctus *or the*

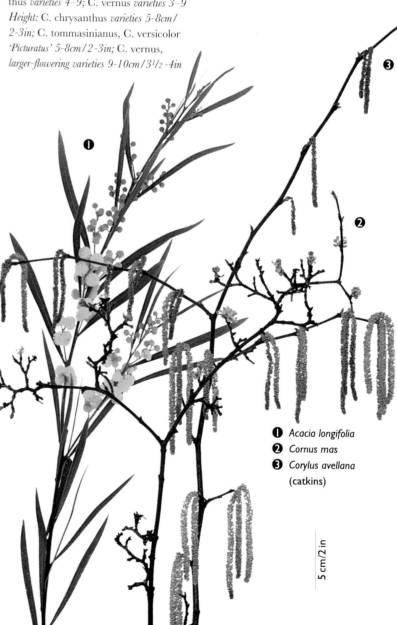

❶ *Acacia longifolia*
❷ *Cornus mas*
❸ *Corylus avellana*
   (catkins)

5 cm/2 in

5 cm/2 in

aptly named 'Brass Band' and the larger-flowering varieties, such as the rich purple C. vernus 'Remembrance'. The delicate and dainty species crocuses are lovely arranged in a small glass on their own where you can inspect their brilliant saffron-yellow and orange stamens, anthers and pollen. I also love C. versicolor 'Picturatus' (see page 151) and the straight-up C. tommasinianus with its chalky-mauve exterior and richer inside. All the larger-flowered crocuses look good combined with other late-winter flowers or floating on their own in a shallow glass bowl as a table centrepiece. They last only two to three days cut, but the pleasure they bring is as intense as it is brief.

Cultivation *Plant autumn-flowering crocus varieties in summer, and winter- and spring-flowering varieties in late summer or early autumn. Plant them 5cm/2in deep and about 8cm/3in apart in well-drained soil or short grass and in full sun.*

I simply buy crocus bulbs and let them spread. You can also propagate in early autumn by seed or by dividing clumps of bulbs if these have formed.

ERANTHIS
Winter aconite
Tuberous perennial Zones: 4–7
Height: 5-10cm/2-4in

Varieties good for cutting *These buttercup-yellow anemone-like flowers with their green ruff of leaves look best on their own either in a short glass or floated in a shallow bowl with dried beech leaves (see page 90). They open up most fully in sunlight but look pretty at night under a table lamp. Choose the large-flowered E. hyemalis Tubergenii Group 'Guinea Gold'.*

Cultivation *Like snowdrops, aconites are best divided and planted while still 'in the green', so beg a clump from a friend. Plant in a heavy, reasonably fertile, moist but well-drained soil. They do best in alkaline conditions, under deciduous trees and shrubs where they can spread undisturbed.*

HAMAMELIS
Witch hazel
Deciduous shrub Zones: 5–9
Height and spread: 2.5–3m/8-10ft × 2.5m/8ft

Varieties for cutting *All the witch hazels, with their spidery frost-proof flowers, like the tentacles of a sea anemone, are lovely cut and last up to two weeks in water. Place three branches in a vase and put it where you can enjoy the faint but delicious scent. H. × intermedia 'Pallida' is the best yellow-flowered form but H. × intermedia 'Jelena' has more delicate flowers (see page 155).*

Cultivation *Plant in moist but well-drained, neutral to acid soil (they will grow on lime but not chalk). Most like a sunny, open site, though H. × intermedia thrives in semi-shade. They are slow growers, but you can propagate by layering in autumn.*

IRIS
Main entry: Winter Blue and Purple, page 158. *The little buttercup-yellow reticulata iris I. danfordiae, with green spots on its falls, goes perfectly with the rich purple species I. reticulata (see page 158).*

LONICERA
Honeysuckle
Main entry: Summer Pink, page 123. *L. × purpusii is another winter-flowerer with an exotic scent. It outdoes both its parents, L. fragrantissima and L. standishii, by more continuous flowering. Strip some leaves to show off the flowers.*

NARCISSUS
Main entry: Spring Yellow, page 109. *Put a few stems of the pretty little bright yellow N. 'Tête-à-Tête' in a jug on the centre of the kitchen table, on their own or mixed with double snowdrops and a few stems of ivy. 'Topolino' is another delightful early-flowerer.*

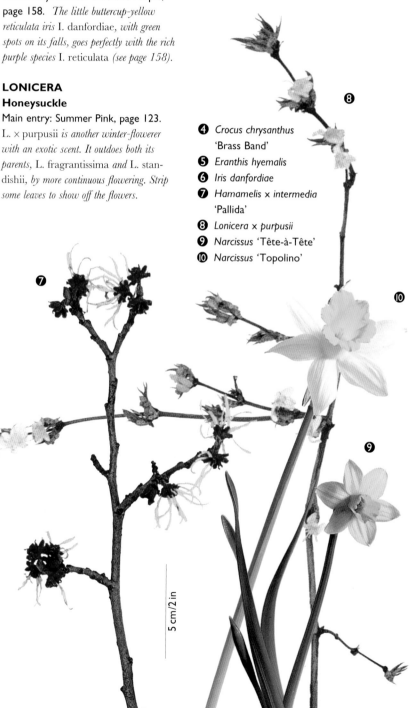

❹ *Crocus chrysanthus 'Brass Band'*
❺ *Eranthis hyemalis*
❻ *Iris danfordiae*
❼ *Hamamelis × intermedia 'Pallida'*
❽ *Lonicera × purpusii*
❾ *Narcissus 'Tête-à-Tête'*
❿ *Narcissus 'Topolino'*

5 cm/2 in

Blue and Purple

CROCUS

Main entry: Winter Yellow, page 156.
C. vernus 'Remembrance', with large purple flowers, is lovely in a multicoloured late-winter posy (see page 93).

HELLEBORUS

Hellebore, Lenten rose

Main entry: Winter Green and Silver, page 149. *I love the fashionable purple, almost black, varieties of* H. orientalis. *Try* 'Queen of the Night' *and* 'Philip Ballard'.

IRIS

Rhizomatous or bulbous perennial, some evergreen Zones: 4–9
Height: I. reticulata *10-15cm/4-6in;* I. unguicularis *20cm/8in;* I. foetidissima *30-90cm/12-36in;* I. sibirica *50-120cm/20-48in; Intermediate Bearded 40-70cm/16-27in; Tall Bearded 70cm/27in*

Varieties good for cutting *In the gloomiest depths of winter irises are an absolute essential of the cutting garden.*

I. unguicularis *in all its colour forms produces flower after exquisite, fresh-looking flower to provide regular bunches for the bedside or your desk. Grow clumps of the sumptuous plush purple-velvet* I.u. 'Mary Barnard' *to mix with a few sprigs of* Cornus mas *or* hamamelis. *Grow too the scented pale lilac* I.u. 'Walter Butt', *which looks best with one or three stems in a simple glass on their own.* I. lazica, *a more robust version of* I. unguicularis, *is also a beauty, flowering from late winter through the spring. Even more delicate is the deep purple, yellow-veined* I. reticulata *that appears towards the end of winter. Another early-spring beauty is* Hermodactylus tuberosus *with its green and bumblebee-brown flowers. In spring and early summer the first of the aristocratic Tall Bearded irises appear. Choose a selection of early, mid-season and late flowers, from the Intermediate or Tall groups, of at least one white, one violet-blue (*'Jane Phillips', *see page 133), one red (*'Ruby Mine', *see page 126), one black (*'Sable'*) and one purple variety.* I. chrysographes, *with flowers of the darkest indigo-violet, and near-black* I.c. 'Black Knight' *are also stunning. In the*

autumn, grow I. foetidissima *for its seed heads (see page 144).*

Conditioning *Stand in deep water after cutting. Remove fading flowers of Bearded irises, and buds will continue to emerge.*

Cultivation *Except for* I. foetidissima, *all irises grow best in full sun. The beardless Siberian irises need moist but not waterlogged conditions, succeeding best in humus- rich, moist, open, sunny sites.* I. unguicularis *prefers a sheltered site and thrives in poor, well-drained, even gravelly soil. Do not feed or mulch these irises, or they will have lovely lush leaves and no flowers.*

Unlike most perennials, irises benefit from summer planting immediately after flowering. Bearded irises, I. unguicularis *and* I. reticulata *all like their rhizomes to be baked in the sun. When planting, dig out a wide shallow hole and make a low mound in the middle, like an earth castle surrounded by its moat. Rest the iris rhizome on this, spreading out the roots into the moat. Plant 13cm/5in apart, with their leaves and buds facing so as to get maximum sunlight. Cover the roots and lower part of the rhizome with soil and firm it down. The central ridge of the rhizome*

5 cm/2 in

❶ *Crocus vernus* 'Remembrance'
❷ *Helleborus orientalis*
❸ *Iris reticulata*
❹ *Iris lazica*
❺ *Iris unguicularis* 'Mary Barnard'

should show above the soil.

Irises will produce more flowers if dug up, divided and replanted every three years. Both after planting and after flowering, cut the leaves to 15cm/6in to prevent the rhizome being dislodged by wind-rock.

Propagate rhizomatous irises by division of the rhizomes after flowering in late summer. Dig up the whole clump, inserting the fork well away from the plant to avoid damaging the rhizomes. Split it into manageable 8-10cm/3-4in pieces. Discard any old rhizomes, detach the new young parts from the clump, and neatly trim off the ends. Dust with fungicide. Trim the long roots by one-third and cut the leaves to prevent rock. Replant as above, firm in well, and water.

Propagate bulbous species, like the reticulatas, by division after flowering in spring.

MUSCARI
Grape hyacinth
Main entry: Winter White, page 152.
The deep blue scented grape hyacinth M. armeniacum is lovely mixed with snowdrops alone, or in a late-winter combination with other tiny gems.

PULMONARIA
Lungwort
Herbaceous perennial Zones: 3–8
Height: 20-40cm/8-16in
Varieties good for cutting *Showy pulmonaria cultivars are far more interesting than the wild species lungworts with their*

slightly muted blue and pink. Most have the characteristic pretty, spotted white and green leaves, hairy stalks and cowslip-like flowers. Since many of the best colours are unnamed hybrids, it is best, as with hellebores, to buy them in flower. Look for the deep resonant blue and purple forms with large flowers and long stems, such as P. longifolia. P. 'Frühlingshimmel' is a pale mauve-blue. Reds include P. rubra 'Redstart' (see page 155), and for white there is P. officinalis 'Sissinghurst White' (see page 152).

Pulmonarias always look pretty arranged on their own, perhaps in a small posy.
Cultivation *Pulmonarias are invaluable as winter-flowerers since they thrive in shade: keep them moist and they will soon self-seed into all your darkest corners. Divide them every three or four years, in autumn or spring.*

ROSMARINUS
Rosemary
Evergreen shrub Zones: 8–9
Height and spread: 2m/6½ft × 2m/6½ft
Varieties good for cutting *I pick rosemary throughout the year to use as foliage, but it is at its best in late winter and through the spring when covered with a haze of blue flowers. With its fragrant and robust leaves, it is a good addition to any table centre. Grow the deep blue forms like R. officinalis 'Sissinghurst Blue'. It is very*

6 *Muscari armeniacum*
7 8 9 *Pulmonaria hybrids*
10 *Rosmarinus officinalis* 'Sissinghurst Blue'
11 *Scilla siberica*
12 *Chionodoxa forbesii*

free-flowering. Use its highly branched structure as your main foliage to mix with fresh whites, yellows, blues and greens or in a brightly coloured bunch with tulips and anemones.

Use the upward-growing, very hardy R.o. 'Miss Jessopp's Upright' for a hedge round your cutting garden. With its unbranched twisting and turning stems it is excellent for adding as the final vertical emphasis in a bunch of flowers, to break up any symmetry and neatness. When the flowers are over the greeny-blue foliage makes a pretty and aromatic combination with lavender and honeysuckle, or mixed with sweet peas.
Conditioning *Strip the leaves that will be below the water line and hammer any very weedy stems.*
Cultivation *Rosemary is a slightly tender shrub, so needs a position in full sun, or against a sunny, protective wall, with dry, well-drained soil. If you get frost damage cut back to healthy wood in the spring. If you have a straggly old plant, cut hard back in spring. It is anyway good practice to prune shoots back to half their length in spring.*

Rosemary is easily propagated from semi-ripe cuttings in summer (see pages 38, 39).

SCILLA and CHIONODOXA
Bulb Zones: 3–9
Height: 10-25cm/4-10in
Varieties good for cutting *These two very similar-looking families of bulbs have clear, azure-blue stars that are perfect for tiny mixed posies in late winter and early spring (see page 93). Choose the bright, intense colour forms, like Scilla siberica 'Spring Beauty' and Chionodoxa forbesii, not the washed-out pale blues. Pink and white forms include C.f. 'Pink Giant', with white petals flushed soft pink.*

To tell the two genera apart, check whether the petals are separate all the way down. If they are, the plant is a chionodoxa. If the petals are fused as they emerge from the centre, it is a scilla.
Cultivation *These are cheap bulbs to buy and quickly become established. Plant them 5-8cm/2-3in deep, in a site that does not completely dry out in summer. The scillas prefer full sun, except for S. siberica which does well in shade. The chionodoxas all thrive in sun or part shade. Top-dress with leaf mould or compost in the autumn.*

Propagate both scillas and chionodoxas by division in late summer or autumn.

5 cm/2 in

Shrubs, Trees and Year-round Foliage

Many of the foliage plants here are used as structural stems in starting arrangements. But there are a few beauty queens, such as callicarpa and spindle berries, to use on their own. Evergreens provide material all year round, but avoid the deadening greens – such as laurel – used by many florists.

ACER PLATANOIDES
Maple

A. platanoides (**1**) *and* A.p. *'Crimson King'* (**2**) *are bright and fresh with their* acid-green and yellow flowers and red or bright green newly emerging leaves. Mix with spring bulbs or anemones. The red and yellow colours of A.p. 'Crimson King' are the perfect complement to bright Parrot tulips (see page 59).

AESCULUS HIPPOCASTANUM
Horse chestnut

The sticky buds of the horse chestnut tree (**3**) *emerge from tight bud into luscious green new leaves. Cut boughs to watch them emerging on their own, or mix them with strong and flamboyant flowers such as the Parrot tulips, which parade their huge, frilly flowers at the same time in spring.*

ALNUS
Alder

During late winter the elongating rich brown-purple catkins and small cones of A. cordata (**4**) *make a lovely structure for any big vase. Mix with sumptuous amaryllis (see page 87) or simply with a great haze of pussy willow. The crinkly bright green leaves will emerge from nothing to appear suddenly one morning when you come down for breakfast.*

CALLICARPA

The tiny pinhead purple berries of C. bodinieri (**5**) *have a brightness and beauty that make them look like a peculiar, poisonous sort of medicine. They are at their best in late autumn when the leaves have been shed, with only the brilliant violet berries remaining on their slim branches. The berries look good on their own in a bright and contrasting orange or turquoise vase but they also mix spectacularly with orange dahlias. They will last for over a month before wrinkling.*

CARPINUS BETULUS
Hornbeam

Whether you pick hornbeam with its early spring catkins or wait until the summer

5 cm/2 in

when its seed cases hang from the tree like
upside down pagodas (**6**), hornbeam is
exciting and unusual foliage to add to any
arrangement. Cut it right down and use the
bright lime-green seed cases as the foliage to
mix with poppies, cornflowers and lavender
in a multicoloured summer swag (see pages
64–7). Or exploit their elegance by cutting
great tall branches to enhance any large vase.

CHOISYA
Mexican orange blossom

Whether you choose the ordinary luscious
shiny bottle-green variety, C. ternata (**8**), or
the bright yellow-green-leaved C.t.
'Sundance' (**7**), Mexican orange blossom has
excellent long-lasting foliage. Pick them in
spring for their scented flowers, too.

CORNUS ALBA
Dogwood

Cornus is an invaluable shrub for the cutting
garden. C. alba colours up beautifully in
autumn (**10**), and you can use its bright bare
branches in winter too. The fresh white-
bordered leaves of C. a.'Elegantissima' (**9**)
are excellent in summer for mixing in a
white and green arrangement. Use its strong
upright habit as your main foliage structure.

DIPSACUS
Teasel

The great spiny spikes of common teasel,
D fullonum (syn. D. sylvestris) as a green
bud (**11**) or with its whorls of pale mauve
(**12**) are impressive sculptural foliage on their
own or mixed with luscious bunches of lilies.

ELAEAGNUS
Oleaster

The silver-leaved, olive-like deciduous
E. angustifolia and E. commutata (**13**)
are beautiful and elegant used in summer or
autumn arrangements. They go perfectly with
my favourite crimsons, lapis-lazuli or sky-
blues and oranges.

5 cm/2 in

EUCALYPTUS
Gumtree

*A multitude of eucalyptus varieties (**1**) is available, providing invaluable foliage through the winter. Use sprigs of eucalyptus to lighten an arrangement of green and white. Cut larger stems to arrange on their own.*

EUONYMUS
Spindle

*The common spindle tree E. europaeus has pink fruits in autumn (**2**), and as the fruits ripen the hanging purses open and reveal the wonderful contrasting orange seeds contained in their vibrant pink fleshy carapace. Arrange them on their own with many large boughs in a jug for the centre of a table, or use them simply as foliage with other pinks and greens.*

HEDERA
Ivy

*The delicate bird's foot ivy, H. helix 'Pedata' (**5**), is my favourite among the ivy family. Trail it across the table for a winter dinner or arrange it twisting and turning out from a tied bunch. In the autumn the black shiny berries of the wild form of H. helix make a useful addition to an arrangement.*

LIGUSTRUM
Privet

*Ordinary privet makes dull foliage but it may be worth planting the golden variety, L. ovalifolium 'Aureum' (**3**) or silver L.o. 'Argenteum' to use as background foliage in large arrangements (see pages 74–5).*

MALUS
Apple, crabapple

*The white-flushed pink blossom of the apple M. 'Ribston Pippin' (**6**) is to me a symbol of spring. Cut a few of its gnarled and knotted branches to have on their own. Crabapple M. 'John Downie' is another beauty, providing pure white blossom. In late summer and autumn this fruit tree family comes into its own again – any of the crabapples such as 'Golden Hornet' (**7**) or even the smaller apples are fine companions to early-autumn flowers.*

PITTOSPORUM

P. tenuifolium, *with its small, wrinkly-edged greyish-green leaves and* P. 'Garnettii' (**4**), *a variegated hybrid with white-flushed-pink margins around the leaves, are a great source of foliage throughout the winter. The deep crimson cultivar* P.t. 'Purpureum' *is a perfect background plant to zingy oranges and acid greens at any time of year.*

PRUNUS

Cherry, plum, blackthorn, sloe

P. 'Taihaku' (**8**), *my favourite tree for spring cutting, is a must if you have room for it. Its huge white saucer-shaped flowers drop a dense cloud of white confetti like a snow storm in spring. The species* P. avium *with its smaller dense collections of flowers* (**12**) *is a lovely companion for any spring flower you care to name (see page 63). The blackthorn,* P. spinosa (**13**), *also has a pretty Japanese-style blossom that is light on the eye. This doubly earns its keep, for in autumn the black-smeared-blue sloes are set against the panther-blue-black of the spiny stems. Combine this with the rich chocolate, oranges and yellows of rudbeckias, sunflowers and autumn dahlias.*

QUERCUS

Oak, red oak

The red oak, Q. rubra (**14**), *with its mixture of green, chestnut-brown, orange and red leaves, is enough arranged on its own in*

a vase in the autumn, or use it as your foliage for any great dahlia, salvia and gladioli arrangement. The copper, brown and ochre leaves of oak trees are excellent as a base for many huge autumn vases (see pages 82–3). The bright green acorns of Q. robur (**15**) *are invaluable mixed with*

crabapples and sunflowers for a glamorous yet relaxed vase (see page 55).

RHAMNUS

The white-margined evergreen R. alaternus 'Argenteovariegata' (**9**) *is unusual in its tolerance of shade and is an invaluable filler for your winter and early-spring bunches.*

RUTA GRAVEOLENS

Rue

Rue (**10**) *is almost alone in its delicacy among the evergreen plants which can provide foliage at the leaner times of year. It can cause skin allergies, so cut and arrange wearing rubber gloves, particularly on a hot sunny day.*

SORBUS ARIA

Whitebeam

The chiselled, deeply veined, silver-grey leaves of S.a. 'Lutescens' (**16**) *are perfect to lighten up any mixed spring vase. Pick them in bud to open out gradually, revealing their fresh grey upper surface and silver underside.*

SYMPHORICARPOS ALBUS

Snowberry

The snowbery, a scraggy shrub (**11**) *usually associated with hedges and wild gardens, has milky white, often flushed pink berries like helium balloons hanging on the end of narrow pliable twigs. Pick them through autumn and on into the winter to freshen up your heavy hot colours (see pages 82–3).*

Index of Plants

Page numbers in *italic type* refer to plans, photographs or their captions. Numbers in **bold type** indicate main entries.

Author's Acknowledgements

I have many people to thank for helping me in the writing and making of this book.

First of all I want to thank Xar Sturges and Anna Ben for getting married. It was at their wedding that my husband Adam Nicolson cornered Frances Lincoln and suggested that, if she wanted someone to write a book about growing and arranging cut flowers, I might be the person she was looking for.

I also want to thank several people for being very generous with plants from their gardens. My mother, Faith Raven, supplied me with the bulk, particularly for the plant portrait section. I also want to thank Robert and Jane Sackville-West, Simon and Antonia Johnson and Peter, Ian and Tony at Baker and Duguid in Nine Elms Market. Thompson and Morgan and Chiltern Seeds supplied me with the seeds for my annuals. I must not forget Nipper Keeley who made the much admired blue onions on top of the gondola posts in the cutting garden.

There are several people who allowed us to take photographs in their houses. Again I thank my mother, Faith Raven, my father-in-law, Nigel Nicolson, and the former administrator at Sissinghurst, Paul Wood. Hugh Raven. Jane Stuart-Smith and Pia Tryde also allowed us to invade their privacy.

There are many people who have, over the time I was writing the book, been a fount of gardening information. My mother and my sister Anna Raven have taught me a lot, as have Christine and Andrew Banbury, David Aitcheson and Sarah Cook, but perhaps most of all I owe thanks to Montagu Don.

There has also been a great team working on the look, the words and the accuracy of this book. Tony Lord has checked the plant nomenclature and hopefully ironed out most of my ignorance. Sally Cracknell, Trish Going, Akio Morishima and Caroline Hillier have made it look so beautiful. Caroline came and held my hand at every one of the photography shoots and, without her and Pia, there would have been many flops. Erica Hunningher, Jo Christian, Alison Freegard and Sarah Mitchell have done equal magic with the words. I always write too much. I am also very grateful to Penny Hobhouse for agreeing to write the Foreword.

There have been many friends and members of my family who have helped out in the crises along the way, with support and advice or help with the children and cooking when I was late on the delivery of a batch of text. Patricia Howie, Alex and Marion Kelsey, Chris Aston (who was the midwife for my daughter Molly), my agent Sarah Lutyens, my partner in 'Garlic and Sapphire' Louise Farman, and of course close friends, Pots and Ivan Samarine, Aurea and Andrew Palmer, and Sarah and Montagu Don.

Perhaps at the top of the list are those that are here from day to day, taking the home and garden pressure off me so I can concentrate on writing. Adam, my twin sister Jane Raven, Ken Weekes, Peter, Will and Feo Clark, and Anna and the entire Cheney family are all owed a huge debt of gratitude.

Sarah Raven
Perch Hill, July 1996

Publisher's Acknowledgements

The publishers thank Valerie Hill for the watercolour plans and illustrations on pages 16-21, 24-25 and 28-29. They are also grateful to the following people for their help in producing this book: Joanna Chisholm, Jonathan Folland, Celia Levett, Peggy Sadler, Richard Schofield and Caroline Taylor.

Editors Jo Christian, Alison Freegard
Art editor Sally Cracknell
Horticultural Consultant Tony Lord
Index Penny David
Production Jennifer Cohen
Editorial Director Erica Hunningher
Art Director Caroline Hillier

HARDINESS ZONES (Z)

Hardiness zone ratings are a rough guide to the appropriate minimum temperature a plant will tolerate. Hardiness depends on factors such as the depth of a plant's roots, its water content at the onset of frost, the duration of cold weather, wind force, and the length of (and temperatures encountered) the preceding summer. These ratings, based on those devised by the US Department of Agriculture, are allocated to plants according to their tolerance of winter cold in the British Isles and Western Europe. In climates with hotter and/or drier summers, as in Australia and New Zealand, some plants will survive colder temperatures; their hardiness in these countries may be one or, rarely, two zones lower than quoted.

CELSIUS	ZONES	°FAHRENHEIT
below -45	1	below -50
-45 to -40	2	-50 to -40
-40 to -34	3	-40 to -30
-34 to -29	4	-30 to -20
-29 to -23	5	-20 to -10
-23 to -18	6	-10 to 0
-18 to -12	7	0 to 10
-12 to -7	8	10 to 20
-7 to -1	9	20 to 30
-1 to 4	10	30 to 40